UNITED STATES
MONETARY POLICY

UNITED STATES MONETARY POLICY

Edited by

Neil H. Jacoby

REVISED EDITION

Published for

THE AMERICAN ASSEMBLY

Columbia University

BOOKS FOR LIBRARIES PRESS
FREEPORT, NEW YORK

INTERNATIONAL STANDARD BOOK NUMBER:
0-8369-5702-4

LIBRARY OF CONGRESS CATALOG CARD NUMBER:
79-164586

PRINTED IN THE UNITED STATES OF AMERICA

Preface

This is the second edition, revised, of *United States Monetary Policy*. Under the editorship of Dr. Neil H. Jacoby of the University of California (Los Angeles), the chapters that follow were written originally as background reading for a series of American Assemblies on monetary policy. The first of these meetings was the Fourteenth American Assembly, held at Arden House, the Harriman (N.Y.) campus of Columbia University, in October, 1958. Three other Assemblies took place in 1959, with the cooperation of Duke University, Town Hall of Los Angeles, and Southern Methodist University. Since 1958, this volume has also been used extensively in college and university courses and by the general reading public.

The opinions found herein are those of the authors and do not necessarily represent the views of The American Assembly or the American Bankers' Association, who generously contributed to the financing of this edition.

The American Assembly

Henry M. Wriston   Clifford C. Nelson
Chairman   *President*

CONTENTS

UNITED STATES
MONETARY POLICY

Introduction: Contemporary Monetary Issues[1]
NEIL H. JACOBY

Six years have passed since *United States Monetary Policy* was published in 1958. That volume was directed to a general audience. The papers it contained, all by respected professional economists, were intended to define the principal issues of monetary policy, to weigh alternative solutions, and to provide laymen with the essential knowledge needed for intelligent discussion of monetary issues in the American economy. The book was designed to fill a void in existing literature, to lower the barrier to public understanding of the workings of monetary policy in a free, democratic society.

Subsequent events have shown that the 1958 volume was timely, and that it fulfilled its mission. The first edition attained an extraordinarily wide circulation. Moreover, the publication of the volume was succeeded by an unprecedented surge of public interest in monetary matters, leading to a spate of popular and professional literature. Probably, no aspect of American economic policy has been treated in so voluminous a body of literature in so short a time. The only comparable collections are the extensive studies of the Temporary National Economic Committee during the late 1930's, and the "three-foot shelf" of volumes emerging from the work of the National Monetary Commission during the years 1907–12.

Events have thus fully borne out the truth of the opening sentence of the 1958 edition of *United States Monetary Policy*— "The money question is again in the spotlight of public attention."

In his comprehensive 1962 review of the development and status of monetary theory and policy, Professor H. G. Johnson cited no

[1] I am grateful to Karl Brunner and J. Fred Weston for helpful comments upon this essay.

1

fewer than 129 significant professional economic publications, more than three-fourths of which appeared subsequent to 1958.[2] Since 1958, the United Kingdom and Canada, as well as the United States, have published the results of massive public inquiries into the institutional machinery and the policies of their monetary and credit systems. The Committee on the Working of the Monetary System appointed by the Treasury of the United Kingdom brought forth its Report in August, 1959.[3] In 1961, the Commission on Money and Credit published its Report on *Money and Credit*, the fruit of a three-year intensive study sponsored by the Committee for Economic Development of the United States.[4] This was followed by eighteen volumes of supplementary studies of particular financial industries and monetary policy problems by seventy-five economists whose work had helped to guide the Commission to its conclusions. Even more recently, in 1963, the Royal Commission on Banking and Finance of Canada published its Report, redefining the role of banking institutions and monetary policy in the Canadian economy.[5]

Nor have the legislative and executive branches of the U.S. federal government neglected monetary issues. Extensive hearings have been held in recent times by the Joint Economic Committee of the Congress on the Recommendations of the Commission on Money and Credit. The Senate Finance Committee labored and brought forth a proposed Financial Institutions Act, which later died in the House. In 1963, President Kennedy appointed three committees—on federal credit programs, financial institutions, and pension funds—to study and report upon the CMC proposals.[6] Meanwhile, the Controller of the Currency sponsored and published a series of banking and monetary studies in

---

[2] H. G. Johnson, "Monetary Theory and Policy," *American Economic Review*, LII, No. 5 (June, 1962), 335–84.

[3] *Report of the Committee on the Working of the Monetary System* (London: H. M. Stationary Office, CMND 827, August, 1959).

[4] Commission on Money and Credit, *Money and Credit* (Englewood Cliffs, N.J.: Prentice-Hall, 1961).

[5] Royal Commission on Banking and Finance, *Report* (Ottawa, 1963).

[6] The reports of the first two committees were analyzed by R. J. Saulnier in *Recent Studies of Our Financial System*. Business Paper No. 9. (Bureau of Business Research, Graduate School of Business, Indiana University, 1964).

commemoration of the centennial of the national banking system.[7]
So far, the tangible products of legislative inquiries have been
modest; but potentially far-reaching changes in policies of charter-
ing and regulating national banks have been instituted, and shifts
in the legislation governing the private financial system appear
probable.

Apart from governmental and quasi-public inquiries into monetary matters, the academic community and research foundations
have been active in this field during the past half-dozen years.
Among the most basic contributions are those of Goldsmith,[8] Gurley and Shaw,[9] Friedman,[10] and Brunner and Meltzer.[11]

In view of this extraordinary spate of literature on many facets
of monetary policy during the past six years, why is a second
edition of *United States Monetary Policy* necessary? The answer
is that nearly all of the recent literature has been either highly
technical, or specialized, or not readily accessible to the layman.
What the intelligent layman needs is an accurate but intelligible,
comprehensive but not encyclopedic, account of monetary policy
issues between the covers of one volume. This need is as urgent
today as it was in 1958.

Even more important is the fact that, despite the widespread
attention given to monetary policy issues by economists, bankers,
and statesmen during recent years, many issues remain "moot."
Although much progress toward understanding has been made,
research has not yet discovered answers to many monetary
problems in which one may repose a high degree of confidence.
Personal "values" and judgments thus continue to play an important role in the formation of monetary policies. These are the

[7] Deane Carson (ed.), *Banking and Monetary Studies* (Homewood, Ill.:
Richard D. Irwin, 1963).
[8] Particularly, *Financial Intermediaries in the American Economy* (Princeton, N.J.: Princeton University Press, 1958).
[9] Especially, *Money in a Theory of Finance* (Washington, D.C.: The
Brookings Institution, 1960).
[10] Especially, *A Program for Monetary Stability* (New York: Fordham
University Press, 1959); and, with Anna Schwartz, *A Monetary History of
the United States, 1867–1960* (Princeton, N.J.: Princeton University Press,
1963).
[11] Brunner and Meltzer's extensive work, part of which has appeared in
articles, will be published in *Monetary Theory and Monetary Policy* in 1965.

stuff of which public debate and discussion is made in a democratic society.

During most of the post-World War II era (strictly speaking,
since the Federal Reserve–Treasury "Accord" of March, 1951),
the federal government has relied upon monetary policy as a
principal instrument for achieving United States economic goals.
The Employment Act of 1946 placed great responsibilities upon
the federal government for maintaining a prosperous economy.
Americans have come to judge the performance of the economy,
and the record of each national administration, by more exacting
standards than have ever before been applied. As a people, we
insist upon more rapid, better sustained, and more widely shared
economic progress than we were accustomed to expect in earlier
times. Because monetary policy could be a primary means toward
these ends, we naturally expect more of it than we once did. We
inquire whether current monetary institutions, processes, and
controls are yielding their full potential values in regulating the
economy. We wonder whether the monetary concepts that guide
the Federal Reserve System's policy have even been adequately
formulated and appraised.

Much of the difficulty of questions of monetary policy arises
from lamentable gaps in our knowledge of basic monetary relationships. For example: What factors determine the "demand"
for money by households or by business enterprises? Is there a
stable relationship between the flow of income into a family or its
stock of wealth, on the one hand, and the amount of money it
desires to hold, on the other? What is the optimal stock of money
in the economy under various circumstances? How do nonbank
financial institutions influence the behavior of the money supply?
What are the rules that should guide the monetary authorities in
adjusting the stock of money and credit through time? What are
the time lags involved between actions of the monetary authorities and the responses of the economy?

Dependable answers to monetary questions will, of course,
require a great deal more fundamental research. But better monetary policy in the future will also require education in and discussion of the monetary facts and relationships discovered by
research. Research and education are indispensible to each other.

Education, without the knowledge revealed by research, can be stultifying. Research, unaccompanied by the education that puts new knowledge into action, can be sterile. Our purpose in this volume is educational—to raise the important issues of contemporary monetary policy in a systematic framework, and to bring to bear upon those issues such knowledge as we possess.

In the present chapter we shall refrain from taking a position on monetary issues: That is done by other contributors to this volume. Being free, for the time being, of the annoying responsibility to answer difficult questions may enable us to concentrate attention upon the formulation of monetary issues in ways that put our minds in motion down the right channels. Proceeding on the aphorism that a question well posed is half answered, let us try to set out in an orderly fashion the monetary problems that beset our economy.

WHAT IS "MONETARY POLICY"?

First of all, what is meant by "monetary policy"? A little thought makes it evident that the phrase can have both a broad, comprehensive meaning, and also a strict and narrow interpretation.

Broadly speaking, "monetary policy" can be conceived to embrace *all measures undertaken by government or by private enterprises to affect the structure and operation of the financial system of the economy or the supply and use of money by the public.* Such measures include the selection of a monetary standard and the organization and regulation of the central bank, banks of deposit, and nonbank financial institutions. They include the constitution and management of federal lending and loan-insuring agencies, such as those in the Housing and Home Finance System, the Farm Credit System, or the Small Business Administration. In this broad conception, "monetary policy" would also include governmental actions with respect to public expenditures, taxation, and the management of the public debt. Indeed, under an inclusive definition a large part of public economic policy can, without strain, be brought under the broad umbrella of "monetary policy."

A much more restrictive concept of "monetary policy" is, however, customary in American economic writing and thinking. The phrase is ordinarily taken to refer to *the regulation of the supply and use of money (currency and bank deposits) by the Federal Reserve System.* "Monetary policy" in this narrower sense is concerned with the objectives and instruments of control of money and credit in the hands of the Board of Governors of the Federal Reserve System and the Federal Reserve Banks. It considers all transactions between the central bank, commercial banks, financial intermediaries, and the public that influence the demand for and the supply of money.

In this volume we are concerned primarily with monetary policy in the strict sense. The major features of the U.S. monetary system, such as a currency unit having a fixed amount of gold and a fractional-reserve banking system, will be taken for granted. We shall put to one side such monetary problems as alternative monetary standards, fixed or variable exchange rates with other currencies, 100 per cent reserve banking, international monetary arrangements, and the financial constitution of the domestic economy. We focus attention upon Federal Reserve policies and instrumentalities of monetary management. The *general* instruments include open-market purchases and sales of government securities, discount rates and policies, and adjustments in the ratios of reserves to deposits that member banks in the System are required to maintain in the Federal Reserve Banks of their respective districts. In addition, the System possesses a *selective* instrument of control in its power to fix the terms of stock-market credit. In the past, the System has also exercised selective control over the terms of installment credit to purchase automobiles; and selective control of home mortgage credit has frequently been proposed.

Although monetary policy in the narrower sense can wield a powerful influence upon the economy, it is inescapably connected with U.S. public policies regarding taxation, expenditure, lending and loan insurance, debt management, and international trade and investment. It cannot be formulated or evaluated apart from policies in these other spheres by other important countries as well as our own in an interdependent Free World economy. The connections of monetary policy to these other policies must be understood before any useful conclusions can be reached about the adequacy of the current machinery of monetary management and the principles that should guide its operation.

A Framework of Monetary Policy Analysis

It is helpful to portray in a flow diagram major causal influences, and their interrelationships, which bear upon the performance of the United States economy. Although much oversimplified, Figure 1 shows the main linkages between monetary policy instruments and economic goals, and the stages in this chain of influence at which nonmonetary forces come into play.[12]

Monetary policy produces its effects upon the performance of the economy *indirectly*—by influencing the aggregate amount and composition of effective demand for goods and services and the interest rates charged for investment funds in the financial markets of the nation. But its influence upon aggregate demand and interest rates is, again, indirect, being primarily upon the size of the stock of money held by households, business firms, and nonbank financial institutions. The money stock, in turn, is controlled mainly by the amount of member-bank reserves. Under our fractional-reserve banking principle, member banks of the Federal Reserve System are required to maintain in the Federal Reserve Bank of their district a specific minimum amount, averaging about 15 per cent, of their deposits in cash. An individual bank is able to make additional loans and investments, thereby creating additional demand deposits for the public, only to the extent that its current balance with its Federal Reserve Bank exceeds its legal reserve requirement. However, the customers of any individual bank will check against the deposits created by its loans to them, and these checks will be deposited mainly with other banks, adding to their excess reserves and lending power. If they, too, add to money stock by making additional loans and creating deposits, some of them will flow back as deposits in the original bank. Thus, in theory the banking system as a whole ultimately

[12] Figure 1 is approximate and ignores feed-back effects in a dynamic model. An alternative flow diagram might show *monetary policy variables and the gold stock* determining the *monetary base* (bank reserves plus currency), which, along with the public's division of money balances into deposits and currency and the banks' division of their assets between loans plus investments and reserves, controls the *supply of money*. Money supply, taken jointly with public demand for money and the public's supply of assets to the banks, determines *aggregate demand* and *interest rates,* which, in turn, determines *real output* and *the price level.* Through time, the latter variables feed back influences to the former.

FIGURE 1

FLOW DIAGRAM OF MAJOR MONETARY AND OTHER INFLUENCES
UPON UNITED STATES ECONOMIC PERFORMANCE

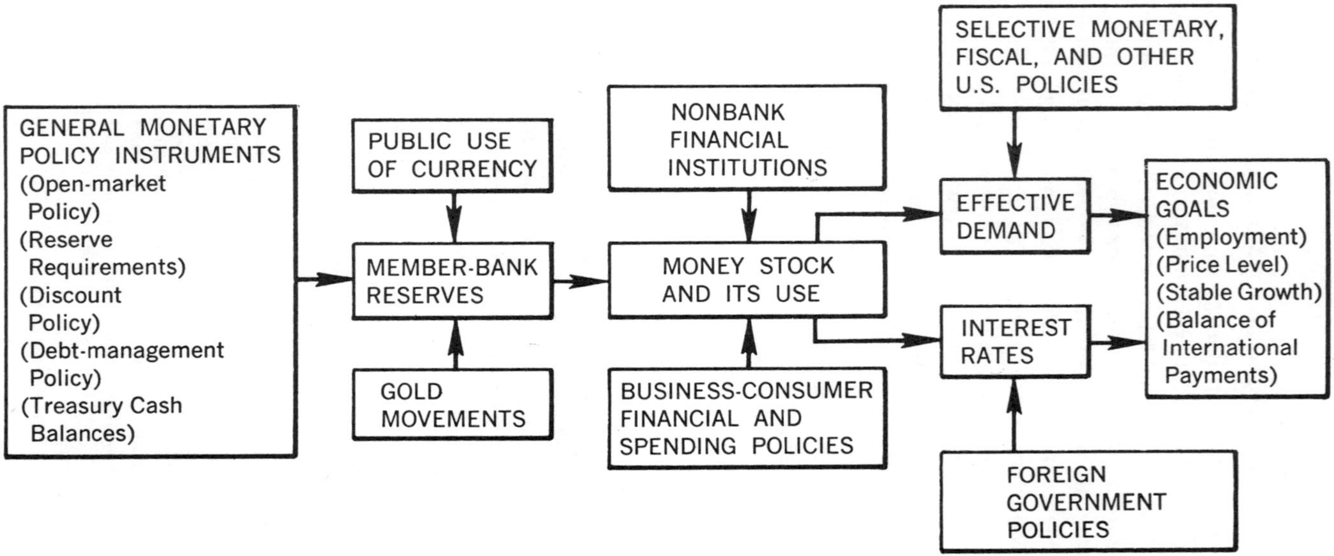

should be able to add about $7 of money for each additional
$1 of reserves. Empirical studies indicate that the actual mul-
tiplier is much smaller—between 2.5 and 3.0—which implies that
a large fraction of new bank credit spills over into additional
currency. By controlling the amount of reserves through open-
market operations, discount rates, and legal reserve requirements,
the Federal Reserve authorities nonetheless can exert a powerful
leverage on the total money supply.

Not only is the influence of general instruments of monetary
policy indirect, but it is *partial and incomplete*. At each stage in
the chain of causation depicted in Figure 1, other important variables come into play, which are outside the control of the Federal Reserve authorities and which may either magnify or offset
the influence of monetary policy. Again, let us start with goals of
economic performance, and work backward.

Effective demand for final products of the economy and the
interest rates ruling in financial markets are a product not simply
of the stock of money (currency and bank deposits) in the hands
of the public. They are also determined directly by selective
monetary policy instruments, and even more importantly by the
taxing, spending, and lending policies of the federal government
which bear upon the net spending power of the public.

It should be observed, in this connection, that only *selective*
monetary policy instruments, such as Federal Reserve control of
the terms on which stock-market credit can be made available to
lenders, exert a *direct* influence upon the amount of effective demand for equity securities. Domestic interest rates depend not
alone upon Federal Reserve adjustments in the money stock, but
also upon the interest rates ruling in the financial markets of
major foreign countries with which the United States maintains
active economic relations. This greatly complicates the task of
formulating monetary policy. It becomes necessary to gear U.S.
monetary policies into U.S. fiscal and other policies bearing upon
aggregate demand, and also to take into account financial relations of the U.S. economy with the rest of the world and the way
in which those relations are being influenced by the policy actions
of foreign governments.

To take a familiar example, attainment of high levels of production and employment at home may call for U.S. monetary policies conducive to the expansion of effective demand and to the lowering of interest rates. But if the U.S. already has a large deficit in its international balance of payments, a liberal monetary policy may well expand U.S. demand for foreign imports and for foreign investments yielding higher rates of return, thus enlarging the deficit in the U.S. balance of payments beyond prudent levels. In this circumstance, a preferable public policy might be to restrain the growth of credit and to maintain higher money rates by a restrictive monetary policy, while expanding domestic demand through tax reduction and liberal fiscal measures.

The amount of effective demand in the economy is determined not only by the stock of currency and bank deposits held by the public, and by its current flow of money income. It is also influenced by the financial policies of households, business firms, and nonbank financial institutions in using the spending power they possess. These are factors beyond the direct influence of the Federal Reserve authorities. They determine what economists call the "income velocity" of circulation of money. Are the habits, preferences, and financial policies of these different groups of money-users relatively stable through time, so that the Federal Reserve authorities may ignore them in formulating monetary policies? Or do they change with such frequency and unpredictability as to call for major adjustments in monetary policies, and perhaps for equipping the Federal Reserve authorities with new, special powers of control over nonbank financial institutions? In technical language, the basic issue is whether the demand function for money is relatively stable through time. Recent studies support an affirmative answer to this question.

To be more specific, do savings and loan associations, life insurance companies, pension funds, and other financial institutions tend to build up idle money balances under some conditions and to deplete these balances in acquiring investment assets under other conditions, thus introducing a disturbing influence in the rate of use of money? This issue has been debated extensively by economists in recent years.[13] Although the weight of evidence and

[13] Professors Gurley and Shaw have proposed that the main nonbank financial institutions, as well as banks, should be required to maintain

opinion currently favors the view that no special new instruments of control are necessary, the issue is by no means settled.

Moving back another step in Figure 1, it is to be noted that the amount of member-bank reserves is depicted as a function of the general monetary policy instruments. Although it is true that the Federal Reserve authorities can dominate the amount of member-bank reserves available for backing up bank deposits and, under a fractional reserve system, can thereby effectively control the potential stock of money, two important qualifications of their power exist. First, although they can make reserves available to commercial banks by open-market operations, discount policy, or adjustment of legal reserve requirements, they *cannot compel* member banks to expand their loans and deposits. Loan and deposit expansion (and thereby increase in the money stock) depends also upon the willingness of banks to lend and of consumers and business firms to borrow. The power of the Federal Reserve authorities to curtail further expansion of the money stock, or to bring about a reduction in the outstanding stock, is clear enough. Faced with a shortage of reserves, a member bank is obliged to call loans or to sell investments. If the whole banking system is short of reserves, all banks must contract loans and the aggregate amount of deposits and the stock of money will shrink. But the ability of the Federal Reserve System to expand the money supply by augmenting the amount of reserves available to member banks is limited and conditional. Even though the amount of reserves made available to member banks is greatly increased, general pessimistic expectations in the economy may inhibit a recovery in the demand for loans. Thus interest rates may fall to very low levels, as they did during the 1930's. Because the cost of being liquid becomes negligible, a liquidity "trap" may develop, manifested in the presence of large excess reserves in the banking system for extended periods of time. Although the reality of this argument has been questioned, this "asymmetry" in the ability of monetary policy to check an inflationary boom in comparison with its ability to lift the economy out of a recession may be an important limitation.

---

minimum legal reserves that are variable in the discretion of the Federal Reserve authorities.

A second qualification of the power of the Federal Reserve authorities to control bank reserves lies in the fact that their amount is partly dependent upon the public's use of currency, and upon inflows and outflows of gold resulting from decisions of foreign central banks and other foreign claimants on the U.S. gold stock. However, these factors are not serious impediments to the operation of monetary policy. The public's use of currency ordinarily varies predictably through the seasons of the year. Gold flows can be controlled, or at least predicted with some confidence, by cooperation between the Federal Reserve Board and central banking authorities of other countries. Hence, the Federal Reserve authorities can take these influences upon bank reserves into account in utilizing the instruments of general monetary policy.

To summarize: It is apparent that one set of issues of monetary policy concerns the magnitude, speed, and leverage of changes in general monetary policy instruments upon the performance of the economy. Another set has to do with the choice of reforms in monetary policy to increase the speed, leverage, and predictability of their effects upon output, employment, and the international balance of payments. To use a mechanical analogy, present monetary machinery is far from being a precision instrument. Rather, it is a complex loose aggregation of shafts and gears that works with so much friction and slippage that the timing and magnitude of its "work" output cannot be closely predicted from its input. Moreover, the monetary machine is only one part of a far larger and more complex economic mechanism, to which the monetary mechanism is not closely geared and which has a different set of controls. Changes in any one of a large number of nonmonetary factors can strengthen or weaken, accelerate or decelerate, the effects of changes in monetary policies. Although a vast amount of time and ingenuity has been expended by economists during recent years in sharpening theories of monetary relationships and testing their validity, a large area of ignorance and uncertainty remains. Within this area, informed judgments must be made by the monetary policy-makers.

With this general framework of monetary policy analysis in mind, we may now state the principal issues of monetary policy that arise in each of a number of contexts.

MONETARY POLICY AND U.S. ECONOMIC GOALS

Perhaps the most fundamental issues of monetary policy have to do with its primary purposes. We assume that monetary measures should contribute to the realization of generally accepted national economic purposes, including full employment, steady growth of output, a stable price level, and long-run balance in U.S. financial relations with the rest of the world. Monetary policy should foster the growth of the U.S. economy at the maximum sustainable rate, while maintaining a dollar of dependable buying power and a satisfactory balance of international payments. And it should do this within an economy giving maximum play to competitive private enterprise, open markets, and individual freedom.

Are the several economic goals compatible with each other? What is the role of monetary policy in achieving each of them? Should the central bank have the single responsibility of trying to maintain a stable purchasing power for the dollar, or should it have plural objectives?[14] Does a conflict exist between full employment and stable growth of production, on the one hand, and maintenance of a stable price level, on the other? If there really is such a conflict, which goal should take precedence in formulating monetary policy? Or must such a conflict be resolved by other public policies that curb excessive powers of labor unions or business corporations over wages and prices, and thus make prices more flexible and resources more mobile than they now are?

Is there a fundamental conflict between the goals of rapid growth of domestic output and employment and long-run balance in the nation's international payments? If so, which goal should monetary policy serve? Is it necessary to seek the solutions to such an incompatibility in *nonmonetary* measures that increase the flexibility and efficiency of the U.S. economy and harmonize and coordinate the economic policies of Free World countries? If wage rates and prices are controlled to a significant extent by

[14] Professor Jacob Viner has argued that the central bank's mission should be restricted to maintaining a stable purchasing power of the monetary unit. See his *Problems of Monetary Control*, Essays in International Finance, No. 45 (May, 1964), (International Finance Section, Princeton University, Princeton, N.J.).

private groups, monetary policy per se will not be an adequate weapon for combating price inflation. It can make its maximum contribution to our economic purposes only in an economy in which competition is effective and in a world in which competitive forces are given reasonably free play in determining international flows of trade and investment.

ROLE OF MONETARY POLICY VERSUS FISCAL POLICIES

A separate and equally formidable set of problems arises in defining the role of monetary policy, as against fiscal (and other) policies, in the total economic policy "mix" that will be optimal for the attainment of economic targets. Here must be noted the existence of two schools of thought among economists and policy makers.

The neoclassical school is inclined to assign monetary policy a leading role in the economic drama, and to regard regulation of the money stock as an active and important force in the performance of the U.S. economy through time.[15] The implication is that *relatively* less importance should be attached to fiscal policy—the regulation of federal taxation, expenditures, and debt management in the effort to attain economic goals. The Keynesian school, on the other hand, is inclined to denigrate the role of monetary policy and to elevate fiscal policy to the stellar role. It regards the indirectness of its influence on spending as a serious fault. It is particularly impressed by the alleged inability of monetary policy to stimulate economic activity in times of recession.

Where does the truth lie between these poles? Most economists will agree that monetary policy can be relatively more effective in curbing an inflationary boom, and fiscal policy relatively more prompt and predictable in stimulating aggregate demand in times of underemployment; but this still leaves a wide area for differences in judgment about the degree to which flexible monetary and fiscal policies should be used under various circumstances. Judgments—no matter how well informed—are never a good substitute for tested and systematic principles.

[15] For a strong elucidation and defense of this position, see Milton Friedman and Anna Jacobson Schwartz, *op. cit.*, chap. 13.

About the need for coordination of monetary, fiscal, and debt-management policies there is no debate. Clearly, it would be folly to expect beneficial results from an expansionist monetary policy if, at the same time, the Treasury is reducing income available for expenditure by the public by cutting government expenditures and/or raising tax rates. Vice versa, an effort by the Federal Reserve authorities to curb the expansion of bank credit could be negated if the Treasury were currently financing rising governmental expenditures by selling government securities to the banking system and providing banks with the reserve basis for expanding their loans and deposits. Does the proper coordination of monetary and fiscal policy require new governmental machinery? Or do present informal consultative arrangements suffice?

In this connection, it is argued that the power of fiscal policy to influence economic performance could be increased by Congressional action to provide for automatic changes in tax rates, based on movements of an index of prices or of the unemployment ratio, or by giving the President limited powers to vary tax rates and federal expenditures on public works. Although President Kennedy requested such powers in his Economic Report of January, 1962, the Congress has not seen fit to delegate any of its prerogatives to the executive.

Finally, what is the role of the vast network of federal lending and loan insuring agencies that has grown up since the Great Depression of the 1930's? How can their activities be made to reinforce, rather than to frustrate, general monetary and fiscal policies? Is it desirable to bring the management of these agencies under closer surveillance of the Treasury and the Federal Reserve System?

STANDARDS OF MONETARY MANAGEMENT—STATUTORY RULE OR DISCRETIONARY AUTHORITY?

As we have observed, students of monetary policy and business cycles hold widely differing opinions regarding the ultimate power of monetary policy to achieve desired ends. They differ not only in their assessment of the potential values of monetary versus fiscal and other policies, but also in their confidence in flexible discretionary management of the money stock by the Federal Reserve System *versus* an inflexible statutory rule for changing the money stock. This has given rise to the well-known "rules versus authorities" debate in economic circles during the past generation. Those who favor the present system of discretionary money management concede its shortcomings, yet they believe that our powers to diagnose and predict changes in the economy are sufficiently good, and that the economic impacts of changes in the monetary instruments can be gauged with enough precision, to make discretionary management produce better results than would a simple statutory rule, such as increasing the money stock by 3 or 4 per cent per annum.

Those who take a dim view of discretionary management argue that economic forecasting is subject to so many errors, and that there is so much uncertainty about the many time lags between identification of a change in the economy and the effective date of corrective monetary action, that *ad hoc* monetary policy is ineffective and may even be perverse. Better results would flow from a fixed rule to increase the quantity of currency and bank deposits in the economy by X per cent a year, to allow for steady growth of output without price inflation. Such a rule, according to its protagonists, would make monetary actions move in the right direction more often than in the wrong, and would prevent monetary authorities from inadvertently worsening the situation.

Would the United States get better monetary regulation under a specific statutory rule than under the discretionary exercise of its powers by the Federal Reserve authorities?[16] While the weight of opinion runs strongly counter to this view, there are a number of related questions about standards of monetary management which are debatable. Is public uncertainty about monetary policy helpful or hurtful to the processes of economic growth and stability? Granted that the Federal Reserve authorities should exercise discretion in using monetary tools, what standards or guidelines should they use in reaching decisions? What weight should they assign to the amount of excess reserves in the system? To

---

[16] Professor Modigliani concluded, on the basis of empirical tests, that during the period 1952–60, "the record appears favorable to discretionary policy, at least in comparison with any of the more commonly advocated

the amount of "free" reserves, i.e., the surplus of excess reserves over member-bank borrowings from the Federal Reserve Banks? To changes in price levels? To the unemployment ratio? What are the circumstances in which a desired economic consequence should be sought by open-market operations, discount policy, or changes in legal reserve requirements?[17] Indeed, are all of the three major instruments of monetary policy needed, or would open-market operations alone suffice, as some have argued?

SELECTIVE VERSUS GENERAL MONETARY POLICY INSTRUMENTS

Another set of issues is concerned with the extent to which selective controls over the credit that can be made available for particular uses should supplement general controls over the amount of bank reserves.

Laissez faire thinkers tend to look askance at selective economic controls of all kinds on the doctrinal ground that they constitute unwarranted interference by government with markets. They argue that, if financial markets are competitive, the relative interest rates and terms of loans available for various purposes will be impersonally determined so as to bring about an optimal allocation of bank credit. Governmental interference with this process, they aver, can only produce an inferior result. Selective monetary controls change primarily the composition of aggregate demand, rather than its amount.

Proponents of selective credit controls argue, to the contrary, that discrimination is inherent in any governmental policy to guide the economy toward national economic goals. Government now intervenes widely in financial markets with *affirmative* measures to expand selected kinds of credit for housing, farmers, small businesses, and other particular groups. Why, in principle, should

---

types of rules" in pursuing a goal of full employment. See Franco Modigliani, "Some Empirical Tests of Monetary Management and of Rules Versus Discretion," *Journal of Political Economy*, LXXII, No. 3 (June, 1964), 243.

[17] The appropriate "mix" of general monetary policy instruments has received wide attention. See especially, Warren L. Smith, "The Instruments of General Monetary Policy," *The National Banking Review*, I, No. 1 (September, 1963); and Neil H. Jacoby, "The Structure and Use of Variable Reserve Requirements," in Deane Carson (ed.), *op. cit.*

it not be free to act *negatively* in restricting the terms and conditions of supply of particular kinds of credit, if and when they threaten to produce destabilizing effects upon the economy? The United States Government has already had a far more extensive experience with selective credit controls than is commonly appreciated.

Apart from doctrinal disputes over the principal of selective economic controls, many thorny issues arise in determining the proper scope of selective controls of commercial bank credit. Apart from its brief restrictions of the terms of automobile installment credit during World War II and the Korean conflict, the Federal Reserve System has had thirty years of experience with the selective control of stock-market credit. Generally, the System has been reluctant to undertake the task of administering additional selective credit controls. Given the great fluidity of bank credit, the task of policing its usage is not an easy one. Should the Federal Reserve System be given specific or discretionary "stand-by" powers to restrict the terms and conditions of consumer installment credit? Of home mortgage credit? Should such powers be exercised by another federal regulatory agency than the Federal Reserve System? Are selective credit controls that operate positively preferable to negative controls? Or are both types needed? For example, with the benefit of hindsight, would the U.S. economy have been better off if governmental restraints upon consumer installment credit had dampened the boom in automobile demand in 1955? Although professional opinion appears to have swung toward a negative position on selective controls in recent years, the issues cannot be regarded as closed.

Limitations of Monetary Policy

We have already observed that monetary measures are not all powerful in attaining economic goals, and are particularly limited in their ability to kindle economic expansion during periods of recession. But other limitations are alleged to exist in both the efficiency and equity with which they operate.

It is said that structural changes in the U.S. economy have reduced the effectiveness of the traditional monetary instruments. Among such changes are: the great burgeoning of governmental expenditures; steep income-tax rates, which blunt the impact of rising interest rates; accelerated depreciation allowances under federal tax laws, which expand the capacity for internal financing by business; the relatively greater usage of long-term amortized loans; the recurring need of the Treasury to borrow money; the large holdings of government securities by the banks; and the growth of nonbank financial intermediaries such as life insurance companies, savings and loan associations, and pension funds. All these factors, it is said, have reduced the responsiveness of the economy to shifts in Federal Reserve policies. Above all, monetary controls of the price level are said to have been rendered impotent by "cost-push" factors, notably wage demands by powerful labor unions and pricing practices of monopolistic corporations.

All of these forces undoubtedly reduce the relative effectiveness of monetary policy; the relevant question is how important is their influence. Are borrowers really insensitive to higher interest rates and lesser credit availability in the boom, and unresponsive to lower rates and easy credit in slack times? Recent empirical research suggests, to the contrary, that monetary measures retain great power to influence economic behavior, although after considerable time lags.

The *equity* of restrictive monetary policies has also evoked much complaint. Restrictions upon bank credit are said to discriminate unfairly against small businesses, home builders, school districts, and other municipal governments, while leaving large corporations and the federal government relatively unaffected. Is there substance to these charges? The empirical evidence is not conclusive.

One fact seems clear. Much of the alleged inefficiency and inequity of monetary policy is due to a lack of adequate competition in financial and product markets, and to a failure to coordinate monetary with fiscal, debt-management, and other governmental policies. This being true, wise public policy calls for remedying these defects, and not for assigning monetary policy a lesser role in the management of the economy.

LESSONS OF POSTWAR MONETARY EXPERIENCE

Many questions arise with respect to the proper interpretation of our experience with a flexible monetary policy since 1951. How large a contribution, if any, has it made to stable economic growth without price inflation? Are the manifest imperfections in the behavior of the economy to be attributed to inadequacies in the tools of monetary management? Or have they been due mainly to the failure of the monetary authorities to act quickly and boldly enough? Is a much more flexible monetary policy indicated for the future? Or a much *less* flexible one? On the other hand, should one assess monetary performance favorably, and look mainly to improvements in fiscal, competitive, and other policies, and to a better coordination of these measures with monetary policy for a more felicitous result in future years? The Commission on Money and Credit gave the Federal Reserve good marks for its behavior since 1951. Its proposals for improving monetary policy related principally to reforms of the financial structure of the U.S. economy and the coordination of monetary with federal fiscal, debt, and credit actions. Although not all students of monetary policy will agree with this assessment, most will assign some credit to monetary policy for the relatively mild business cycles and the containment of inflation during the past dozen years.

The postwar experience of the United Kingdom with a flexible monetary policy is especially worthy of study by Americans, since the position of the United States has moved much closer to that of Britain in recent times. Both countries provide the "reserve currencies" for financing world trade, and both are obliged to operate under the constraint of avoiding long-term deficits in their balances of international payments. What monetary tools has Britain used in its effort to attain its national goals? How were its monetary policies fitted into a general strategy for growth without inflation? The United Kingdom has recently incorporated the American instrument of variable legal reserve requirements into its monetary arsenal. What lessons can we learn from British experience?

STRENGTHENING MONETARY CONTROLS

Even after structural impediments to the efficiency and equity of their operation have been removed, opportunities certainly exist to strengthen monetary controls of the economy.

Some reformers hold that monetary controls should be exercised by the U.S. Treasury, or at least placed in the hands of a governmental agency not under the influence of commercial bankers. They seek to terminate the so-called independence of the Federal Reserve System from the executive branch of the federal government, and to place monetary policy directly under an authority answerable only to the President of the United States. Others propose the establishment of a National Economic Council as a coordinating agency. It would be analogous in its field to the National Security Council in matters of defense. The President would be chairman, and the heads of the principal economic agencies of the government, including the Board of Governors of the Federal Reserve System, would be members. Although the Commission on Money and Credit was inclined to regard present organizational relationships as satisfactory, one may properly inquire whether they cannot be improved. Organizational considerations are of practical importance in determining the answers to several issues. To what extent, if at all, should the debt-management activities of the Treasury influence Federal Reserve monetary actions? Is the interest cost of carrying the public debt a pertinent consideration for monetary policy?

At another level, how can the present instruments of monetary policy be sharpened? Perhaps the most important issue regarding open-market policy has been the "bills only" doctrine. Should the Federal Reserve directly intervene in the medium- and long-term sectors of the government security market, as well as in the short-term market for Treasury bills, on the ground that changes in the rates and availability of short-term credit are not propagated to the medium- and long-term sectors rapidly enough? The Federal Reserve authorities have advocated a policy of "bills preferably" rather than "bills only," but some skeptics remain unsatisfied even with this degree of liberalization.

The instrument of variable legal reserve requirements has been a much debated issue. Opinions vary from those who hold it to be a disturbing and unnecessary tool of policy which should be replaced by a fixed and uniform reserve ratio, to those who believe that it has unique and valuable functions to perform and should be retained and improved. The idea has been plausibly defended that Federal Reserve control of the economy could be enhanced by basing legal reserve requirements upon the turnover, i.e., the rate of use, of bank deposits held by banking offices rather than, as at present, upon the geographical location of such offices. Many other reforms of the reserve machinery have been suggested from time to time, including the payment of interest on reserves by the Federal Reserve Banks, or permitting banks to satisfy part of their reserve requirements by depositing interest-bearing government securities instead of cash in Federal Reserve Banks. These latter proposals imply that current commercial bank earnings and capital accounts are inadequate. A more radical proposal is to extend Federal Reserve control over nonbank financial institutions by requiring them to maintain minimum legal reserves, variable in the discretion of the authorities. The Commission on Money and Credit recommended only a uniform reserve ratio against demand deposits in all banks and a "sparing" use of variable reserve requirements in countercyclical policy. However, its reasoning has not been persuasive to all students of banking.

Finally, the device of deposit insurance merits attention. In one sense, it is an instrument of monetary policy, because the insurance by a federal agency of up to $10,000 of deposits in each bank account is a vital bulwark of public confidence in the American banking system, and a powerful deterrent to any future deflationary shrinkage of bank loans, deposits, and money stock, such as that which shook the U.S. economy to its roots in the 1930's. In view of the fact that the price level has more than doubled since the $10,000 limit on insurance per account was fixed in 1934, is it now time to raise the insurance limit substantially? And should deposit insurance, now available to depositors in commercial banks and share owners in savings and loan associations, be extended to those entrusting their money to federal credit unions?

CONCLUSION

A short essay affords inadequate space even to state all of the contemporary issues of monetary policy, let alone to analyze or solve them. "The monetary problem stands out today as the great intellectual challenge to the liberal faith." More than a generation has passed since Henry Simons began, with these words, his celebrated article on "Rules Versus Authorities in Monetary Policy." Despite the great advances that have been made in our monetary knowledge and the institutions that embody it, these words remain true today.

Although most of the gaping faults and fissures in the U.S. monetary system of the 1930's have long since been closed, subsequent world economic developments have raised new monetary problems. The enormous expansion of Free World trade and investment since World War II, combined with a much slower growth of Free World monetary gold stocks and the persistent balance-of-payments deficits of the United States and Britain, have recently raised serious questions about the adequacy of present international monetary arrangements. Will balance-of-payments difficulties of the key countries and a deficiency in the amount of internationally acceptable means of payment erect barriers to the future expansion of Free World economies? If so, what should the United States, in cooperation with other free nations, do about these problems? These issues go beyond United States monetary policy per se and cannot be explored here. They do exemplify the need for unremitting examination of our monetary machinery, and constant readiness to make timely reforms.

The role of the monetary system, in the United States and in the whole Free World economy, has rightly been likened to that of the heart and circulatory system of the human body. No free economy based on private initiative and open markets can survive without a healthy monetary organism. It behooves us, therefore, to avoid monetary arteriosclerosis, and to keep the system vital and flexible, in order to serve the economic needs of our own and other free societies of the world.

1. Tools and Processes of Monetary Policy*

RALPH A. YOUNG

The primary responsibility of the Federal Reserve System is to manage the money supply of the U.S. economy in the public interest. In a growing economy, this responsibility involves regulating the expansion of money balances held by the public in relation to the expansion of real output so as to minimize both price inflation and general deflation and keep the economy's transactions with other countries in sustainable balance. In other terms, the special concern of U.S. monetary policy is to foster a financial climate favorable to forces of economic growth while maintaining a relatively stable domestic purchasing power and a stable international value for the dollar.

Economic activity under modern private enterprise proceeds at an uneven rate that gives the over-all appearance of a cyclical rhythm around an upward growth trend. When spending by the public in relation to offerings of goods results in inflationary demand pressures in markets generally, monetary management has the task of restraining the expansion of bank credit and money balances. When spending falls short of market supply and deflationary symptoms are present, the job is to encourage expansion

* Associates on the staff of the Division of Research and Statistics, Board of Governors, Federal Reserve System, have generously assisted in the preparation of this chapter. Acknowledgment is made especially to Robert Solomon, Associate Adviser to the Division, for his help in shaping the text for the first edition, and to Stephen H. Axilrod for his suggestions for improving the text of the revised edition. The chapter's present version has benefited particularly from the author's collaboration in preparing a fiftieth anniversary edition of the Board's booklet, *The Federal Reserve System, Purposes and Functions,* published in December, 1963. The description of system tools and processes set forth here is generally consistent with that presented in this booklet.

of bank credit and money balances. The fact that this task can never be perfectly performed by monetary policy should not be deplored unduly, for continuing adaptation to the economy's undulation, a characteristic having many causes, helps a private enterprise economy to maintain its dynamism.

Basic Factors in Monetary Management

A modern monetary system is a complicated mechanism, with its foundation in credit transactions. In the United States, each commercial bank that is a member of the Federal Reserve System is required to keep and maintain a reserve balance with the Federal Reserve Bank in its district. This reserve balance must be kept equal to specified percentages of the bank's demand deposits and its time deposits, as defined by law or regulation.

The required reserve balances of all member banks are the fulcrum of monetary management. With a given level of reserve requirements, changes in the volume of member-bank reserves, permitted or brought about by monetary management, affect directly the ability of member banks to extend credit to customers and to assume the deposit liabilities to the public that result from these credit extensions.

In its monetary operations, then, the immediate concern of the Federal Reserve monetary policy is with the volume of member-bank reserves. The commercial banks that are Federal Reserve members hold about 85 per cent of the deposits and earning assets of all commercial banks. Many of these member banks, through interbank correspondent relationships, are in turn depositories for reserve balances of nonmember banks.

Thus, the reserves of member banks, the bulk of which are kept as balances at the Reserve Banks, serve as the effective reserve base of the entire banking system. The Federal Reserve regulates member-bank reserves through operations that initially affect its own assets—that is, Federal Reserve credit, primarily in the form of U.S. government securities held or of loans to member banks. As the System makes its credit available, the total amount of bank reserves is affected. This in turn exercises a powerful influence on the total flow of commercial bank loans and investments. And these are an important element in the total supply of credit and the dominant element in the volume of bank deposits, which is the major element in the U.S. economy's money supply.

Fluctuations in the volume of member-bank reserves, however, are brought about by a number of other factors than the amount of Federal Reserve credit which the System has extended. These other factors include:

Gold flows. The U.S. monetary mechanism, together with that of the other major countries, may be described as a managed gold standard. The U.S. dollar is defined by law as a given weight of gold, and an ounce of gold has a stabilized official value of $35. Furthermore, Federal Reserve holdings of gold currency set a formal limit to the expansion of Federal Reserve credit, since, by statute, the Reserve Banks must ordinarily hold 25 per cent of their note and deposit liabilities in this form. Movements of gold into and out of the monetary mechanism mainly reflect variations in the nation's balance of international payments.

The U.S. Treasury either buys or sells gold primarily in licensed transactions with the monetary authorities of other countries. Through these transactions, gold is either monetized or demonetized at $35 per ounce. Assume, for instance, that a foreign monetary authority sells $10 million of gold to the U.S. Treasury and that the proceeds are used to purchase goods in this country.

The first step is that a foreign account in a Federal Reserve Bank goes up $10 million and the Treasury account in the Reserve Bank goes down $10 million. Then, when the projected purchases of goods are made, dollars are sold by the foreign authority to importers in its country who pay for them with a draft drawn in favor of an American exporter. The exporter deposits the draft with his bank, usually a member bank, which in turn deposits the draft in its reserve account at a Reserve Bank. The Treasury, which originally bought the gold, replenishes its Federal Reserve Bank account by issuing an equivalent amount of gold currency to the Reserve Bank.

In this way, the gold stock of the Treasury, the gold currency reserve of the Reserve Banks, the reserve balances of member banks, and the bank deposits of the sellers of the goods are each increased by $10 million. Hence, changes in the economy's monetary gold stock are directly registered in the amount of member-bank reserve balances.

Foreign deposits at Federal Reserve Banks. Deposits of foreign monetary authorities, foreign governments, and international agencies in the Federal Reserve Banks are primarily for operating purposes. They represent a part of the dollar resources available to foreigners to make payments in this country, or to meet temporary shortages of dollars in exchange for foreign currencies. They also serve in part as monetary reserves of foreign central banks. When dollar payments are made from any such balance at a Reserve Bank, the recipients of the payments deposit them with member banks, which in turn add them to their reserve accounts at Reserve Banks. In effect, dollars are shifted from Reserve Bank balances of foreign holders to Reserve Bank balances of member banks. When foreign deposits are being built up—for example, as a result of a balance of international payments favorable to foreign countries—a corresponding drain on member-bank reserves results.

Currency in circulation. The public may hold its active money balances in the form of currency in pocket or in a bank deposit, or in both forms, but it ordinarily chooses to hold the bulk of them in bank deposits repayable on demand. While considerations of convenience, safety, and custom tend to establish a fairly stable relationship between these two forms of money balances—with currency amounting to about one fifth of the total—the division of money holding between them varies from time to time. In particular, balances held by the public in the form of currency fluctuate sharply with seasonal spending patterns.

Shifts in the form in which the public holds money, even though little or no change may occur in the total money supply, cause changes in member-bank reserves and affect monetary management. As commercial banks supply currency in response to the needs of customers, they draw down their reserve balances, first, in the form of cash on hand, and second, in the form of deposits at the Reserve Banks; as customers return currency to the banks, the banks in turn deposit amounts in excess of vault cash needs in their reserve balances at the Reserve Banks.

Treasury cash balances. U.S. government check payments are made by the Treasury from its accounts with the Federal Reserve Banks. The Treasury also keeps deposit accounts with approved commercial banks for the receipt of certain taxes and of proceeds from the sale of securities to the public. The Treasury maintains a scheduled flow of funds from its balances at commercial banks to its balances at the Reserve Banks. This scheduled inflow is designed to counterbalance the outflow of check payments made by the federal government and to keep the Treasury balances at Reserve Banks at a level that is consistent with the Treasury's current transactions needs. Treasury cash transactions, however, run into billions of dollars each month, and, despite careful supervision of its accounts, abrupt fluctuations in Treasury balances at the Reserve Banks will frequently occur. These fluctuations will cause corresponding changes in the level of member-bank reserves.

Federal Reserve float. Float represents Federal Reserve credit extended to member banks in connection with the check-collection process. One of the tests of a good monetary system is that the means of payments shall circulate freely at par in every region that the system embraces. The par check-collection mechanism of the Federal Reserve Banks is designed to help attain this end. Its effective functioning requires each Reserve Bank to credit the reserve balances of the banks in its district that forward checks for collection in accordance with an established schedule. The present schedule provides for a maximum deferment of two days. When, for mechanical reasons, checks are not actually collected within this time schedule, a Federal Reserve Bank extends credit to the member bank and float arises. For the Federal Reserve System as a whole there is always some volume of float outstanding. The amount fluctuates within each month and over the year, primarily in consequence of variations in the volume of check transactions, but also as a result of weather and other factors affecting the speed of collection by mail.

Interplay of factors. The Federal Reserve System must maintain detailed records concerning each factor affecting member-bank reserves in order to be fully informed about its past behavior, and to keep its current behavior under careful observation. Any potential change in member-bank reserves that may be brought

FACTORS AFFECTING BANK RESERVES

Weekly averages of daily figures   Billions of dollars

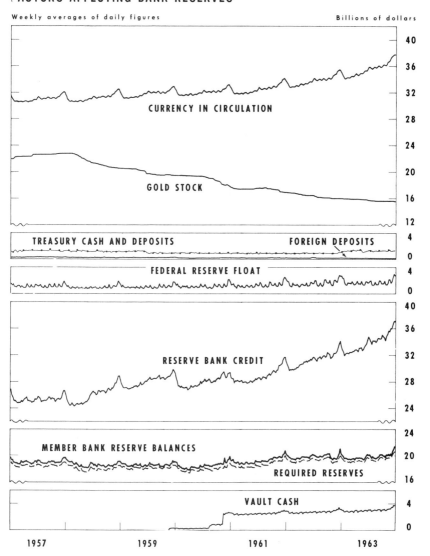

CURRENCY IN CIRCULATION

GOLD STOCK

TREASURY CASH AND DEPOSITS   FOREIGN DEPOSITS

FEDERAL RESERVE FLOAT

RESERVE BANK CREDIT

MEMBER BANK RESERVE BALANCES

REQUIRED RESERVES

VAULT CASH

1957   1959   1961   1963

about by any factor, or combination of factors, needs to be promptly identified by monetary management so that a decision may be made whether the change should be permitted to affect member-bank reserves or whether it should be offset. As is true of any dynamic mechanism, this process of administering the level of member-bank reserve balances must work with a margin of tolerance for unpredictable day-to-day fluctuations.

From the standpoint of an observer of the credit market or of a participant in it, a significant change in member-bank reserves brought about by one or more of the five factors described above can be just as indicative of monetary policy as a change brought about by overt reserve banking action. In the one case, the observer or participant infers that monetary management has permitted a change to occur; in the other case, that overt action has caused it to occur.

Although what is most important to the market observer or participant is that the quantity of reserves has changed, the way in which the change was brought about does influence the observer's view as to whether the change reflects a deliberate policy decision or was a chance occurrence of no policy significance. It also influences his view as to the likely market effects—in terms of extent and duration—of changes in bank-reserve positions.

INSTRUMENTS OF FEDERAL RESERVE POLICY

In regulating the reserve base of the commercial banking system, the Federal Reserve System relies on three interrelated instruments: open-market operations, discount operations, and changes in reserve requirements. System policy has one objective —to promote maximum economic growth over the longer run, while preserving the domestic purchasing power of the dollar and maintaining its value internationally. In carrying out policy directed to this objective, the System uses these three instruments in a complementary fashion to affect the supply of reserves and their cost to member banks.

Besides these general instruments, the System has one selective authority for influence on credit markets—the regulation of stock-market credit. This is a special-purpose instrument, designed to prevent the excessive use of credit in the stock market.

Open-Market Operations

Open-market operations generally consist of Federal Reserve purchases or sales of readily marketable asset claims in the open market. Regardless of who may sell the claims purchased or who may buy the claims sold by the Federal Reserve, these transactions have a direct impact on the volume of member-bank reserves. A distinctive aspect of open-market operations is that they are undertaken at the initiative of the Federal Reserve System and, therefore, are an active reflection of prevailing monetary policy.

Explanation of operations. Open-market purchases or sales of the Federal Reserve are made by the manager of its open-market account—who is an officer of the Federal Reserve Bank of New York—under instruction of the Federal Open Market Committee, the System's central policy-setting body. These transactions are in United States government securities primarily, but they may include bankers' acceptances in relatively small amounts and foreign currencies as directed by the Committee. The purchase or sale orders are placed through the open-market account manager with dealers who buy and sell on their own account as well as for others, and who are prepared to permit the execution of orders to affect their own inventory of such assets.

The established dealers in the government securities market, where the bulk of Federal Reserve open-market transactions takes place, number about a score. Placement with them of orders for securities by System account is usually preceded by competitive bidding among the dealers and is typically on the basis of the best price offered or bid by them.

When the Federal Reserve, via the manager of the open-market account, places an order with a dealer for a given amount of government securities, the dealer either buys the securities in the open market or sells them from his own portfolio. In payment the dealer receives a check on a Reserve Bank, which he deposits in his own account with a member bank. The member bank then deposits the check in its reserve account with a Reserve Bank. Federal Reserve purchases of government securities thus add to the reserve balances of member banks. Conversely, sales of securities reduce reserve balances. The resulting changes in reserve positions affect the ability of member banks to make loans and to acquire investments.

Sometimes System purchases of securities are made under agreement that the selling dealer will repurchase the securities within a specified period of fifteen days or less. These arrangements provide reserves on a temporary basis—put-out reserves with a string on them, as it were. This type of operation also provides dealers in government securities with temporary financing of their inventories when funds are not freely available in the market except at interest rates significantly higher than yields on their inventories.

Evolving practices. Between 1953 and 1960, Federal Reserve open-market operations were largely confined to short-term government securities—primarily to Treasury bills maturing within ninety days—a practice that came to be dubbed by System observers as "bills only," or "bills preferably." This practice derived from the fact that short-term securities are the closest to cash of any market instrument, and also have the most active and continual trading of any sector of the market. Transactions in these securities, therefore, affect bank reserves with a minimum of direct effect on the market supply of and demand for securities and so on market prices and yields.

Various factors account for the active and continual trading in the short-term end of the government securities market. Most important is investment by commercial banks as well as other financial institutions of the bulk of their operating or secondary reserves in short-term government securities. Likewise, large commercial and industrial corporations invest in them much of their excess cash balances and funds accumulating for large payments, such as taxes and dividends. Short-term government securities are, in effect, a haven in which liquid funds of the financial and business community can earn an interest return until they are needed for operating purposes. Sales and purchases made daily by thousands of banks, other financial institutions, and businesses in adjusting their operating positions make for a steady stream of trading in short-term securities.

During and for a period following World War II, the Federal

SYSTEM HOLDINGS OF U.S. GOVERNMENT SECURITIES

Weekly averages of daily figures

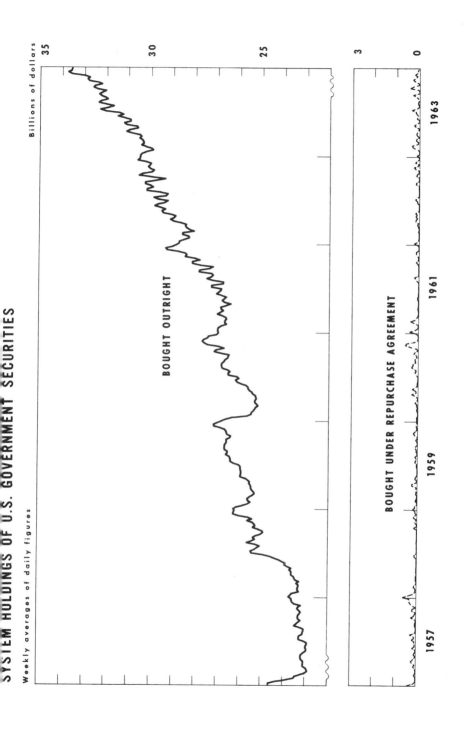

Billions of dollars

BOUGHT OUTRIGHT

BOUGHT UNDER REPURCHASE AGREEMENT

Reserve supported the entire market for U.S. government securities; that is to say, for the general purpose of stabilizing prices and yields, it bought and sold freely government securities of all maturities. As a result, all maturities of government securities had the same market liquidity.

This experience demonstrated that System use of open-market operations to stabilize market prices and yields of federal securities precluded their use to regulate the reserve position of the banking system. Indeed, the market was free to expand commercial bank reserves simply by selling more securities than would be purchased without Federal Reserve intervention. In stabilizing the market, the System functioned as residual buyer, automatically creating bank reserves in the process.

This operating dilemma came into sharp focus when the Korean crisis in 1950 brought a resumption of inflationary trends. To resolve the dilemma, an accord was reached with the Treasury early in 1951 that the Federal Reserve would discontinue stabilization of prices and yields on government securities and henceforth conduct its open-market operations with a view to keeping to a minimum the conversion of government securities into bank reserves through Federal Reserve open-market operations in support of the bond market. Two years later, the Reserve System decided that open-market operations would henceforth be directed solely to effectuating the objectives of its credit and monetary policy.

Other reforms of open-market practice. The relationship of open-market operations to Treasury debt-management operations was also modified early in 1953. During World War II, the Reserve System used its open-market instrument to facilitate Treasury borrowing operations. These activities, which continued after the war, involved System open-market account transactions in maturing issues, in when-issued securities, and in outstanding issues of maturities comparable to those being offered by the Treasury in a particular refinancing. One effect of such operations was that the System, with its virtually unlimited resources, competed against the market in such transactions. Market traders, in consequence, tended to limit their own trading during the period of the refinancing, obliging the Federal Reserve to release more of its credit than was perhaps desirable at the time. Accordingly, to avoid having a market too dependent on Federal Reserve credit and to limit the System's market participation to a purely monetary objective, this kind of operation was discontinued.

Even though this reform relieved the System of responsibility for supporting Treasury financings, it did not eradicate the risk to their success deriving from concurrent monetary actions. Over a period of time, the reality of this risk led the System to avoid abrupt changes in conditions of bank credit availability and cost just before, during, and immediately after Treasury financing operations. This practice has come to be called "maintenance of an even keel" during periods of Treasury refinancing or new cash borrowing, other than through auctions of Treasury bills. While at times the shifting of desirable monetary action to periods before or after Treasury financings may be disadvantageous, such shiftings are apt neither to be frequent nor to have much adverse effect on a monetary policy consistent with the goal of economic stability.

An additional change in Federal Reserve open-market methods was made in 1953. In the late 1930's the System began to state in official publications that maintenance of orderly conditions in the money and securities markets was one aim of its open-market operations. During and immediately after World War II, this objective was extended to mean a firm stability of prices and yields for all sectors of the market. Since this experience demonstrated that open-market operations conducted for market orderliness ran the risk of becoming operations to stabilize market prices and yields and of adding to or subtracting from bank reserves without regard to the economy's needs for more or less money, some other guideline for System interventions was sought. After extended study, it decided to limit its intervention in the market for purposes of coping with its day-to-day instabilities to the correction of disorderly conditions, should such conditions develop.[1]

Debate over operations in short-term securities and its outcome. The Reserve System's general practice during the 1953–1960 period of confining open-market operations to the short-term sector of the market eventually came under sharp attack. According to critics, the practice prevented the System from fostering economic stability by directly influencing long-term interest rates.

Interest rates on government securities, these critics argued, are pivotal rates in the U.S. capital market. Because there is no risk of default on U.S. government securities, their market yields run lower than yields on other securities, but by a fairly consistent margin that reflects the constant appraisal by investors of the worth to them of the risk differential. It was thus contended that System transactions in long-term government securities could affect the market supply as well as the volume of funds available to the whole long-term market and consequently the prices and yields in that market. By affecting market supply, prices, and yields in this way, the argument ran, the System could influence significantly the volume of long-term financing and thereby the volume of the economy's investment activity.

Against this criticism, the defenders of limiting System open-market operations to short-term securities contended that such operations exerted their main effect on the credit and capital markets via bank reserve positions.[2] Under the percentage reserve system, additions to or subtractions from commercial bank reserves have a multiple expansive or contractive effect on bank lending and investing power. Thus any given change in System holdings of securities is typically accompanied by a change several times as large in commercial bank portfolios of loans and investments. Consequently, the major influence of System open-market operations on market prices and interest rates stems not from the operations themselves, but from commercial bank transactions in securities to expand or contract their loan and investment portfolios. In other words, the direct effect on market prices and interest rates resulting from an increase or decrease in Federal Reserve holdings of particular securities and a corresponding decrease or increase in their market supply will be minor, while the indirect effects resulting from changes in commercial bank portfolios will tend to be large. And in evaluating this contention, it should be kept in mind that the size of System open-market operations is ordinarily very small in relation to the volume of any category of securities outstanding in the market.

The defenders of the so-called "bills preferably" doctrine further argued that commercial banks are unique financial institutions, combining both monetary and savings functions. In this dual role, they acquire assets having maturities distributed throughout the range of the market. Thus, changes in the level of their combined reserve balances give rise to resulting bank portfolio transactions in all sectors of the market, and so exert a pressure on long-term interest rates as well as on short-term interest rates.

Moreover, other investors in government securities, especially savings institutions, maintain a distribution of maturities of their portfolio holdings adapted to their needs. The professional managers of these portfolios must be constantly alert to changes in the various supply-and-demand factors in the market, including the changing reserve-and-asset position of the commercial banks. Their alacrity in adapting their portfolios to changes in market factors, it was contended, thus helps to spread the effect of changes in bank reserve positions on interest rates through the entire market.

Whatever the merits of these respective arguments as to the technique best suited for the conduct of System open-market operations in government securities, developments during the late 1950's and early 1960's in the U.S. balance of payments and in relationships between the U.S. credit market and credit markets in other major trading nations abroad put the issue in a quite new perspective. For most of the postwar period, the United States balance of payments had been in moderate deficit, but this was at a time of general dollar shortage with widespread restrictions by foreign countries on currency convertibility and capital flows.

In the late 1950's, the period of so-called dollar shortage seemed to end—as exports of foreign countries became increasingly competitive in world markets and as the international liquidity positions of major industrial countries were restored from their low postwar levels—and restrictions on convertibility and capital flows were substantially reduced. One sign of the end of the dollar shortage was the emergence of a large and, as it turned out, persistent deficit in U.S. international transactions, which was reflected in a substantial decline in the U.S. gold stock. The emergence of close interrelationships among conditions in leading world financial markets also influenced the United States international position. Accordingly, balance-of-payments deficits in the early 1960's came to reflect enlarged outflows of capital from the United States to foreign countries.

Experience in 1959 and 1960 in particular demonstrated that shifts in relative levels of interest rates here and abroad could quickly activate sizable flows of credit between the U.S. and foreign markets. In 1960, domestic interest levels declined relative to those abroad as economic activity in the U.S. receded, partly because of contracting borrowing demands and partly because of Federal Reserve action to encourage accelerated bank credit expansion. The result was that short-term capital outflows sharply increased from their 1959 volume, when interest levels were much higher.

In these circumstances, the Federal Reserve was confronted with a problem of minimizing downward pressures on short-term interest rates in domestic markets. Accordingly, it began, early in 1961, to conduct part of its open-market operations in medium- and longer-term securities whenever such operations could relieve such pressures on the short-term market and be carried out without undue price and yields effect. For over-all credit and monetary policy, a necessary consequence of this decision was to make evident that the cost of money in credit markets, and particularly the cost of short-term money, would henceforth be a secondary element of concern of open-market operations.

Operations in the foreign-exchange market. The extension of Federal Reserve open-market operations in government securities through the range of maturities outstanding in the market was not the only effect on System practices of the enlarged deficit in U.S. international payments. In early 1962, the System commenced to buy and sell foreign currencies in the exchange markets and in direct transactions with foreign central banks as one aspect of its open-market instrument. In formalizing its assumption of a foreign-exchange role, an officer of the New York Federal Reserve Bank was designated to be special manager of the System open-market account in charge of executing System foreign-currency transactions.

In undertaking such operations, the Federal Reserve set forth the aims of smoothing out abrupt changes in exchange rates for the dollar and also the prevention of fluctuations in U.S. gold reserves or dollar liabilities due to temporary forces acting in markets. The Federal Reserve also established three broader aims: first, to supplement the international exchange arrangements provided by the International Monetary Fund; second, to strengthen cooperation in currency convertibility among central banks and international agencies; and third, to help resolve the longer-run problem of the inadequacy of gold in meeting the world's needs for monetary reserves.

Federal Reserve foreign-currency operations, by their nature, are not apt to have a big effect on the availability conditions for bank reserves. For one thing, they are not likely to be large in any given period. For another, such bank reserves effects as they do have, if not in a desired direction, may be readily offset by System operations in government securities.

Also, by their nature, foreign-currency operations themselves could scarcely have far-reaching effects on factors ultimately responsible for the U.S. payments deficit. In this respect, monetary policy makes the bulk of its contribution to balance-of-payments stability through encouragement of price stability domestically and through attempts to minimize outflows of interest-sensitive liquid capital. Nevertheless, System operations in foreign currencies do provide an additional instrument for defending the dollar from short-term speculative payments flows and consequent outdrains of gold. In this way, they are an immediate aid in sustaining world confidence in the dollar.

Although System foreign-currency operations were initially expected to be limited in size, it seemed expedient to enter into arrangements whereby large operations could be undertaken in case of need, so that this possibility would itself be a deterrent to speculative disturbances in exchange markets. Accordingly, a network of stand-by reciprocal currency arrangements was entered into with the central banks of eleven principal trading nations and with the Bank for International Settlements, in a total amount exceeding, at the end of 1963, $2 billion of foreign currencies.

Under these arrangements, known as currency swaps, either of the agreeing parties can obtain on call a stated amount of the other's currency for an equivalent amount of his own. In the event of a drawing, the balances acquired have to be repaid by the time agreed at the same exchange rate. This protects both parties from loss in the event that one currency in the interim depreciated. The acquired balances may be invested at a pre-agreed interest rate or at any time sold in the exchange market or to the other party to the swap. If both parties concur, the agreements may be renewed any number of times.

Discount Operations

Provision of facilities for lending to commercial banks is a traditional function of central banks. In the United States, lending by the Federal Reserve Banks to member banks has come to take the form chiefly of advances secured by U.S. government securities. While commercial and other business paper of prime quality and short maturity are eligible for discounting, borrowing against government securities as collateral is more convenient and time saving for the borrowing bank, since the collateral is riskless and instantly appraisable.

From the viewpoint of the individual member bank, a decision to borrow is ordinarily prompted by the desire to avoid a deficiency in its legal reserve. Such a deficiency is likely to result from a drain of deposits and therefore of reserves to another bank. In adjusting to such a reserve drain, the individual bank has the alternative of selling an asset or borrowing at the Federal Reserve or from another bank.

When a member bank borrows or discounts at a Reserve Bank, the proceeds of the loan are added to its reserve balance on deposit at the Reserve Bank. Conversely, when the indebtedness is repaid, the amount of repayment is charged against the indebted bank's reserve balance. Federal Reserve advances to or discounts for member banks are usually of short maturity—up to fifteen days. The interest rate paid by member banks for this accommodation is known as the discount rate.

Described in this way, the discount facilities of the Reserve Banks appear as little more than a convenience to member banks, enabling them to adjust their reserve positions to shifts in deposits. The fact is, however, that use of the discount facilities, as will be explained later, puts member banks under pressure to limit their loan expansion.

Discount administration. Federal Reserve Bank discounts of member-bank paper are not automatic; the discount facilities are made available to member banks as a privilege of membership in the System and not as a right. Under Regulation A of the Board of Governors, applicable to the discount process, all of the Federal Reserve Banks in accommodating member-bank applications for discount credit adhere to the following guiding principles set forth in the regulation:

> Federal Reserve credit is generally extended on a short-term basis to a member bank in order to enable it to adjust its asset position when necessary because of developments such as a sudden withdrawal of deposits or seasonal requirements for credit beyond those which can reasonably be met by use of the bank's own resources. Federal Reserve credit is also available for longer periods when necessary in order to assist member banks in meeting unusual situations, such as may result from national, regional, or local difficulties or from exceptional circumstances involving only particular member banks. Under ordinary conditions, the continuous use of Federal Reserve credit by a member bank over a considerable period of time is not regarded as appropriate.
>
> In considering a request for credit accommodation, each Federal Reserve Bank gives due regard to the purpose of the credit and to its probable effects upon the maintenance of sound credit conditions, both as to the individual institution and the economy generally. It keeps informed of and takes into account the general character and amount of the loans and investments of the member banks. It considers whether the bank is borrowing principally for the purpose of obtaining a tax advantage or profiting from rate differentials and whether the bank is extending an undue amount of credit for the speculative carrying of or trading in securities, real estate, or commodities, or otherwise.

Member-bank reluctance to borrow. Federal Reserve Bank discount standards are in practice reinforced by a tradition among this country's banks against operating on the basis of borrowed reserves—at least for any extended period. This tradition does not mean that member banks feel reluctant to rely on Federal Reserve lending facilities to meet temporary or unusual cash drains. But it does mean that under normal conditions member banks will make a practice of limiting their resort to Reserve Bank borrowing to necessary occasions, and that once in debt, they will seek to repay promptly. Continuing pressures on their reserve positions and other special developments may, at times, weaken this reluctance, but it nonetheless persists as a factor affecting member-bank borrowing.

Member-bank attitudes toward operating with borrowed funds vary from bank to bank. Many banks never borrow from a Federal Reserve Bank, preferring to make reserve adjustments in other ways. Reluctance to borrow, as well as incentive to repay promptly, results from the disposition of depositors, especially business and financial depositors, to be critical of the liabilities assumed by temporary borrowing, since, in case of insolvency, they take precedence over the claims of depositors. Another consideration is that such borrowed funds are generally more expensive than funds obtained through deposits.

Federal funds market. In a banking system made up of as many independent units as that of this country, and with as widely varying banking conditions, individual banks will at times be deficient in reserves and at other times have excess reserves. Since total reserve funds are limited in supply, a fairly well-organized market has developed, known as the federal funds market, in which banks with balances in excess of needs offer to lend them on a day-to-day basis to banks deficient in reserves. Such transactions, when they are arranged, rarely occur at rates above the Reserve Bank discount rates, but can and do take place at rates below the discount rate when the supply of reserves is running well ahead of the demand for them.

Conditions of supply and demand in the federal funds market, and also the proximity of the federal funds rate to the discount rate, necessarily vary directly with general credit conditions and influence member-bank borrowing from the Reserve Banks. When funds are readily available in this market, use of the discount facility by member banks is reduced, largely because fewer banks are experiencing reserve deficiencies, but also because the federal funds market is a cheaper source of temporary funds.

The discount rate. Technically, the discount rate is the publicly announced charge applied by the Federal Reserve Banks on discounts or advances to member banks. And as a matter of statutory requirement, each Federal Reserve Bank must establish its discount rate, subject to review and determination by the Board of Governors in Washington, every fourteen days. Because there has been a close interrelationship between the level of Reserve Bank discount rates and short-term money rates in the market, and because the establishment of the rate entails a Federal Reserve judgment as to whether the current flow of bank credit and money is consistent with the country's transactions and liquidity needs, discount rate changes are commonly viewed as an important index of the direction of Federal Reserve policy.

The founders of the Federal Reserve System contemplated that Reserve Bank discount rates would be set in accordance with regional financial conditions. They expected that variations in regional conditions would lead to variations in discount rates among the twelve banks. In recent decades, the tendency has been for rates to be uniform, although there have been periods in which different rates have temporarily obtained. Basically, this modern tendency towards uniformity reflects improvement in the facilities and speed of communication and transport as well as further industrial, commercial, and financial integration.

Credit is the most fluid of resources and flows promptly to the market of highest yield. Growth in the number and assets of regional and national enterprises that are capable of meeting their financing needs readily in the cheapest market has increased the mobility of demand for funds. The highly sensitive markets for Treasury bills, for readily negotiable paper such as bankers' acceptances and commercial bills, for other government securities, and for federal funds provide a mechanism through which these forces of fluid supply and mobile demand ultimately converge, giving rise to pressure for equality of discount rates among the Reserve Banks. Thus, over the years, it has become increasingly appropriate to think of System discount-rate policy in terms of "the discount rate" rather than in terms of twelve Reserve Bank rates.

Relation of discount rate to market rates. The Federal Reserve discount rate and market rates on prime short-term paper are interdependent. From the viewpoint of the individual member bank, reserve adjustments can be made either by borrowing at the Federal Reserve (or from other banks) or by selling short-term assets in the market. The margin of preference as between one form of reserve adjustment and another is in part affected by relative cost. The cost of adjusting a reserve position by selling securities is measured by the interest earnings foregone. Thus, the margin of preference as between discounting and selling securities is influenced by the relationship between the discount rate and the market yields on types of securities that are likely to be held by banks as liquid assets or a second line of reserves. Prominent among these are U.S. Treasury bills and other short-term government obligations.

In a period of monetary restraint, short-term market rates tend to rise in response to demand for funds and also as a result of bank sales of Treasury bills and other prime paper of near maturity. As short-term market rates rise above the discount rate, the Reserve Banks are likely to raise the discount rate in order to maintain the discipline of the discount mechanism as a deterrent to bank loan expansion.

On the other hand, as the discount rate rises above market rates, banks are likely to shift away from discounting toward selling government securities or other prime paper as a means of reserve adjustment, in view of its lower cost. But this in itself, by increasing the market supply of short-term securities relative to the demand, tends to drive up short-term interest rates toward or above the discount rate. Thus, in a period of credit restraint, short-term market rates tend to cluster around the discount rate and they are likely to rise together in a series of upward adjustments, until the need for restrictive monetary policy has passed.

No simple rules govern the interpretation of changes in the discount rate. In some circumstances, a change in the discount rate may express a shift in direction of Federal Reserve policy toward restraint or ease. In other instances, it may reflect a further step in the same direction. In still other cases, a change may represent merely a technical adjustment to market rates designed to maintain the existing degree of credit restraint or ease.

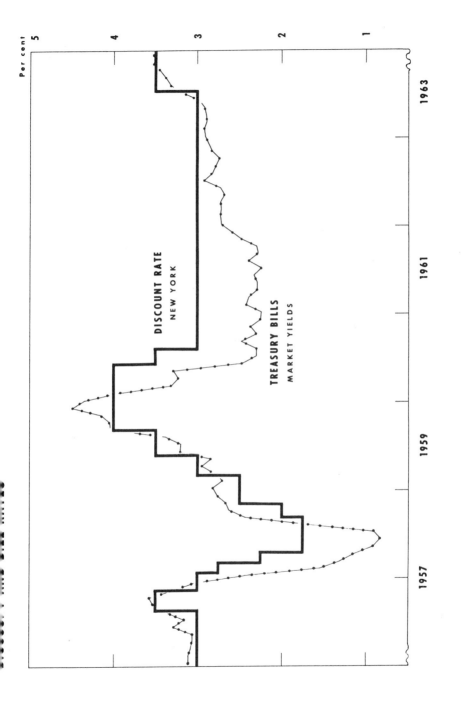

Per cent

DISCOUNT RATE
NEW YORK

TREASURY BILLS
MARKET YIELDS

1957   1959   1961   1963

Changes in Reserve Requirements

Federal Reserve authority to vary the required reserve percentages for commercial banks is a relatively new instrument of reserve banking; it was first made available through banking legislation in 1933 and 1935. The Federal Reserve System may vary within specified limits the required reserve percentages for each of the two classes of banks—reserve city banks and country banks—and for two kinds of deposits—demand and time. The permitted changes in requirements may be applied to one or both classes of banks at the same time, but they must be kept within the limits set for each class and must be uniform for all banks within a class.

The range of Federal Reserve discretion over reserve percentages and the percentage requirements in effect as of January 1, 1964, are shown in the accompanying table. The table also shows the number of member banks in each reserve class and the percentage of total member-bank deposits accounted for by each group of banks.

MEMBER-BANK RESERVE REQUIREMENTS
(As of January 1, 1964)

	Statutory range of requirements (Percentage)	Requirements in effect (Percentage)	Number of member banks in class[a]	Percentage of member-bank deposits held by class[b]
Net-demand deposits				
Reserve city banks	10 to 22	16 to ½	220	60
Other banks	7 to 14	12	5,884	40
Time deposits				
Reserve city banks	3 to 6	4	220	55
Other banks	3 to 6	4	5,884	45

[a] End of November, 1963.
[b] Average for November, 1963.

Action to change the level of reserve requirements does not affect the amount of member-bank reserve balances, but it does affect the amount of deposits and, therefore, of loans and investments that member banks can legally maintain on the basis of a given amount of reserves. A given amount of member-bank reserves, in other words, can be made to do more or less bank credit and monetary work according to the level of reserve percentages.

Two things happen when the required reserve percentages are changed. First, there is an immediate change in the liquid asset or secondary reserve position of member banks. If reserve percentages are raised, banks that have no excess reserves must find additional reserve funds by selling liquid assets in the market or by borrowing from other banks or from the Reserve Banks. If reserve percentages are lowered, individual banks find themselves with a margin of excess reserves available for investment in earning assets and for debt repayment. Since banks maximize their earnings by keeping debt free and their own resources as fully invested as possible, their usual response to a lowering of reserve requirements, after retiring indebtedness, is to acquire earning assets. Initially they are likely to purchase short-term market instruments of high liquidity as assets for temporary holding.

Second, there is a change in the rate of multiple expansion of deposits for the entire banking system. For simplicity of explanation, suppose a bank has only one kind of deposit and that the required reserve percentage is 20 per cent. Then $1 of reserves will support about $5 of deposits. If the percentage requirement is reduced to 15 per cent, $1 of reserves will support about $6.67 of deposits. The 15 per cent requirement, thus, will support one-third more deposits than the 20 per cent requirement.

The authority to make changes in required reserve percentages has sometimes been described as a clumsy and blunt instrument of monetary control. For one thing, such changes affect at the same time and to the same extent all member banks subject to the action, regardless of their individual reserve needs on the occasion. For another, even small changes in reserve requirements, say, of one-half or one percentage point result in relatively large changes in the total available reserves and in the liquidity positions of member banks as a group. If, to avoid a large reserve effect, a change is limited to a particular class of banks, a difficult and perplexing problem of equity between classes of banks is presented.

Moreover, changes to a new level of reserve requirements cannot be spread over a period of time, but must become effective on some selected pre-announced date. The credit market is fore-warned that on this date either demand or supply pressures will be accentuated, with the risk of disturbance and instability in the prices and yields on securities at the time.

Finally, there is the consideration that a bank's reserve percent-age serves as an anchor for current and forward management de-cisions. Abrupt change in the weight of this anchor can have an upsetting influence in the portfolio programs of individual—par-ticularly smaller—banks.

For these reasons, the reserve requirement instrument of mone-tary policy is not readily adaptable to day-to-day and short-run operations. Since the authority to change reserve requirements be-came available, its use has been restricted to situations calling for reserve changes of more than temporary import. Increases in re-serve requirements have been made either under conditions when excess reserves of member banks were large and widely distrib-uted, or when reserves were freely available to member banks in consequence of Federal Reserve support of the government secu-rities market. Decreases in reserve requirements have been mainly associated with efforts during recession to avert credit and mone-tary contraction and to stimulate resumption of economic growth.

Structural adjustment, nevertheless, has also been a motive for some reserve-requirement changes. Postwar decreases during re-cession periods, for example, have reflected in part a transition from high early postwar requirements to levels more consistent with earlier peacetime standards. Again, adjustments in 1960 had the purpose of unifying requirements among city banks and of offsetting the inclusion in required bank reserves of vault cash as permitted by legislation enacted the year before. Further, a reduc-tion in requirements against time-and-savings deposits in 1962 represented an adaptation largely to relieve downward pressures on money rates at a time when capital flow abroad induced by money rate incentives was tending to worsen the U.S. balance-of-payments problem.

Regulation of Stock-Market Credit

Since 1933, the Federal Reserve System has been enjoined by law to restrain the use of bank credit for speculation in securities, real estate, or commodities. Since 1934, the System has been specifically directed to curb the excessive use of credit for purchasing or carrying equity securities by regulation limiting the amount that brokers and dealers in such securities and banks may lend on securities for that purpose. At brokers and dealers, the regulatory limitation applies to any type of security; at banks, it applies only to corporate stocks registered on national security exchanges. The regulatory limitation does not apply to any loan for other purposes, even though the loan may be secured by stocks.

The mechanism of stock market credit regulation is not widely understood. The amount that lenders will loan against securities will always be less than the current market value of the securities to be pledged as collateral. The lender calls the difference between the two the customer's margin. For example, if a loan of $7,500 is secured by stock worth $10,000, the customer's margin is $2,500, or 25 per cent. Thus, by prescribing the customer's margin, the loan value of the securities may be controlled; the greater the margin required, the less the amount that can be lent. In recent years, the upper limit of the margin required by Federal Reserve regulation has been 90 per cent, the lower limit 50 per cent.

Federal Reserve regulation requires the lender to obtain the specified margin in connection with the purchase of the equity securities. If the collateral security for the indebtedness subsequently declines in value, the regulation does not make it necessary for the borrower either to put up additional collateral or to reduce the indebtedness. However, the banker or broker making a loan may require additional collateral if he deems it necessary.

Regulation of stock-market credit by the margin requirement, though bearing directly on the lender, puts restraint on the borrower and thus dampens demand for this credit. A very important aspect of this restraint is the limitation it places on the amount of pyramiding of borrowing that can take place in a rising market as higher prices create higher collateral values and permit more borrowing on the same collateral. In such periods, an increase in the required margin may be indicated in order to limit acceleration of stock-market credit expansion resulting from tendencies toward pyramiding.

The purposes of regulation through margin requirements are to

STOCK MARKET

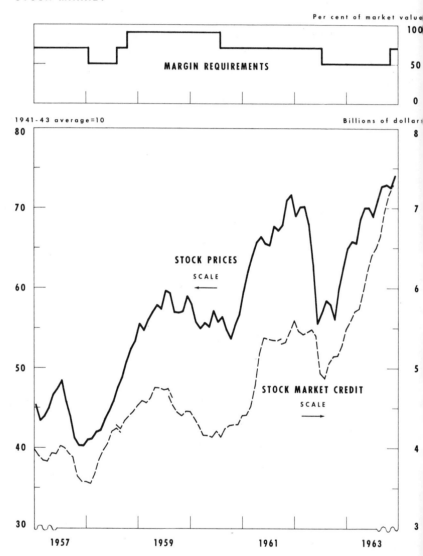

Per cent of market value

MARGIN REQUIREMENTS

1941-43 average=10

Billions of dollars

STOCK PRICES

SCALE

STOCK MARKET CREDIT

SCALE

1957   1959   1961   1963

minimize the danger of excessive use of credit in financing stock-market speculation, and to prevent the recurrence of speculative stock-market booms based on credit financing, such as culminated in the price collapse of 1929 and the subsequent severe credit liquidation. A stock-market boom followed by collapse is always possible, but without excessive feeding by credit it is not likely to assume the proportions or to have the effects that it had in earlier periods.

Other Special-Purpose Instruments

Under special conditions of national emergency, or exceptionally strong inflationary pressures, the bank-reserve instruments have been temporarily supplemented by two other selective tools —regulation of consumer credit and regulation of real-estate credit. Consumer credit was subject to regulation during World War II and for two years following, and again in two later periods of strong inflationary tendencies, including the post-Korean War period. Regulation of real-estate credit was specially authorized during the post-Korean War period. The authority for this regulation was divided between the Housing and Home Finance Administrator with respect to governmentally aided lending and the Federal Reserve System with respect to other construction lending.

These types of regulation, though effectuated through the lender, accomplished their purposes by making the conditions of borrowing more restrictive to the borrower, thereby dampening his demand for credit. They limited the amount of credit that might initially be granted by a lender in relation to the value of the property being financed, or they limited the time that might be agreed upon by borrowers and lenders for the repayment of obligations, or they did both. All grantors of credit of the types specified under these regulations were subject to them, were required to register under them, and could be penalizd for their violation.

In postwar years, these two regulations were imposed under special and temporary authority provided by the Congress. Although statutory authority for their application has not been available in recent years, public discussion of the desirability of such authority has recurred from time to time, especially with regard to regulation of consumer credit. In 1956 and 1957, the Board of

Governors of the Federal Reserve System, at the request of the President and the interested committees of the Congress, undertook a comprehensive investigation of consumer installment credit with a view to the advisability of a continuing authority for its regulation, when appropriate, in periods of inflationary pressures. The evidence assembled through this study concerning the desirability of such an authority was inconclusive, and, consequently, no statutory enactment was either recommended or provided.

The regulation of consumer credit and of real-estate credit presents much more difficult problems of administration, compliance, and enforcement than arise in regulating stock-market credit. These problems grow partly out of the large numbers of lenders, in addition to banks, that are affected by regulation. They also stem, however, from the diversity of financing practices and circumstances that characterize these credit fields. These instruments, consequently, are less flexible and adaptable selective tools than is the margin requirement instrument.

COORDINATION OF MONETARY POLICY INSTRUMENTS

In its monetary management operations—seasonal, cyclical, and growth—the Federal Reserve System's major tools are those affecting the reserve position of member banks. Open-market operations are the most flexible and constantly used instrument, and hence the principal means of coping with short-term forces influencing member-bank reserves, including those associated with seasonal variations in the public's uses of currency, in Federal Reserve float, and in business, farmer, and consumer use of bank credit. Discount operations, while they play some part in cushioning seasonal pressures on individual banks or on groups of banks in communities subject to special seasonal fluctuations, perform their main role as a complement to open-market operations in dealing with cyclical swings in credit demand and money balances.

Provision of bank reserves for meeting the economy's need for growth in the supply of money is accomplished in part by open-market operations and in part by changes in reserve requirements. Use of the latter instrument for growth purposes may be made during economic recessions, in order to gain whatever stimulative effects on the economy monetary expansion may have at that time. Reserve requirement levels may also be changed in special situations where large changes in the volume of reserves, such as result from sizable international movements of gold, need to be offset or cushioned.

Regulation of stock-market credit, a special-purpose instrument as mentioned earlier, functions as a supplement to the bank-reserve instruments. By providing a means of dealing directly and selectively with a highly volatile type of credit, it serves to moderate the strength of general credit action that might otherwise have to be taken as a result of stock-market speculation and credit use. Since these aspects of stock-market activity fluctuate with general business conditions, changes in the margin requirement are similarly correlated.

The main cyclical work of monetary management is carried out by complementary reliance on open-market and discount operations. The ultimate effect of the joint use of these instruments in a growing economy is on the rate of expansion of member-bank deposits and assets. When monetary policy is operating restrictively in a period of boom, there will be a retardation in the rate of expansion of total bank deposits and assets and of the active money supply—demand deposits and currency. Under a stimulative monetary policy in periods of recession, sooner or later there will be an increase in the rate of expansion of these magnitudes. Situations that require monetary action to induce an actual contraction in these strategic quantities will seldom arise.

Interrelationship of Tools in Periods of Monetary Restraint

The interplay of open-market operations and discount operations in regulating the rate of expansion of bank deposits, bank assets, and active money balances needs brief explanation. When the volume of the economy's transactions is expanding rapidly and inflationary pressures develop (as active spending financed by credit, especially bank credit, presses strongly against the availability of productive resources), restraint on monetary expansion will be called for. On the basis of historical patterns in these circumstances, the Federal Reserve undertakes open-market operations that provide a smaller amount of reserves than the banks are seeking as they attempt to satisfy the many and varied demands for credit.

As a result of this action by monetary management, individual banks will find it necessary to sell government securities in the market in order to obtain funds with which to meet demands for loans by their customers. Although such sales of securities provide additional reserves to individual banks, they do not add to over-all bank reserves unless the Federal Reserve purchases the securities. As each bank sells securities, it draws reserves from other banks, whether the securities are purchased by other banks, by businesses or individuals, or by other financial institutions.

As a policy of monetary restraint continues or is accentuated, there will be more frequent and more widespread reserve drains among member banks. This will lead an increasing number of banks to borrow temporarily at the discount window of the Reserve Banks in order to maintain their legal reserve positions. For each bank, the borrowing will be temporary, but the repayment by one bank draws reserves from other banks, which in turn will have need to borrow at a Reserve Bank. Thus, restrictive monetary action leads to a larger volume of member-bank borrowings, as more banks find their reserve positions under pressure more often.

It can be said that a Federal Reserve decision to limit the volume of member-bank reserves is, in a sense, a decision to put member banks as a group under pressure to borrow reserve funds. A higher level of member-bank borrowings, representing increasig frequency, amount, and duration of discountings by a growing number of banks, is a normal and an expected reaction to a restrictive monetary policy.

Since borrowing at the Reserve Banks adds to member-bank reserves, it may seem that use of the discount facility is more an offset than a supplement to restrictive monetary action. The discount mechanism in these circumstances serves, it is true, as a safety valve, providing banks with a temporary means of reserve adjustment. Use of the safety valve, however, does not afford an escape from monetary restraint.

In the first place, an increase in member-bank discounts does not necessarily increase on balance the total of member-bank reserves. Federal Reserve open-market operations (sales of government securities) will offset, at least in part, the increase in discounts; the rise in discounts, in fact, will be a result of restrictive open-market operations. Second, the cost of using the safety valve is likely to be increased as Reserve Bank discount rates are raised. Third, individual banks that are in debt to the Reserve Banks tend to use any free reserves that come into their possession to repay their debts rather than to make additional loans and investments, and thus restrict their own credit expansion. Meanwhile, continued Federal Reserve restriction of the supply of reserve funds requires member banks in the aggregate to maintain a large volume of borrowings.

In summary, in periods of monetary restraint member banks find it necessary or desirable to borrow to avoid reserve deficiencies. After they have borrowed, their lending policies tend to become more stringent because they are under pressure to repay their indebtedness. Yet, efforts of the individual banks to free themselves of debt to the Reserve Banks cannot free member banks as a group from indebtedness so long as the Federal Reserve maintains pressure on reserve positions. Hence, member-bank attitudes toward lending and investing will remain conservative and even become cautious.

Interrelationships in Periods of Monetary Ease

When boom in economic activity loses momentum and slacks off, correction of the excesses and distortions of the boom period may set in motion contractive forces, with the result that a period of downswing in economic activity ensues. As recession symptoms appear, the objectives of monetary management will shift from restraint to stimulation of credit ease. The Federal Reserve will supply reserves more actively through open-market operations and, if such action is deemed consistent with longer-term monetary needs, the System may supplement open-market action by reducing the level of member-bank reserve requirements.

The first response of the banking system to these actions, experience shows, will be a reduction in member-bank indebtedness to the Reserve Banks; that is to say, the initial quantity of reserve funds supplied will be promptly absorbed by the efforts of indebted banks to pay off their borrowing. When this phase has passed—and its duration will depend in part on the aggressiveness of Federal Reserve action—the funds supplied will flow into bank loans and investments, with an accompanying expansion of bank deposits.

Net-Reserve Position

The immediate focus of the Federal Reserve's policy instruments is such that the credit market partly gauges the direction of System monetary policy by observing closely the net-reserve position of banks—the difference between the aggregate of member-bank reserves in excess of requirements and member-bank borrowing at Reserve Banks. While the amount of reserves held in excess of requirements by member banks as a group will fall or rise to some extent with monetary restraint or ease, the movement of excess reserves is generally rather small. The volume of member-bank borrowing, on the other hand, moves with greater amplitude in response to changes in monetary policy.

As an index of monetary policy, the net-reserve position of member banks has various defects. For one thing, it is subject to fairly wide day-to-day and week-to-week fluctuations resulting from unpredictable changes in the various monetary factors discussed earlier in this chapter. For another, the long-run behavior of the reserve position may not be fully revelatory of monetary action, because it reflects both changes in monetary action to make reserves available and changes in bank preference for reserves. There is, in short, no unique relation between the level of free reserves and the amount of expansion in bank credit and money.

Over a period of months, though, a fairly steady upward or downward movement in free reserves will tend to reflect adaptations in the use of monetary instruments to current credit and economic developments. When, for instance, existing reserve pressure or ease is greater than is consistent with appropriate growth in the economy's supply of bank credit and money, it is, of course, desirable that such pressure or ease be moderated, and this is likely to be reflected in changes in the amount of bank borrowings and hence in their free reserves. But while the combined

Billions of dollars

EXCESS RESERVES

BORROWINGS

NET RESERVE POSITION

1957   1959   1961   1963

impact of the several instruments of monetary management is registered in the net bank-reserve position, the ultimate focus of policy is on the expansion of money balances in relation to expansion of real output, and this ultimate focus needs constantly to be kept in mind.

RESPONSE OF THE ECONOMY TO MONETARY ACTIONS

The impact of System monetary measures is transmitted to the economy at large through the commercial banking system. Their immediate effect is to influence the availability and cost of credit at commercial banks. After a short lag, reactions from the initial impulse pervade the whole credit market, affecting not only borrowers and lenders but to some degree the spending and saving decisions of all households and business enterprises that participate in the financial process.

Measures taken by the Federal Reserve to regulate the total of bank loans and investments will of necessity be reflected in the total of bank deposits or liabilities. Thus, the monetary response to System actions may be regarded from the viewpoint of either bank credit or bank deposits, or both.

Response of Bank Loans and Investments

The ability of commercial banks to extend a greater or smaller amount of credit has widespread effects on businesses, consumers, governmental units, and financial institutions. In an expansionary situation in which over-all demands in the economy are rising more rapidly than the capacity to produce, monetary policy may seek to temper the expansion of bank credit. The reaction of the commercial banks to this policy was outlined earlier; here we may note some of the effects on borrowers, spenders, and investors.

Direct impact on borrowers. As banks come under increasing reserve pressures—indicated by a rising level of member-bank borrowings at Reserve Banks in relation to excess reserves—they will dispose of government securities in order to obtain funds with which to meet the loan demands of their customers. Thus their secondary reserve positions will decline and this fact, along with their indebtedness to the Reserve Banks, will foster more caution in extending new loans or adding to their investment portfolios.

As banks begin to restrict the expansion of their assets, some marginal borrowers whose credit requests are rejected or trimmed will find it necessary to curtail their spending plans. In time, this will somewhat curtail growth in business inventory and capital expenditures, insofar as business concerns are dependent on bank financing for such outlays. The willingness of banks to acquire mortgages and to lend to consumers for the purpose of acquiring durable goods will also be lessened. As banks raise their loan standards, their willingness to lend to other financial institutions engaged in mortgage or consumer financing is likely to be reduced. In this way, monetary restraint will have an impact on the financial positions and policies of other lenders—notably, mortgage lenders and consumer finance companies.

The brake on spending that results directly from the lessened availability of loan funds at banks will be reinforced by rising rates of interest on bank loans. Higher loan rates to customers will discourage or divert some credit demands. Under strongly expansive conditions, credit demands and interest rates in the market will generally also have been advancing; this will require that banks raise their rates as one means of rationing their credit supply among the most pressing and credit-worthy borrowers.

Expansion in spending of consumers and businesses generally will be slowed as banks limit the pace at which their assets expand. The impacts on spending will differ in timing and degree from one household or business to another, varying with the dependence on credit financing and the sensitivity to higher interest rates and other credit changes.

At times when Federal Reserve policy is attempting to encourage rather than restrain credit expansion and spending, the effects will be just the reverse of those described above. As their reserve positions improve, banks will undertake to utilize additional reserves in acquiring securities and in making loans. Under these conditions, as market interest rates decline and banks compete for borrowers, customer loan rates will be lowered. The increased availability and reduced cost of bank loans will directly encourage credit-financed expenditures, with secondary effects tending to increase cash spending.

Effects on other credit markets. Apart from directly affecting the availability and cost of loans to borrowers at banks, monetary policy has significant influences on other credit markets. In periods when a tempering of monetary expansion is appropriate, banks will find it desirable to sell government securities in order to expand loans. As they do so, they absorb funds from the money and capital markets at the very time when demands for loanable funds in those markets by businesses, consumers, and governments are increasing. Thus the tendency for interest rates to rise and for capital values to decline is accentuated.

These interest-rate and capital-value movements have important effects on investment activity and on saving. Rising interest rates, particularly on long-term securities, affect directly the ability and willingness of businesses, consumers, and state and local governments to borrow in order to undertake capital investments. Here again, the impact is likely to be on marginal spending plans, and will not be uniform among borrowers and sectors of the economy. Some borrowers and areas will be more sensitive to interest-rate movements than others, reflecting greater structural reliance on credit financing.

In addition to the restrictive effect of rising interest rates on investment outlays, the reduction in market values of existing securities in the portfolios of investors and financial institutions will also inhibit spending and lending. A holder of a security whose market value falls may be deterred from selling it in order to undertake an expenditure or to lend to someone else. But even if he decides to sell, his proceeds will be less, and therefore he will be able to spend or lend less, than when market prices of securities are higher.

In periods when monetary policy is designed to encourage, rather than to restrain, credit expansion and spending, commercial banks will be in a position to supplement the supply of funds reaching the money and capital markets from other sources. The resulting conditions will contribute to declining interest rates and rising capital values, thus encouraging borrowing and spending. The main impact will be on credit-financed spending, but increased cash spending will be a secondary result.

Response of the Volume and Turnover of Money

The volume of money that is appropriate to the U.S. economy at any given time depends on many factors, including the volume of transactions to be financed and the desire of the public to hold money balances for one reason or another. There is no simple automatic relationship between the amount of money outstanding and the amount of total spending. A given volume of money can be associated with higher or lower levels of total spending, depending on the frequency with which money is used. Just as a railroad with a fixed number of cars can increase the number of passengers carried by increasing the speed of its trains or reducing their turn-around time, so a given amount of money can finance more transactions if its turnover rises. The turnover, or velocity, of money indicates how much work each unit of money does in financing transactions. It is measured by dividing the total value of transactions by the quantity of active money.

The quantity of active money is nothing more than the sum of cash-and-demand deposit holdings by all businesses, consumers, financial institutions, governments, and other units in the economy. The amount of money each money-user decides to hold has an important bearing on monetary velocity. In fact, the reciprocal of velocity represents cash balances held per dollar of transactions.

Cash balances are held for a variety of reasons. A large part of their total represents transaction balances; that is, sums of cash held as demand deposits and currency for the purpose of financing regular purchases. The need for such balances varies in part with the time gap between receipts and expenditures. For example, people who are paid each week have a larger cash balance at the beginning than at the end of the week. For people who are paid on a monthly basis, the spread between the beginning-of-month and end-of-month balance will be much wider and their average cash balance higher. The size of transaction balances also varies with income. The higher a person's income and expenditures, the larger his transaction balance is likely to be.

Cash balances are held for other reasons. They are built up as savings out of income, in anticipation of future expenditures or investments in financial assets. In many cases, they are held as contingency funds, or as provision against a rainy day. Cash balances are also held for speculative reasons, in expectation of a reduction in price of a security or a commodity.

The size of cash balances that businesses and individuals find it desirable to hold for all these purposes depends partly on the level of interest rates. When interest rates are low, the sacrifice involved in holding cash rather than an interest-bearing asset is relatively small. The higher the level of interest rates, the greater the sacrifice in holding idle cash instead of a financial asset that earns interest. A time deposit in a bank is such an asset. The form in which precautionary, contingency, or speculative balances in particular are held—whether as demand deposits or as time deposits at banks—is highly sensitive to the interest return. And in evaluating the adequacy of the economy's existing money supply, consideration has to be given to the public's preferences for near-money assets—not only time deposits, but also savings-and-loan shares, mutual-savings-bank deposits, and short-term U.S. government securities.

What is the response of the economy to changes in the rate at which the supply of money is growing, under the influence of monetary policy? At each level of incomes and interest rates, there will be an amount of money that the public wishes to hold for transactions purposes and for the other purposes indicated above. Suppose that the actions of the Federal Reserve result in a smaller volume of money than this. The result is likely to be a rise in interest rates and a reduction in expenditures as the public attempts to establish the desired level of money balances. On the other hand, a volume of money in excess of what the public wishes to hold leads to reductions in interest rates and increased spending.

As interest rates rise or fall in these circumstances, they influence spending decisions. In addition, however, such changes in interest rates interact with the demand for money balances. At any given level of income, a rise in interest rates will lead people to feel satisfied with smaller cash balances. Thus there is an accommodation, through changes in interest rates, to the available volume of money.

This type of accommodation reveals itself in variations in monetary velocity or turnover during business swings. In periods when demands for credit are strong, expansion of bank credit limited, and interest rates advancing, incentives to economize on cash balances become important and velocity will tend to rise. When these conditions are reversed, velocity will tend to decline. Although changes in velocity represent normal financial behavior, their effect is to offset in part Federal Reserve efforts to influence spending by retarding or stimulating expansion in the quantity of money.

To what extent do swings in money turnover negate the actions of monetary management? A reply to this question must be based on the recognition, in the first place, that changes in velocity in a given period of expansion tend to be self-limiting. Especially on the upside, there are limits beyond which velocity cannot be increased without great inconvenience. In other words, there is a basic minimum below which cash balances of the public at the time are not likely to be reduced, without also reducing spending.

Secondly, monetary action can influence in some degree, but only in some degree, the speed with which velocity approaches its maximum. And not always can it take full account of the effects of increasing velocity. If, for example, domestic and international conditions permit vigorous and persistent monetary action, then the sooner and more completely will such action be able to offset any countervailing changes in the use of cash balances.

Effects in Stimulating and Restraining Demand

In popular discussions of monetary policy, there are frequent admissions of its effectiveness in restricting inflationary pressures, but doubts as to its effectiveness in stimulating demands in periods of economic deflation. In view of the experience over the past century of the U.S. economy with recurrent recession and several periods of severe depression, these doubts are understandable. They overlook, however, that each of these interruptions of growth was followed by revival and expansion to new high levels of output and purchasing power. Easy credit conditions were associated with these successive recovery periods. While easy credit conditions, of course, did not determine the occurrence of recovery, their presence was an indispensable factor in it. This whole matter may be clarified by considering just what happens in the economy at large in consequence of tight or easy credit conditions.

Credit conditions tend to tighten when employable productive resources are intensively used, and demand pressures, fed in part by credit-financed spending, are very strong and potentially inflationary. Restriction on credit financing will check the expansion of money payments among businesses and to consumers at a time when additional money income would merely add to market demand and perhaps prices without expanding the supply of goods available for purchase. Curtailed spending for goods and services will have a dampening effect on the demand for the producer's equipment and machines required to make consumer goods and on the demand for other finished goods necessary to production. As expansion in spending tapers off, pressures of demand against the supply of goods generally abate. Businessmen, investors, and consumers may anticipate these developments and, through their attitudes and actions, bring them about more promptly and in greater degree. After periods of active boom and inflationary threat, this process of adjustment tends to restore stability in the economy.

In a period when total demand tends to be deficient, the advent of easy credit conditions will mean greater liquidity for the economy, partly in the form of increased cash balances. This will encourage spending. It will be supplemented by heightened incentives for credit-financed spending as interest rates decline and credit becomes more readily available. Those types of spending that are particularly sensitive to interest-rate movements and credit availability—such as residential construction outlays, long-term investment expenditures such as by public utilities, and projects of state and local governments—are likely to lead the way in this respect. The initial stimulation of spending resulting from these developments will be multiplied as businesses enlarge their money payments and consumers increase their spending. Increased total spending will thus add to the money income available for more spending and as income rises the basis for further borrowing will be established. Accordingly, the demands of consumers for goods and services will be further expanded and the ability of businessmen to improve and add to production facilities further strengthened. These conditions will give impetus to recovery and favor resumed economic growth.

This brief description of economic adjustment in a vigorous and possibly inflationary boom and potentially deflationary recession is of course oversimplified. Nevertheless, it suffices to suggest the powerful economic forces that are set in motion by tighter and easier credit conditions. Monetary policy, to be sure, will be only one factor in any given economic situation; how large a factor it becomes will depend in considerable degree on the timing and strength with which it is pressed. Monetary policy is a potent means of public policy in furthering attainment of greater domestic stability and closer international-payments balance, but, as often pointed out, it is not omnipotent.

ORGANIZATION FOR UNITED STATES MONETARY MANAGEMENT

The Federal Reserve System is a specially designed institution, planned to be a blend of public and private interest and regional and national interest. The System is coordinated by a federal government body—the Board of Governors—in Washington. A graphic view of the System's structure, in relation to its several instruments of monetary action, is shown in the accompanying chart.

Division of Responsibility for Use of Monetary Instruments

Decision-making with respect to open-market operations is vested in the earlier mentioned body, the Federal Open Market Committee. The membership of this Committee is made up of the seven members of the Board of Governors, the President of the Federal Reserve Bank of New York, and presidents of four other Reserve Banks, who serve one-year terms in rotation. All of the Reserve Banks are thus represented in the membership of the Committee in the course of three years.

The Chairman of the Board of Governors, by tradition, serves as Chairman of the Committee and the President of the New York Federal Reserve Bank serves as its Vice Chairman. The Committee has a specially designated staff, who are also members of the staffs of the Board of Governors or the Reserve Banks. The

FEDERAL RESERVE ORGANIZATION
FOR POLICY-MAKING

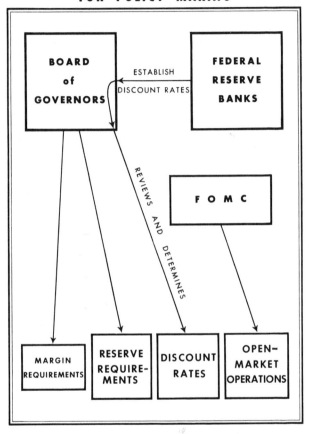

Committee's operations are conducted through the agency of the New York Federal Reserve Bank, and, as stated earlier, officers of that bank serve as manager and special manager of the open-market account.

Authority over discount operations is shared among the directors of the twelve Reserve Banks and the Board of Governors in Washington. Administration of member-bank borrowings is a responsibility of each Reserve Bank, subject to the standards for discounting set forth in regulations of the Board of Governors and subject to the Board's general supervision. Authority over the discount rate is shared by the directorates of the Reserve Banks, which establish the discount rate, and the Board of Governors, which reviews and determines it. The Board of Governors, however, may initiate discount-rate changes at the various Reserve Banks as well as act on proposals submitted to it for review and determination.

Decision as to changes in member-bank reserve requirements is the responsibility of the Board of Governors alone. So, also, is regulation of margin requirements on stock market collateral.

Coordination in policy-making. Coordination of the use of the Reserve System's tools of monetary policy has gradually come to be a function of the Federal Open Market Committee, which operates as the central clearing mechanism for over-all discussion of the interrelated policy instruments. The Open Market Committee now meets every three weeks. These meetings are regularly attended by the seven members of the Board of Governors and by the five Reserve Bank presidents who are currently members. Nonmember presidents are invited to attend, and usually do.

The formal policy decisions made at these meetings relate exclusively to open-market actions in domestic securities and foreign currencies. However, the entire credit and economic situation in the various regions, in the country as a whole, and in the international area is reviewed both in relation to open-market operations and in relation to the use of complementary instruments. This central forum of discussion enables the related policy bodies to make their respective judgments in the light of a shared economic intelligence.

Independence of the Federal Reserve System

The Federal Reserve System may be thought of as an independent instrumentality of the federal government. Both its pattern of organization and its position in the governmental structure are unique. In order to assure a nonpolitical—perhaps more accurately, bipartisan—administration of the money supply, its organization, which is a blend of public and private participation, is fortified with safeguards against domination by any special-interest group.

Its independence is not a matter of independence from government but of independence within the structure of government. In this position, its operations necessarily are consistent with the broad objectives of national economic policies. What independence means, then, is that the Federal Reserve System has independent responsibility for applying its best judgment within its technical field of monetary management.

In describing the organization and position in the federal government of the Federal Reserve System before the Committee on Finance of the United States Senate, the Chairman of the Board of Governors, in 1957, drew the following pertinent analogy of the Federal Reserve System to a public trusteeship:

> Broadly, the Reserve System may be likened to a trusteeship created by Congress to administer the nation's credit and monetary affairs— a trusteeship dedicated to helping safeguard the integrity of the currency. Confidence in the value of the dollar is vital to continued economic progress and to the preservation of the social values at the heart of free institutions.
>
> The Federal Reserve Act is, so to speak, a trust indenture that the Congress can alter or amend as it thinks best. The existing System is by no means perfect, but experience prior to 1914 suggests that either it or something closely approximating it is indispensable.

Liaison with Other Government Agencies

It is necessary and important that the Board of Governors in Washington maintain an active liaison with the other agencies of government and with the interested committees of the Congress. The maintenance of this liaison is a primary responsibility of the Chairman of the Board. It is effected on a day-to-day basis through his constant communication with the Secretary of the Treasury, the Chairman of the Council of Economic Advisers, and other officials of the executive branch, and also through his contacts with the chairmen of the Banking and Currency committees of both the Senate and the House. On the international side, it is effected through his membership on the National Advisory Council on International Financial and Monetary Problems. Regular and active interchange of information and technical intelligence, domestic as well as international, among the staffs of the government agencies serve to reinforce liaison at the top level.

MONETARY POLICY GUIDES

In the U.S. economy, all individual and group activities are affected by the use of money. Monetary management, therefore, will reflect all phases of economic life and, directly or indirectly, will influence all of them. The goal of monetary management—sustainable economic growth with a stable purchasing power and foreign-exchange value for the dollar—means a climate in which employment opportunities increase as the labor force expands, while the average of prices at which the growing national produce is sold on domestic and international markets remains relatively stable.

The objective of growth and the objective of price-level stability may, on occasion, seem in conflict. In the short run, output might be made to rise more rapidly at the expense of inflation. And for a while, when output is depressed, prices might not on the average decline and so fail to function as a stimulant to revival. In the longer run, however, without a relatively stable price level, and particularly without that expectation on the part of the public, it is most unlikely that orderly economic growth at the maximum sustainable rate would be attainable. Similarly, without growth, price-level stability would be endangered by the absence of growth forces to cushion recession and lend strength to revival.

To carry out its responsibilities, the Federal Reserve must keep informed about the great variety of economic and financial factors that bear on the current and prospective movement of the U.S. economy. For this purpose, the System maintains a research staff at the Board of Governors' headquarters in Washington and at each of the Reserve Banks, to sift current information from all available sources—regional, national, and international, private as well as public. This current information is then compared with past data so that future developments may be anticipated. The System's operating divisions are an important source of banking statistics, and its supervisory officials are an important source of

SELECTED ECONOMIC INDICATORS

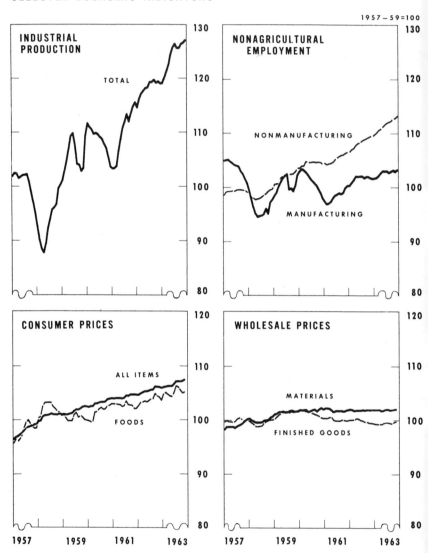

1957—59=100

INDUSTRIAL PRODUCTION

TOTAL

NONAGRICULTURAL EMPLOYMENT

NONMANUFACTURING

MANUFACTURING

CONSUMER PRICES

ALL ITEMS

FOODS

WHOLESALE PRICES

MATERIALS

FINISHED GOODS

1957   1959   1961   1963   1957   1959   1961   1963

intelligence on the credit standards prevailing at banks and related institutions and on the soundness of trends in credit use.

No single indicator tells when and by how much the volume of commercial bank reserves, and the quantity of money, should be changed. The various informational guides that are available are often conflicting in their indications. Therefore, it has become the practice of the System to seek a view of the developing economic situation, domestic and foreign, that is both comprehensive and balanced. To the extent practicable, this view is presented in quantitative form. Thus, a moving image of a dynamic economy is provided so that the shifting importance of underlying monetary supply-and-demand forces may be observed and identified as objectively as it is humanly possible to do.

From an operating standpoint, the System's role in the economy is to help regularize the flow of funds in the credit and capital markets that partly finance demands for goods and human services. Hence, the emphasis of System intelligence efforts is on how all of the known forces of production, employment, income, and prices bear on the volume of credit and the trend in money balances, and how financial forces, as reflected through these magnitudes, are reacting in turn on aggregate levels of production and purchasing power. In the last analysis, it is only through the functioning of the credit and capital markets that monetary policy can influence the course and stability of general economic activity.

Federal Reserve actions to influence the flow of loanable funds are always a means to an end that serves the public interest. At all times there will be both known and unknown forces at work, and seldom will the course that System policy should follow be unequivocally clear. The System must continuously evaluate and re-evaluate existing forces, using objective criteria and facts as a basis for exercising its best judgment as to the current and prospective situation. Reflecting its established process of continual evaluation, a policy of restraint or of stimulation will not take definite form as of a single date, week, or month, but will usually represent a succession of adaptations in a more or less consistent direction over a period of time.

Monetary policy is the one instrument of national economic policy that can respond promptly and flexibly to the balance of domestic and international forces—either on the restrictive or tempering side or on the stimulative side. Its posture and actions, moreover, can be readily redirected if this balance has been misjudged, or when the balance of forces has changed. Monetary policy is never static, but is always in a state of adaptation. Its basic purpose, however, is invariant: namely, to provide the volume of bank reserves, and thereby of bank credit and of money balances, consistent with sustained economic growth and stability of the value of the dollar.

2. Money Supply and Stable Economic Growth
EDWARD S. SHAW

Our purposes are to discuss the meaning of "money" and to review American experience with money. We shall also consider a proposal for monetary policy that only a corporal's guard of economists will defend, namely, that monetary policy be added to the array of built-in economic stabilizers, taken off discretionary control, and put under automation.

DEFINITIONS OF MONEY

Everyone Rolls His Own

It is almost true that everyone rolls his own definition of money and has his own rules for measurement of the money supply. To confuse matters further, some people do not think that the definition matters. Others insist on attaching restrictive adjectives, so that one has to cope, for example, with "high-powered money," "fiat money," "token money," "inside money," "outside money," and "near-money." Sometimes an object is counted as money when it is held privately in the country of issue, and not-money when it is held by government or by people abroad. The Chairman of the Board of Governors of the Federal Reserve System is not optimistic that the confusion will settle: "I think all of us have to study a great deal more before we can say positively and precisely that this is what constitutes the money supply."[1]

On page 74 is a table, in Federal Reserve terminology, from which is concocted now one, now another, definition of money with measurements to match. The figures apply to a date chosen at random, October 30, 1963.

MONEY OR NOT?

Item	Amount (Billions of Dollars)
Money supply	
Currency component	31.1
Demand deposit component	119.5
Related deposits	
Time	
Commercial banks	109.9
Mutual savings banks	44.0
Postal Savings System	0.5
Foreign	1.2
U.S. Government	
Treasury cash holdings	0.4
At commercial and savings banks	3.8
At Federal Reserve Banks	0.8

"Money," as the composite of some items above, increased in amount over the preceding year at a very modest pace. "Money" comprising a different combination of these items increased more rapidly than usual. If you suspect that growth in money was under tight restraint, you can tailor a definition to your suspicion. If you prefer to think that restraint was mild, you can be right again—with a different definition.

There is authority for counting as money only the hard core of the first two items in the list above—that part balanced by the banking system's stock of gold and of claims on the federal government. There is authority, too, for extending the list to include traveler's checks issued by the American Express Company. One can find enumerations of "money" that include anything called a "deposit" in anything called a "bank" along with "shares" in savings and loan associations and credit unions.

The definition in common usage begins with the dictum "A dollar is a dollar." A unit of money bearing the price, or face value, of $1 today bears the same price tomorrow and next year. It discharges a debt for $1 any time, and it always buys something else with a price tag of $1. No one haggles over money's price.

This definition is not quite as rigorous as it may seem, because it would count in money not merely the "currency component" with legal-tender quality but the "demand-deposit component" as well. The latter does depreciate a little in price, subject as it is to service charges. It would appreciate a little, if Congress once again permitted interest credits on checking balances. This definition is flexible enough to admit nearly everything that people use as money—as a means of payment.

Modern money is a debt, differing from other forms of debt in that its price does not vary. It is a debt of the monetary system —the commercial banks, the Federal Reserve Banks, and the Treasury monetary accounts. It is issued to other sectors of the economy in payment by the monetary system for purchases principally of nonmonetary securities and monetary metals. It is an IOU even though there is nothing that it promises to pay, no interest yield to the holder, and no maturity date.

THE SUPPLY OF MONEY

At any moment the supply or quantity of money, according to our preference among definitions, is the monetary system's aggregate of fixed-price debt. It is the sum of all legal tender in pockets and tills (except bank tills) together with the sum of unused credits to checking accounts (except interbank accounts).

An observation at a moment of time does not give as accurate a "fix" as is necessary for precision in relating the supply of money to, for instance, national income for a year. Instead of a momentary measurement, one needs an average figure for money outstanding. Normally, too, this raw statistic for money should be cleansed of its very short-run or seasonal fraction and used in "seasonally adjusted" form. Then one cannot confuse a change that is quickly reversible with a change that has come to stay for a while.

An average supply or quantity of money may be outrageously inflationary if it is spread over a small community, grossly deflationary if the community is much larger. Especially in a growth context, it is often the money supply per capita that one needs for analytical purposes. This is not a datum regularly accessible in official tabulations or elsewhere, possibly because most of us are preoccupied with the behavior or misbehavior of money in the short run, too few of us with monetary phenomena in periods long enough for significant change in the population of money-users.

The money we are discussing is *nominal* money—the face value of the monetary system's debt. In the belief that money-users are not blinded by money-illusion and are concerned with money because of its value and not because of its price, economists suppose that it is *real* money, rather than nominal money, that affects patterns and levels of economic activity and economic welfare. Real money is the purchasing power of nominal money. The supply of real money is the supply of nominal money deflated by some one or other index of prices for things that money buys. These with experience in monetary analysis are ruefully aware that no price index is quite right for measurement of the real money supply and of changes in it. Perhaps this explains why the Federal Reserve does not publish the data on real money balances.

As one puts the quantity of money into one statistical disguise after another, he can get very different impressions of its behavior. The quantity of nominal money increased from the annual average of $143.4 billion in 1961 to $146.8 billion in 1962. Quantity grew, it seems, by 2.4 per cent. But did it? If we deflate the data for nominal money by a price index based on 1954, it appears that real money increased a bit less than 1 per cent. And real money per capita, for our noninstitutional population, declined by 0.7 per cent. Was there monetary expansion in 1961–62 or monetary contraction? Was the Federal Reserve "easy"or "hard"?

The "supply of money" that central banks manipulate, that people hold most of the time and spend once in a while, that economists investigate is not, then, a simple concept. It can be a figure so transformed in the statistical beauty parlor as to be hardly recognizable by its closest friends. There is more than meets the eye in any measurement of the supply or quantity of money.

ELASTICITY IN THE SUPPLY OF MONEY: TOO MUCH ELASTICITY AT THE WRONG TIME

It was a common complaint, before passage of the Federal Reserve Act in 1913, that our monetary system was inelastic.

Limitations on its ability to expand the money supply or to adjust the relative amounts of currency and deposits made it vulnerable to shock in short periods and restrictive of economic growth over the long run. The Federal Reserve Act and its amendments put elasticity into the monetary structure. Administration of the act put elasticity into monetary policy.

Partly out of conviction, partly to incite controversy, we are going to argue that the monetary system now is too elastic. Moreover, its expansions and contractions have often been ill-timed. The old monetary system had its flaws, but the new monetary system too has been guilty of permitting or even promoting short-run economic stability, and it has infrequently hit on the right degree of elasticity for economic growth. The optimal monetary system still eludes us.

The Statistical Record

The table below roughly traces our monetary experience during 1900–62. It measures growth in nominal money over the entire period and during eight subperiods. The subperiods begin with 1900–14, when the old monetary system was running out its last miles under critical inspection by a bevy of monetary commissions, public and private.

In four of the subperiods after 1914, policies of the new monetary system were stipulated primarily by the Treasury Depart-

STOP AND GO IN MONETARY POLICY

Period	Change in nominal money (Billions of Dollars)	Annual rate of change (Percentage)
1900–14	5.7	5
1914–19	11.9	15
1919–29	2.9	1
1929–33	− 6.6	− 7
1933–41	28.4	12
1941–45	54.2	21
1945–51	20.3	3
1951–62	25.2	2
1900–62	142.0	5.5

ment. These Treasury intervals were 1914–19, 1933–41, 1941–45, 1945–51. In two of these intervals, the monetary system was conscripted for war finance. For the greater part of 1933–41, the broad objective of policy was to restore liquidity in an economic system that had been parched and seared by deflation. The Treasury's concern for the marketability of its debt distinguishes the years 1945–51.

There were three subperiods when monetary policy was stipulated by the Federal Reserve Board, alias the Board of Governors of the Federal Reserve System. These interludes of board tenure were 1919–29, 1929–33, 1951–62. The first and third of these periods opened with a palace revolution, in the federal executive, against the Treasury's excessive concern for the marketability of its debt at low and steady rates of interest. The first culminated in a shift of power within the Federal Reserve and in adoption of policies that led directly to the disaster of monetary moratorium in 1933. The third period continues, with the Federal Reserve in high repute despite the gathering, from time to time, of vigilantes into monetary commissions.

In 1900 the nominal supply of money was at the near-microscopic level of $5.9 billion. At the close of 1962, the nominal supply of money was 25 times larger, or $147.9 billion. The average annual compound rate of growth was approximately 5.5 per cent. One had no need for a microscope to see the money supply at the end of 1962.

For perspective, the growth rate of 5.5 per cent in nominal money may be compared with the more modest growth rate of about 3 per cent in real value of money. Evidently prices rose at the average annual rate of 2.5 per cent. It may come as a mild surprise that this degree of price inflation has been our method of repudiating about $105 billion in nominal money: nominal money increased by $142 billion; real money by perhaps $37 billion in 1900–62. In terms of its purchasing power, the dollar has shriveled with age.

The Model-T Period

Let us consider the pre-Federal Reserve years 1900–14 a little more closely. In correspondence with accelerating growth in physical production and in the nation's real income and wealth, the money stock grew at the average rate of 8 per cent in 1900–6. After 1906 the tempo of growth slackened throughout the economy, the annual rate of growth in money falling to a little less than 3 per cent. The money supply declined in one year (1907); and it rose in each year of depression, including the dismal year of 1908. From year to year during 1900–14, variation in money's growth rate was less than during four of the seven subsequent intervals.

Waving aside the seasonal stresses of the old monetary system, which were amenable to treatment on the principle of the Aldrich-Vreeland Act, one is tempted to shed a nostalgic tear for our monetary experience in the decade and one half prior to the Federal Reserve Act. The monetary system was Model-T, but it bounced along with surprising efficiency.

Drag-racing the Monetary System

The Federal Reserve Act multiplied the horsepower and brake power in the monetary system. Since 1914, effective control of the system has alternated between Treasury and Federal Reserve Board. The Treasury takes out its aggressions on the throttle of the new machine. The Board reaches for the brakes. And the money supply lurches along a saw-toothed course of growth.

In 1914–19, the average annual rate of growth in nominal money was accelerated to 15 per cent. Then the brakes were put on. In 1920–21, money was contracted by 14 per cent. After rising 2½ per cent, as an annual average, in 1921–29, money sank again in 1933 and touched on a level previously passed in 1918. This is not a profile of monetary stability.

During two of the years in the period 1919–33, the Federal Reserve Board presided over a decline of more than 10 per cent in nominal money. In both years, 1921 and 1931, the monetary brakes were applied to an economic system that was already on the skids of deflation. In seven of the fourteen years there was not monetary contraction, and in six of these seven years monetary contraction was superimposed on other depressing circumstances. It is true that during two years of cyclic recession—1924 and 1927—the Board followed the precedent of the old monetary system in increasing liquidity. But these were years when such a stimulus was less urgent than in five of the six years when the Board departed from the pre-1914 tradition.

The Board's license to drive the monetary system was, in effect, suspended in 1933, when the Treasury took over the controls. Probation was granted in 1936–37, but once more the Board applied the brakes too hard in reducing the money supply by 7 per cent during the fourteen months after March, 1937. The United States economy slid into the recession of 1937–38, and again the Board's license to drive was lifted.

Over fourteen years, 1919–33, the board had "managed" the creation and destruction of $9 billion in nominal money. Over the next eight years, apart from the interlude of 1936–37, the Treasury chauffeur reversed monetary policy and subjected the economic system to an absurdly high rate of monetary expansion. By 1941, the prestige of monetary management was, properly, very low indeed.

In reaction to the monetary experience of 1919–33, the Congress added to the monetary system's capacity for both acceleration and deceleration in the series of reforms that appeared in 1933–45. Retrospectively, it seems that the rational thing to do was to minimize chances for pilot error in managing money, even to the extent of putting the monetary system on automatic pilot and disengaging manual controls. Instead, new opportunities were approved for discretionary action by the monetary authority, whether Treasury or Board. The principle of reform was to create still more latitude for mistakes of policy.

The mistakes came quickly, first on the part of the Board in its deflationary tactics of 1936–37, then on the part of the Treasury during wartime. This is not the occasion to debate wartime economic controls. One may simply offer the opinion that the rate of growth in nominal money during 1941–45, on the order of 21 per cent annually, is a blemish on our record that no amount of rationalization can erase. We expanded the nominal money supply at a rate surpassing by a wide margin even the requirements for rapid real growth in wartime, then deputized thousands of price policemen in OPA and WPB to patrol the channels of money flow. The money accelerator was pushed to the floorboard, and police-men were deployed in droves to keep the public out of the way of the money juggernaut. The new monetary system was a high-powered vehicle for our folly.

Leaning Against Winds and Maintaining Even Keels—
for Sustainable Growth

Until the Accord between Board and Treasury was sealed, in March, 1951, nominal money continued to grow as rapidly as was necessary to support market prices of federal securities. It was the Board that sensed the inflationary implications of Treasury policy and insisted on resuming monetary control. The Board's chronic disposition to restraint was tempered until spring, 1953, by exigencies of the Korean War. Then the foot shackled since 1936–37 was freed and instinctively stepped on the monetary brakes again. The ensuing screech of complaint in the security markets announced the recession of 1953–54.

The foot is never far from the brake: There was contraction of nominal money by 0.7 per cent in 1957 and 0.6 per cent in 1960. The foot is never hard on the accelerator: The maximum in year-to-year rates of growth was 3.9 per cent, in 1958. Growth in money during 1953–62 averaged 1½ per cent in annual data—the lowest rate for any period of prolonged prosperity during the century.

A little probing behind annual data discloses continual adjustment by the Board in money's growth rate. Growth at 1½ per cent annually seems to have qualified as "sustainable" growth: It is the Board's way of "leaning against the winds" of inflation in prices and of deficits in the balance of payments. But holding the economic system to an "even keel" requires somewhat more instability in money's accumulation than annual data reveal. From mid-1953 to mid-1963, quarterly variations in nominal money, expressed as annual rates of change, followed this pattern:

Annual rate of change (Percentage)	Number of quarters
Negative	6
0–1.0	10
1.1–2.0	9
2.1–3.0	4
3.1–4.0	4
4.1–5.0	6
5.1	1

The extremes of quarterly variation in nominal money, expressed in annual rates of change, have been contraction of 3.4 per cent and expansion of 5.1 per cent. When does judgment call for acceleration? The answer is that seven of the eleven quarters in which expansion exceeded 3 per cent followed business-cycle troughs by three quarters or less: Acceleration comes when cyclical recessions are over and recoveries are setting in. When does judgment call for the brakes? The answer is that five of the six quarters in which money contracted came in the immediate vicinity of business-cycle peaks: Deceleration in money, along with other factors, terminates booms. Monetary management within years is a reflex to cyclical instability. It has cultivated booms in their youth, helped to cut them off in their maturity.

One may probe still deeper to find money management in daily, even hourly operations at the trading desk of the New York Federal Reserve Bank. The buying this morning and selling this afternoon are "defensive" tactics against the perturbations that might divert accumulation of money along tangents that do not meet the Board's specifications, in its "dynamic" policy, for cyclical reflexes and secular growth. Money-management is a full-time occupation: If there is a moment to spare from leaning against the wind, it must go to keeping an even keel.

A HALF-CENTURY OF ELASTICITY

Monetary reform in the Federal Reserve Act and its amendments did put elasticity into the monetary system, as much elasticity as the money-manager might wish, within some broad constraints. One of two money-managers, the Treasury, set one standard of elasticity that permitted average annual growth in money of $4.9 billion in twenty-three years. The second money-manager, the Board, permitted no net monetary expansion in 1919–33, reduced money in 1936–37, and during 1953–62 provided money-growth at the average rate of 1½ per cent while now and again decreasing money at short-cycle peaks. In the present regime of the Board, money grows slowly in the long run, varies cyclically within a rather narrow range, and is sheltered against passing instabilities by continual intervention.

DISCRETION OR AUTOMATION—MANAGER OR ROBOT

There are alternative designs for a monetary system. The design that this country has hit upon builds into the system enormous capacity for both inflation and deflation. How to use this capacity depends on the judgment or discretion of the money-manager. Our experience with managed elasticity has been reviewed in recent years by critics singly, in committees, in commissions, and in assembly, the consensus being an endorsement of managed elasticity as applied by the Board of Governors.

Still, a few dissident voices are faintly heard to suggest that an alternative principle could hardly have done worse in the past half-century and might do better in the next. This is the principle of the automatic pilot, of rules rather than discretion. Starting from a money stock that is not obviously subversive of full employment at a relatively stable price level, it would expand money by formula. Various formulae have been suggested, the pure gold standard among them or a composite commodity standard. The formula we discuss below may be called the "demand standard" for monetary control.

The Demand Standard

Feed this rule into an automatic money pilot: Increase the stock of nominal money, continuously and not by fits and starts, at the secular rate of increase in demand for real money. Perhaps the rate should be the 1½ per cent that the Board adopted in 1953–62, but probably not, since the American economy developed symptoms of chronic monetary restraint. The rate of 5½ per cent would not do, since we tried it in 1900–62 and found it inflationary. As a first approximation, split the difference at 3½ per cent.

What are the premises of the demand standard? One is that the real stock of money a community desires to hold in its asset portfolios increases secularly at about the same rate as real income, given rates of interest that affect choice between money and other assets. Another is that real income grows along a stable trend line, associated with secularly stable rates of interest. A third is that deviations in growth of nominal money from growth in desired real money induce price-level changes in the long run and output changes in the short run that may impede economic development. Satisfy stable growth in demand for real money with stable growth in supply of nominal money, and the result is to minimize money mischief.

There could be more complex rules for the money robot than the steady-rate rule. If real money demanded (when employment is full) does not rise secularly along a straight percentage path, automatic alarms might be rung to put the robot on a new course. If the community wishes a possible tonic of secular inflation, growth in nominal money could be accelerated a little to overshoot growth in full-employment demand for real money. The objection now to complex rules of growth in nominal money is that they overtax our knowledge of growth in desired balances.

The idea that demand should be the target for supply is familiar for any other good than money. In the case of money, it does raise eyebrows. "Demand for money" is not a concept in popular use. There is no mention of it in the Federal Reserve Act. One small tabulation remotely akin to it is published in the *Federal Reserve Bulletin*. What is it, and why is it a plausible target for money supply?

We know that money has a fixed price. It can always be sold, with no delay, at the fixed price: It is liquid, as nothing else is. This quality justifies holding money as an asset rather than a like amount of less liquid assets with unstable prices. And a rational calculation of the best portfolio mixture of money and other assets is made in terms not of money's nominal value but instead in terms of money's purchasing power. Demand for money is demand for liquid purchasing power in asset portfolios.

There are three ways of adapting a nominal supply of money to the desired real supply. If nominal money is short, more may be issued so that demand is satisfied. Or, the excess demand evaporates as income and wealth are depressed by the public's attempt to accumulate money through reducing purchases and increasing sales of other things. Eventually, price deflation can increase the real value of the money supply into balance with full-employment demand. The simple adjustment between supply and demand, that does not punish the community with short-run depression and long-run deflation, is the first one of issuing more nominal money.

Similarly, there are three ways of correcting an excess supply of money. One is to issue less nominal money. The second is short-run booms in real income and wealth that culminate in the third solution, price inflation. The simple adjustment is the first one. Demand for money is a relevant standard for control of supply because excess demand or excess supply forces the public into wasteful adjustments of income, wealth, and prices.

But What About the Short Run?

Central banks have fallen into the habit of "high-level busy work," as at the trading desk of the New York Federal Reserve Bank, poking and prodding the money supply even though no one can know, from day to day, whether money is in excess supply or excess demand and even though day-to-day adjustments of demand to supply are easy for the public to make. The demand standard would forbid continual nudges of accelerator and brake.

Seasonal patterns of change in real balances demanded can be estimated and are stable. Instructions to the robot could be written for emission of money in seasonal rhythm. Then there would be little danger that seasonal excesses of supply or demand could provoke excessive and cumulative adjustments in output, employment, and prices.

Apart from theology, few credos are immutable. Apparently one of them is that monetary management can be a delicate, pervasive, and powerful instrument for smoothing the short business cycle. What basis of dissent is there for the advocate of automatic control to stand on? Principally, that the short cycle is so short. Allowing for the ambiguity of cycle indicators, for lags in response of money management to them, and for the lag between money stimulus and cyclical effect, there just is not space in the short cycle for turnarounds of monetary policy. That is why, in our recent experience, money expands in time to accelerate a cyclical recovery and contracts at the peak or after. That is why, in making amends for previous error, monetary management adjusts nominal money by fits and starts.

Monetary control in the cycle has been romanticized. It is an illusion, one may argue, that men of refined intuition, alert to the daily flux of economic statistics, resolving their differences by majority poll can anticipate the need months hence for a change in nominal money now. They cannot compete with the automaton whose steady rate of growth in nominal money supplies more than is demanded in recession and so limits the recession, or supplies less money than is demanded in a boom and so limits the boom.

The Demand Standard in Action

By the rule of the demand standard, the nominal supply of money would be increased at a constant rate compounded, perhaps, with seasonal wavelets of issue. The rate might be adjusted only with Congressional assent, since full and free debate on the matter of long-run inflation or deflation is no less important than full and free debate on such issues as tax burdens, foreign aid, or ventures into space.

Money would continue to be the debt of the monetary system. And the monetary system as it stands would be no less efficient in supplying money at a steady rate than it is in supplying money at variable rates to the taste of Board or Treasury. The purchasing power that the monetary system commands by issuing money could be spent, as it is now, on credit instruments or gold or bank buildings of glass and aluminum. Monetary expansion could be continuous spending of money created for the purpose, the objects of this spending by the monetary system being determined by the community's choice among alternative uses of the savings that accumulate in real money balances.

The demand standard is a break from monetary tradition in the United States and not only because it would substitute rule for authority. In addition, it bans "credit needs" of the community as a criterion for monetary policy. The monetary system would have credit to dispose of in the sense that presumably it would buy securities as the technique of money issue though it might be instructed to buy something else, possibly stockpiles of raw materials or highway construction. Its role as a credit institution would be derivative from its role as a supplier of money, and credit extended would be merely one possible application of the purchasing power represented by money issue.

The Federal Reserve Act is not the constitution of a monetary system. It is a body of rules about credit. The Board has concerned itself predominantly since 1914 with the behavior of security markets, the allocation of credit between markets, and the quality of credit. The Treasury has intervened in money management to secure high prices and low yields on its own credit instruments, with excess money supply as a by-product. A new monetary charter should contain a Section I, specifying the growth rate of money, and a Section II, specifying uses of the purchasing power that money issue confers on the monetary system. A preamble would state unambiguously that Section II is ancillary to Section I.

ANOTHER BUILT-IN STABILIZER

This country takes pride in its built-in stabilizers, the economic balance wheels that automatically limit our deviations from normal growth. Serious consideration has been given to formula flexibility in taxation. It is hardly a radical proposal that monetary control should be added to the measures that go into action, without forethought or discretion, against disturbances in the growth process. Two lines of argument favor the proposal. One is that discretionary control of money has not done well. The other is that automatic control can do better.

The Positive Case for Automatic Control

The case for automatic control does not rest only on disillusionment with discretionary control. There are five principal ways in which stable growth in nominal money can increase economic welfare.

1. Stable growth in money lays the foundation for a solvent and efficient payments mechanism. In inflation, bank capital is reduced relative to bank deposits. Deflation undermines bank capital, through deterioration in asset quality.

2. Stable growth in money removes one hazard of private and governmental economic planning. That is the uncertainty about the length of the monetary yardstick that planners use to measure prospective costs and revenues. Our yardstick, the value of the

dollar, has been rubberized, stretching in each deflation and snapping back in each bout of inflation.

3. Stable growth in money and stability in the price level create a favorable environment for flexible individual prices and price relationships. Each inflation and deflation spawns its own brood of price ceilings and escalators, or price floors and subsidies. Flexibility of the price level promotes rigidity of price relationships. Insofar as a private-enterprise society relies upon flexible price relationships to allocate resources and guide demands, flexible price levels reduce its productive potential.

4. Steady growth in money avoids inflations that distort the form of real capital, and it relieves the economic system of the interruptions in capital formation that result when deflation is applied as the remedy of inflation. Monetary restraint does not correct damage done by excessive monetary ease: It compounds damage. During inflation, savings are misapplied to capital projects that are made to seem worth while by advancing prices. During deflation, savings are destroyed by underemployment of men and resources. Savings misapplied or lost are never recoverable.

5. Steady growth in money and stability in the price level contribute to development of orderly financial arrangements throughout the community. Deflation creates its distinctive pattern of debt, financial assets, and financial institutions. Inflation gives rise to a different pattern. Costs and risks of allocating loanable funds are increased when the financial system is subjected alternately to the shocks of inflation and deflation. Stop-and-go growth in money is a nervous tic in the economic system that the financial structure amplifies, sometimes dangerously, for continuity in the saving-investment process.

An Inning for the Opposition

Antiautomation and prodiscretion have swept the polls of opinion among laymen and economists alike. On what grounds can managed money attract so devoted a following? The list below is short, and its exposition concise, but it may indicate why prolonged indulgence in monetary management is habit forming.

1. Changes in the growth rate of nominal money can be the

antidote for instability initiated outside of the monetary system. If money's growth rate were frozen, the economy would be easier prey to nonmonetary disturbances.

Rejoinder. The antimanagement brief does not deny that monetary policy *could* perform miracles, promoting stable growth and fending off shocks to growth. But our experience contains no miracles. Management skills are not equal to the job of realizing the potentialities of monetary policy.

2. The first half-century of our experience with discretionary management has not been a fair test. It has been distorted by two world wars and their aftermath in crisis and disaster. The Treasury and the Board have done notably well under the circumstances. In a tranquil world the Federal Reserve Act would be a sound charter for sound money.

Rejoinder. Peace and tranquility are not on the horizon for the next half-century. It is just as well to take the pessimistic view that temptations to misuse the monetary system will recur. There will be occasions when the Treasury will insist on borrowing cheaply in disregard of monetary stability. There will be occasions when the Board will deem it wise to disappoint the inflationary expectations that Treasury policy has generated. Now is the time, while there is still relative peace and tranquility, to take precautions against mismanagement in the future.

3. Monetary management is now on an unprecedented level of sophistication. The Board, perhaps even the Treasury, understands that the monetary system's proper target of control is money. It has set for itself the goal of stable growth in nominal money and can achieve as much automation as is safe.

Rejoinder. We are in an era of relative monetary stability. The Board and the Treasury are dedicated men applying exceptional skills to their tasks. Yet, with monetary management at its best, discontinuities occur in monetary growth that are not easy to rationalize. The cessation of growth in money for two years, in 1959–61, was a mistake. The expansion of $8 billion in nominal money during the succeeding two years may be interpreted as confession of error. Stop-go in monetary growth is an expensive school for monetary management.

4. Disarming monetary policy as a contracyclical weapon would put a burden on fiscal policy that it is not qualified to bear. Our experience with fiscal policy in the cycle is not reassuring. Congress moves too deliberately when there is opportunity for adjustments in rates of taxation and spending: The opportunity always slips by. In contrast, the Board can move sensitively to cyclical impulses, adjusting the monetary pedal to cyclic tempo. Fiscal policy is inflexible, monetary policy flexible.

Rejoinder. The cat-and-mouse game with the short business cycle has been lost. Monetary and fiscal policy are as likely to induce and aggravate short cycles as they are to stifle them. Built-in stabilizers have a superior record. Automatic money can be a built-in stabilizer, mechanically creating excess money supply in recession, excess money demand in booms. It has no intellect to be tricked into right responses at wrong cycle phases.

5. The economy is doomed to inflation by cost-push. As the price level is raised by nonmonetary market forces, nominal money must accommodate to it in order that production and employment can be sustained. Money is not an independent source of inflation or deflation.

Rejoinder. The monetary theory of inflation has been locked in battle with nonmonetary theories of inflation for generations. Apparently no finite number of demonstrations that cost-push starts in the wake of monetary expansion and stops in the wake of monetary contraction will break the lineage of structuralism.

6. Demand for real money does not grow along a simple trend line. It follows that growth in nominal money along such a line would be destabilizing, tending to induce inflation when demand for real money slows down, deflation when demand for real money speeds up. The demand standard is a fickle standard.

Rejoinder. Undoubtedly there is no simple, infallible rule for growth in nominal money. Yet, historical evidence seems to be that a simple formula for monetary expansion would have averted the liquidity crisis of 1929–33, or 1936–37, or spring, 1953, or spring, 1958. The demand standard invokes a naïve rule for growth in money, but knowledge about demand for money is not yet sufficient to justify a more sophisticated rule and is even less adequate for discretionary management.

7. If growth in money is stabilized, the economy may still suffer from unstable growth in money substitutes. Perhaps the forces that now result in uneven accumulation of money will shift their impact to other financial assets so that little will be gained by automating money only.

Rejoinder. Our blackest experiences with nonmonetary financial assets have resulted from monetary instability. The collapse of nonmonetary financial institutions in the 1930's is one case in point, the monetization of federal securities in 1941–51 another. If monetary stability were to be sabotaged by financial instability from nonmonetary sources, there are or could be automatic restraints that would bring the saboteurs into line.

8. The demand standard is provincial. It would isolate the American economy behind a fluctuating foreign-exchange rate or it would induce gross instability, behind a stable foreign-exchange rate, in international balances of payments. A domestic rule for growth in nominal money is a "Fortress America" rule that violates our international responsibilities.

Rejoinder. The transition from dollar shortage on foreign-exchange markets to dollar surfeit is hardly evidence that managed money means a stable balance of payments. Damage is done in international monetary relationships by the changes in direction that typify discretionary policy. The automatic dollar standard would dispel uncertainty, among this country's trading partners, as to its monetary policy and reduce their incentive to regional monetary coalitions.

9. Money does not matter. If, in some sense, there is too little of it, higher velocity will compensate, and no consequences for the economy are to be anticipated. If, in some sense, there is too much of it, lower velocity will drain it into a liquidity trap with no wear and tear on important things such as production and employment. Do as you like with money.

CONCLUSION

Monetary economics was dormant, but that phase is past. Its "gentle breezes of inquiry" blow up storms of controversy. One storm has thundered around the topic of automatic money and moved on, with discretionary policy ascendant. The prestige of the Federal Reserve as an instrument of social welfare emerged from the controversy stronger than ever. Yet, automatic money was not disgraced. Both the Federal Reserve and its kibitzers will measure the performance of discretionary policy against the demand standard. (See accompanying table, which shows the annual values of real output, money supply, price level, and real money in the United States from 1900 to 1962.)

GROSS NATIONAL PRODUCT, MONEY SUPPLY,
AND PRICE LEVEL OF THE UNITED STATES,
1900–1962

	M[a] (Billions of Dollars)	P[b] (1929 = 100)	M/P[c] (Billions of Dollars)	T[d] (Billions of Dollars)
1900	5.9	50	11.8	37.4
1901	6.5	50	13.1	40.9
1902	7.0	51	13.7	41.5
1903	7.2	52	13.8	43.6
1904	7.8	51	15.3	43.2
1905	8.7	52	16.8	45.9
1906	9.2	56	16.4	50.9
1907	8.9	59	15.1	52.4
1908	9.1	55	16.5	48.7
1909	9.6	56	17.1	56.3
1910	9.7	59	16.4	56.2
1911	10.4	60	17.3	55.2
1912	10.7	64	16.7	55.5
1913	11.1	64	17.4	57.8
1914	11.6	64	18.1	55.5
1915	13.4	65	20.6	60.6
1916	15.6	72	21.7	67.3
1917	18.3	87	21.0	74.2
1918	20.8	98	21.2	78.9
1919	23.5	110	21.4	77.4
1920	23.1	125	18.5	73.3
1921	20.6	105	19.6	68.7
1922	22.8	99	23.0	72.8
1923	22.9	102	22.5	84.0
1924	24.4	101	24.2	85.4
1925	26.1	102	25.6	88.0
1926	25.4	103	24.7	93.8
1927	25.7	100	25.7	95.1
1928	26.4	101	26.1	96.1
1929	26.4	100	26.4	103.8

(*Continued*)

	M^a (Billions of Dollars)	P^b (1929 = 100)	M/P^c (Billions of Dollars)	T^d (Billions of Dollars)
1930	24.9	96	26.0	93.9
1931	21.9	87	25.2	86.9
1932	20.3	78	26.0	74.1
1933	19.8	77	25.7	72.3
1934	22.8	82	27.8	79.2
1935	27.0	83	32.5	86.7
1936	30.9	83	37.2	98.9
1937	29.1	86	33.8	104.0
1938	31.7	85	37.3	99.5
1939	36.0	84	42.9	107.7
1940	41.9	85	49.3	116.7
1941	48.2	93	51.8	135.9
1942	62.6	104	60.2	155.4
1943	79.9	113	70.7	175.0
1944	90.7	116	78.2	187.7
1945	102.4	118	86.8	184.1
1946	107.6	130	82.7	160.2
1947	113.1	145	78.0	160.0
1948	111.5	154	72.4	166.2
1949	111.2	153	72.7	166.7
1950	116.2	154	75.5	180.5
1951	122.7	167	73.5	195.3
1952	127.4	171	74.5	202.8
1953	128.8	173	74.5	212.1
1954	132.3	174	76.0	208.0
1955	135.2	176	76.8	224.2
1956	136.9	182	75.2	229.0
1957	135.9	189	71.9	233.4
1958	141.2	193	73.2	229.8
1959	142.0	196	72.4	245.2
1960	141.2	199	71.0	251.6
1961	145.7	202	72.1	256.3
1962	147.9	205	72.1	270.0

[a] Adjusted demand deposits *plus* currency. Sources: 1900–14, Raymond W. Goldsmith, *A Study of Saving in the United States*, I, 382–83; 1915–46, Milton Friedman and Anna Jacobson Schwartz, *A Monetary History of the United States 1867–1960*, pp. 708–18; 1947–60, Board of Governors of the Federal Reserve System, *Supplement to Banking & Monetary Statistics*, sec. 1, pp. 20–22; 1960–62, *Federal Reserve Bulletin.*

[b] Deflator for gross national product, with 1929 as base year. Sources: 1900–29, Goldsmith, *op. cit.*, I, 377; 1930–62, *Economic Report of the President*, January, 1962, p. 178.

[c] Column 1 divided by column 2.

[d] Gross national product in 1929 prices. Sources: 1900–29, Goldsmith, *op. cit.*, III, 429; 1930–62, *Economic Report of the President*, January, 1962, p. 172.

3. Uses of Selective Credit Controls*
ARTHUR SMITHIES

This discussion is concerned with the possible uses of selective credit controls in achieving continued economic growth and avoiding inflation or recession in the course of growth. By "selective control" is meant action by the governmental authorities to control the terms and conditions on which credit is made available for particular purposes, such as the purchase of consumer durables, housing, inventory accumulation, or industrial plant and equipment.

Historically, selective controls as herein broadly defined have arisen in three different ways. In the first place, since 1917 the federal government has, directly or indirectly, extended credit to *stimulate* particular kinds of activity or to assist particular classes of borrowers. Such measures have usually originated in time of depression or war; but in important areas, particularly housing and agriculture, have now become permanent features of the economy. These programs, once in effect, can be used to provide additional stimulus or special restriction to the activity concerned.

Secondly, the Federal Reserve System is empowered, or has on occasion been empowered, to regulate the terms and conditions on which private loans can be made. As a result of the 1929 stock exchange collapse, the Board of Governors acquired during 1934 permanent power to prescribe margin requirements for stock-exchange credit. During World War II and the Korean War, it was given temporary power to regulate loans for the purchase of consumers' durable goods and housing. Such controls have been considered purely as an emergency restrictive device. But, if per-

*Since this article was written (1958), there has been virtually no discussion of selective controls, even by the Commission on Money and Credit. Because the author continues to hold the views presented in the paper, it is being published in its original form.

manently in force, they could be used to provide either a stimulus or further restriction.

Thirdly, selectivity can result from the exercise of supposedly general controls. If the Federal Reserve System reduces the liquidity of member banks, its action has different effects on different types of loans. Further, the current theory according to which the Federal Reserve System operates only at the short end of the market for government securities—the "bills only" doctrine—means that its action affects short-term more than long-term borrowers.

In view of the pervasiveness of selective controls in one form or another, they are not something that one can be unequivocally for or against. The issue is not whether, but how, they shall be used.

The discussion will center on two main questions: *First,* have selective controls any role to play in determining the desired speed and character of American economic growth? No country is interested in the rate of growth simply as an aggregate; it is also concerned with the distribution of the national product, say between durable and nondurable consumption, between agriculture and industry, or between construction and other forms of investment. Furthermore, in the modern world, countries are not merely interested in the fact that growth should be steady, but that it should proceed at some desired average rate. To achieve such a complex objective, the government must use a variety of tools, and selective credit controls should be considered in that connection.

Second, can selective credit controls serve as an instrumentality of policy to stabilize the rate of economic growth? No country can reasonably hope to set its course on a steady path of growth and remain on it without exercise of economic controls. Either the growth process, itself, technological change, or "disturbances" from the outside may produce persistent tendencies toward, or particular episodes of, inflation or deflation. While these tendencies probably cannot be removed entirely, the growth process itself may suffer if they are allowed to accumulate.

Economic Growth—A General View

As a preface to the discussion of these main questions it is useful to look briefly at the general aspects of the growth problem. A striking feature of national attitudes toward economic growth in the postwar period has been that countries have aimed at rates of growth almost invariably higher than those that would occur in the normal course of events. This is in sharp contrast to attitudes toward growth in earlier periods. This country, for instance, has always attached great importance to expansion, but has usually allowed the rate to be a by-product of the pursuit of other objectives, such as the maintenance of a vigorous private-enterprise economy, or, more recently, short-run full employment.

The United States has come to give explicit attention to economic growth, largely as a result of planning for World War II and its aftermath. It was quickly discovered during the war that mobilization objectives could be achieved only through economic expansion, and that diversion of resources from existing uses would itself fall far short of meeting the requirements of war. Similarly, in the postwar period this country has discovered that it cannot give full effect to its security objectives and its social objectives unless it expands. Because it is not feasible to expand public consumption at the expense of private consumption, if public consumption goals are to be achieved, public and private consumption must expand together.

In the underdeveloped half of the world, the raising of mass consumption standards has become a prime objective of policy. The possibilities of achieving that end by redistribution of income are extremely limited, and expansion of the total product is the only way by which total consumption can be substantially increased. As a first approximation, therefore, most countries are faced with the need to increase both public and private consumption at some given percentage rate. There can be little doubt that nondefense public consumption must increase; and so long as international tensions continue, the same seems to be true of national resources devoted to defense in most countries of the world.

The desired increase in public and private consumption requires corresponding increases in productive capacity, and these can be achieved only through the continued accumulation of capital. Thus the consumption objectives imply an objective for capital investment. A certain proportion of the annual net national product must be devoted to increasing productive capacity for future years. The historical record seems to indicate that to achieve a 3 per cent rate of growth, about 15 per cent of the GNP must be devoted to gross capital formation every year. If the desired rate of increase is 4 per cent, the proportion invested must be raised to about 20 per cent. On the other hand, if a 2 per cent growth rate is sufficient, the required proportion is only 10 per cent. These percentages are affected by changes in technology; but it would be rash to assume without specific knowledge that future technological change will greatly reduce capital requirements per unit of output.[1]

The growth problem now appears in two parts. The first requirement is that, whatever level of net national production is achieved, the required proportion must be withheld from consumption and made available for capital formation. The second requirement is that incentives to invest must be such that the amount saved, when resources are fully employed, will in fact be devoted to capital formation.

In a private-enterprise economy, the main methods whereby resources are withheld from consumption are private saving and taxation. The general level of taxation should be such that, taking into account the amount of private saving, the ratio of public and private consumption to GNP will equal the prescribed percentage. If, for instance, the required gross savings rate is 20 per cent, the total consumption must not exceed 80 per cent of the GNP. Depending on all the factors involved, this may require a deficit or surplus in the government's budget. So long as the world is beset by the Cold War, the luxury of deficits seems unlikely from the long-run point of view.

If general tax policy is used primarily to achieve the required rate of saving, credit policy must be used to provide incentives to invest. In general terms, the rate of interest must be established at the level that will induce business to undertake investment at the increasing rate desired, which rate will correspond to the increasing savings yielded by a growing national income.

In practice, things don't work out as simply as this. In no country is taxation regarded simply as a method of curtailing consumption. In some countries, considerations of equity seem to demand that profits be taxed at a higher rate than other incomes, and this may require that additional incentives to investment be provided by other methods. Again, the tax system itself is frequently designed to give special incentives to investment, usually in the production of particular raw materials or in industries important for defense.

On the credit side, monetary policy does not simply retard or encourage investment, but, with the advent of consumer credit, has a pronounced effect on consumption as well. Easing of credit may therefore tend to counteract the restrictive effects of taxation on consumption. Credit policy also has pronounced effects in the area of housing, which is intermediate between consumption and investment.

These considerations indicate that the exercise of purely general economic controls in the shape of, say, changes in central bank reserve requirements or uniform changes in tax rates, may not be enough to accomplish national policy objectives with respect to economic growth. This raises immediately the question of selective controls. For completeness, selectivity should be considered with respect both to taxation and to credit. While the following discussion will be concerned with selective credit controls, the alternative of selective tax treatment should be continually borne in mind.

Selective Credit Availability and the Character of Economic Growth

There can be little doubt that the nature of the credit market has influenced the pattern of economic growth, and that, in important instances, its operation in this respect has been influenced by government policy. Future policy, therefore, is more likely to involve modifications of existing policy rather than entirely new departures in principle.

Perhaps the most striking illustration of the influence of the availability of credit on the growth of a particular sector of the economy is the field of consumer credit. Consumer credit is largely provided by a new group of financial institutions that have grown up for the purpose of extending it. These commercial institutions are financed partly by bank borrowing and partly by borrowing from nonbank holders of funds. They are controlled only partially and indirectly: through the government's control over the commercial banks. So far, the government has not been willing to impose the same type of controls upon these institutions that are imposed as a matter of course upon commercial banks. There seems no reason in economic logic why the one group of financial institutions should be subject to fairly rigid controls while the other is not.

There can be no doubt that the availability of consumer credit has had an important effect on both the character and the rate of economic growth in the United States. While the amount of other types of consumption expenditures may have been rather narrowly limited by current income, consumer credit has to an appreciable extent freed purchases of durable goods from that restraint. Furthermore, the durable consumer-goods industries have provided opportunities for investment that are hard to imagine in the nondurable fields.

Consumer credit has not only been free from special controls, but it also seems to be less affected by general controls than other types of credit. The preoccupation of the purchaser with the amount of the monthly payments, which depend on the repayment period as well as on the interest rate, has meant that consumers are prepared to pay much higher rates of interest than other borrowers. This, in turn, has meant that lending directly to consumers or to credit intermediaries is very profitable for commercial banks. Consequently, general restrictions imposed on bank lending are likely to have less effect on consumer credit than on other types of lending.

Without the institution of consumer credit, it is doubtful whether the total rate of growth over the last generation would have been as rapid as it has been. We might well have had a slower rate, with greater emphasis both on nondurable consumption of goods and services and on collective consumption. It can readily be agreed that consumer credit has been necessary for a kind of growth that has been found nationally acceptable. Nevertheless, there is no reason to believe that the haphazard growth of consumer-credit institutions necessarily has yielded optimum growth from the social point of view. In particular, the neglect of education that is now engaging so much attention can be ascribed in part to the competition of durable goods for the consumer's attention.

The second area where credit has been particularly important and where the government has exercised selective controls is in housing. While statistical proof is not available, there is little doubt that the government guarantee of mortgage credit for veterans and insurance for mortgage loans to nonveterans has had a great deal to do with the national movement toward individual home ownership and the dispersion of the cities into the suburbs. In this connection the favorable tax treatment given to home owners, through the ability to deduct property taxes and mortgage interest from taxable income, has also been a contributing factor. Without these special facilities, the housing pattern might have been very different, with an emphasis on rental building and city apartment houses.

The social and political effects of the change are matters of great importance and interest. From the purely economic point of view, the effect of home ownership on national capital requirements is of considerable interest. Here again statistics are not available. I suspect, however, that if everything were taken into account—not only houses, but the highways, automobiles, and community facilities that go with city dispersal—it would be found that there has been a pronounced trend toward a way of living that is capital intensive in comparison with the alternative of greater concentration in cities. Whether or not this is a factor that should influence policy depends on the extent of total capital requirements in the years to come.

The third area where government intervention in credit markets has been important is agriculture. It seems doubtful whether the revolution in agricultural techniques during and since the war would have been feasible without the provision of liberal credit and relief for the farmer from the hazards of credit provided by purely private institutions.

The modern small farm involves a capital investment of at least $20,000. The substitution of capital for labor has meant striking increases in the productivity of agricultural labor; the farm population has been rapidly decreasing and the release of labor from the farm has provided the manpower to facilitate the growth of industry.

Finally, the character of the credit market has influenced the pattern of industrial investment for a variety of reasons:

1. A large part of industrial investment comes from reinvestment of funds accumulated internally by the investing firms—either savings out of profits or depreciation allowances. These funds are more readily available than funds obtained from the market, and their availability increases the ease with which such firms can raise supplementary funds in the market. Consequently, existing businesses, and particularly those with high profits, have a preferential position compared with new businesses that must raise all their capital in the market.

2. Connected with the first point, government regulation of stock exchange credit affects new businesses more than existing businesses.

3. The government, both in times of depression and defense emergency, has provided loans directly to businesses, especially those particularly vulnerable to depression or particularly important to defense.

A selective device that was used in the two world wars and in the Korean War was the provision of accelerated amortization for tax purposes. Accelerated amortization permits a business to write off its investment facilities at a more rapid rate than that dictated by the expected useful economic life of the facility. During war periods, accelerated amortization has been a measure of tax relief, since it has enabled businesses to take their deductions while excess profits taxes were in force. However, if this device is used at a time when profits taxation is unchanging, it operates as an interest-free loan from the government. The tax liability is merely transferred from an earlier year to a later year. Consequently, if accelerated amortization is used in normal times it should be considered as a selective credit control.

Since experience with selective credit controls for industry has been largely confined to wartime, the effectiveness and usefulness of the device is hard to assess. Industrial investment in those periods has been greatly affected by the availability of materials; also, fairly clear criteria have existed concerning the industries that should be encouraged or restrained. Whether or not we yet have sufficient knowledge of interindustry relations to use selective credit controls in the industrial area as a regulatory policy for normal times is open to question.

SELECTIVE CONTROLS TO INFLUENCE THE PATTERN OF GROWTH

We can now consider whether selective controls should play a *permanent* role in influencing the pattern of economic growth.

One school of thought holds that, on doctrinal grounds, no such controls should be exercised; that the differences in credit conditions prevailing in different parts of the money market reflect risk differentials; that the normal operation of the market produces a desirable allocation of resources; and that government interference involves unwarranted discrimination in favor of, or against, particular classes of borrower.

This extreme point of view can be readily rejected. In the first place, as we have seen, the market is by no means perfect. To an appreciable extent funds tend to flow in traditional channels, so that particular parts of it may be oversupplied while others are undersupplied.

Second, lenders' risks are to some extent an institutional matter. The risk of holding a few local farm mortgages to a small country bank is obviously much greater than what would be incurred if risks of many mortgage loans were pooled over a wide geographic area and a wide variety of farms. Government guarantee or insurance arrangements involve such a pooling of risks, at no real cost to the government.

Third, the absence of selective control, rather than its presence, may be discriminatory. For instance, the government may be restraining consumption through taxation, but may be unwilling to tighten general credit conditions for fear of discouraging investment. In the absence of selective control over consumer credit, the total policy would discriminate in favor of consumer purchases or durable goods as opposed to nondurables.

Fourth, some discrimination is inherent in any policy for economic growth. If national policy requires that growth be accelerated, consumption must be curtailed in favor of investment, and, in a sense, consumption as a whole is discriminated against. There is no reason in economic logic why consumption should be treated as a homogeneous aggregate, and why durables should not be distinguished from nondurables. If the national policy is not to accelerate growth but to increase consumption, there is similarly no economic reason why durables should not receive preferential treatment. The purchasers and sellers of durables have no vested interest in the institutional credit conditions prevailing at the particular time. In short, the notion of discrimination, if broadly and uncritically defined, can be used as an argument against any kind of government control.

Whether or not efforts should be made to change the pattern of economic growth in the future through exercise of selective controls or through any other means is a practical, rather than a theoretical, question. The practical issue likely to be decisive in the next ten years or so relates to defense requirements. If defense expenditures are destined to absorb an increasing proportion of the national product, it will be important not only to accelerate the total rate of growth, but also to economize on the use of capital for purposes unrelated to defense. Such a policy may call for permanent restrictions on consumer credit, and for some modification of the present policy of giving preferential treatment for residential building. Whether or not mechanization of agriculture should be carried still further depends on whether the greatest shortage confronting the country is capital or manpower. In the latter event, further capital investment in agriculture may be warranted in order to continue the flow of manpower from agriculture into industry.

The requirements of defense, if sufficiently great, may also warrant the use of selective controls in industry, however difficult they may be to apply. Accelerated amortization may be needed in a few identifiable industries where expansion is particularly important.

Whether or not defense needs increase, the need for increased investment in areas such as education and urban renewal is now widely recognized; and special credit arrangements may be useful to achieve these purposes. If the federal government is required to participate, extended use of loans to public and private institutions may be preferable to outright subsidies.

If defense requirements do not increase in relationship to the national product, there seems to be no compelling argument for the modification of the present pattern of growth. And if by some miracle defense requirements decrease greatly, one possible way for the economy to adjust would be to adopt policies intensifying the use of capital in the form of houses and the accompanying durable goods.

SELECTIVE CONTROLS AND THE CONTROL OF INFLATION OR RECESSION

There has been much debate in the last few years about whether inflation is of the cost-push or of the demand-pull variety. My own opinion is that, in the inflationary problems currently confronted by the United States, both factors are likely to be present. Cost-push inflation cannot occur without at least permissive action on the part of the monetary authorities. For inflation to occur, total demand must be allowed to increase sufficiently to validate the increased level of costs and prices that result from a push. On the other hand, inflation arising initially on the demand side is likely to be intensified by autonomous tendencies for wages and prices to increase.

Whatever the precise diagnosis, the fact remains that any kind of inflation can be restrained, if not eliminated, by the exercise of appropriate controls of aggregate demand. But these controls may involve contraction of demand in some directions, and expansion in others.

One possible source of inflation is that a long-run growth policy may itself be subject to inflationary or deflationary biases. The absence of such biases would mean that the economy was nicely adjusted, so that total demand, productive capacity, and the labor force were all increasing at the same rate. In an economy subject to rapid technical change, such a situation is unlikely to be achieved without adjustments of long-run policy.

If demand is tending to grow more rapidly than industrial capacity or the labor force, or both, it will have an inflationary bias, and in the opposite situation the bias will be deflationary. Or there may be mixed situations where demand is increasing more rapidly than capacity but less rapidly than the labor force, or vice versa.

If the economy faces a labor shortage and the rate of growth in real output is to be maintained, one way out of the difficulty is to take steps to increase the rate at which the productivity of labor is rising. Such steps may involve organizational changes in industry that will achieve a better utilization of labor; they are also likely to require a diversion of investment to areas where investment is needed to facilitate increases in productivity. Such a policy would probably require the exercise of selective credit controls. Accelerated amortization may be applied to the industries to be stimulated, while general tax or credit restraints may be applied to investment in general. Or particular forms of investment that do not contribute materially to productivity increase may be discouraged. Or, alternatively, the best solution may be to slow down the total rate of growth but to ensure that the slowing down does not take place in the sectors whose expansion is essential from the national point of view.

If the inflationary bias arises mainly from a shortage of productive capacity, the appropriate remedy is to increase the rate of saving and, at the same time, to maintain the rate of investment. Such an adjustment could be accomplished by the use of general controls, for instance, a general increase of taxation combined with a general relaxation of credit. Or the desired increase in saving could be achieved by increasing restrictions on the use of consumer credit combined again with general credit relaxation elsewhere.

If the tendency is toward a deflationary bias of the economy and growing unemployment, these measures all would need to be applied in reverse.

Even if the preceding biases are removed, a persistent inflationary tendency of the cost-push variety is still possible. In that event, the most effective but also the most difficult policy to follow would be to alter the structure of the labor and product markets so as to increase competition. If those possibilities are not available, the government may be faced with the alternatives either of submitting to upward price trends or of interrupting the process of growth from time to time. This latter course means that a long cyclical upswing in real output may be deliberately interrupted in order to create uncertainty in the minds of labor and business executives whether wage and price increases will be validated by government policy. The desired degree of uncertainty probably requires recessions of the scale of those of 1949 and 1953, but not necessarily one of the 1957–58 scale.

To create a small recession and to keep it small is a delicate matter. The characteristic of the small recessions of 1949 and 1953 is that they consisted largely in declines in inventory accumulation, while business expenditures on plant and equipment were maintained. In contrast, the reason why the 1957–58 recession had serious aspects was that those expenditures declined noticeably; and the recession, even with more vigorous recovery measures than were being undertaken, was too severe to be considered a normal feature of economic life.

If the government does attempt to end an inflationary trend, it should exercise the type of control that is least likely to have adverse effects on plant and equipment expenditures. Fiscal measures are as a rule too clumsy for the purpose, although there are possibilities of controlling the rate of such expenditures through administrative action. The main burden of the task must be borne by credit policy, on a general or selective basis. Here again a selective approach is needed. To avoid adverse effects on plant and equipment investment, long-term interest rates and credit availabilities should not be affected; restrictive monetary action should be confined to the short end of the market in the hope that a subsequent reversal of the restrictions will bring about recovery. Ironically from some points of view, application of the "bills only" doctrine is the type of selective action that is needed. This is the doctrine that the Federal Reserve authorities should limit their open-market purchases and sales to short-term securities, primarily Treasury bills maturing within ninety days.

Inflation can arise not only from biases in long-run national economic policy, and from persistent tendencies for wages and prices to increase, but also from shorter run or partial disturbances of the economy. To correct such tendencies, selective controls may have an important part to play. Three instances will illustrate this point.

The general credit restrictions imposed in 1929 were undertaken largely, if not exclusively, in an effort to curtail speculation on the stock exchange. In fact, the stock exchange was the only part of the economy that was then subject to inflation. Had selective controls over stock-exchange credit then been available, stock speculation could have been attacked directly without hampering investment; and some of the worst features of the Great Depression might have been avoided. The use of selective instead of general controls could in any event hardly have made matters worse.

Another case of partial inflation was the boom of 1937. At that time general recovery was far from complete, but rapid wage increases followed passage of the Wagner Act and speculative price increases occurred in commodity markets. To check these increases, the government resorted to a general policy of fiscal and monetary restriction. The most important factor probably was the effort to bring federal receipts and expenditures into balance. The action of the Federal Reserve in reducing excess reserves in 1937 might also have had an effect that was mainly psychological but none the less real. It seems reasonably clear that the combined fiscal and monetary action of the government contributed in turning a boom, which may have been precarious, into a severe depression. Perhaps in retrospect no restraining action was called for. But if action had to be taken, it should have been restricted to the area of short-term credit that had a bearing on commodity speculation. Such action might have been feasible without impeding the general course of recovery.

To take a more recent instance, the upsurge in the demand for automobiles in 1955, fed by available installment credit, apparently had a good deal to do with the generation of the boom psychology of that and the following year, with the accompanying expectation that wage and price increases could go on indefinitely. Under these circumstances, the monetary authorities had no alternative but to try to stop the inflation by the use of general controls; and this action necessarily worsened the recession.

Had consumer credit controls been available, there was a clear case for their use in 1955 and 1956. This would have meant less inflation and fewer drastic efforts to cure it. A recession was probably inevitable, but it might well have been milder and more manageable than the 1958 one turned out to be.

If selective action is taken to restrain inflationary disturbances, this action should naturally be terminated or reversed when the inflation is brought under control. On the other hand, if selective action is not taken during a phase of economic expansion, but a general depression results from the exercise of general controls, selective credit relief may not be an appropriate recovery measure. For instance, in June, 1958, it was doubtful whether any particular stimulus should be provided for the purchase of consumer durables. If the economy was temporarily overstocked with automobiles, measures designed to stimulate demand generally would have been more appropriate.

In the case of identifiable disturbances, such as the foregoing examples, the usefulness of selective controls can hardly be disputed. The next question to consider is whether selective controls should be used to reduce the scope of general economic fluctuations that are not exaggerated by speculative tendencies or characterized by special distortions.

Even though long-run economic policy may be well designed, fluctuations in production and employment are very likely to occur unless they are corrected by short-run policy adjustments.

The character and scope of business fluctuations are intimately connected with the purchase of durable goods by producers and consumers and the institution of credit. On that everyone can agree. Whatever the initial causes of departures from the path of steady growth, acceleration effects, lags, and miscalculations in the purchase of durable goods account, in large measure, for the subsequent fluctuations. The question then arises whether stabilization policy should be aimed to influence total employment and output, or whether particular attention should be paid to durable-goods purchases.

One point of view is that economic policy should aim at keeping the value of the national income and the money supply growing at rates determined by the prospective or desired rate of economic growth, and within that framework the market economy should be allowed to make its own short-run adjustments. If, under such a policy the demand for durables rises or falls, the demand for nondurables and services will necessarily move in the opposite direction.

This approach has much to be said for it. It sets up the conditions necessary for the functioning of a market economy and prescribes fairly simple rules for government action. While it should furnish an important general guide to policy, as a complete prescription it runs into fatal difficulties.

In the first place, the policy implies that general increases in wages and prices should not be "financed" by increases in the money supply. If such an increase in wages and prices does occur, the government should "stick to its guns," and the result will be either unemployment or a reversal of the price-wage increase. Under modern conditions of price-wage rigidity the former outcome is the more probable, and it is unlikely to be acceptable. It is not feasible to proceed in this direction farther than to recognize the need for occasional small recessions. Secondly, the policy requires radical changes through time in federal expenditures and taxation. To carry it out the executive would need discretionary power to make temporary changes in tax rates, and a variable system of family allowances might also be needed. While there is much to be said for reforms on these lines, no one in authority shows the slightest interest in them.

In practice, therefore, aggregate demand is likely to expand in response to an increase in demand in any sector. To some extent a credit policy based on "the needs of business" is inevitable. Consequently, an increase in the demand for durables is unlikely to be accompanied by compensating decreases in the demand for nondurables. It is more likely to have multiplier effects that will increase all kinds of demand. Stabilization policy, therefore, must pay direct attention to cyclical changes in the demand for durables. Perhaps this is a policy of "second best," but we do not live in a world where optimum solutions are generally available.

Assuming that the demand for durables should be controlled, should the control be on a general or a selective basis? Those who set great store by simple policies will automatically say that general credit control is the appropriate remedy. But this simple-minded approach overlooks the fact that we have no single control applying generally and uniformly to all forms of credit. To have "general" effects, controls must be applied selectively. But should the objective be uniformly of incidence in some sense or should special durable goods areas be singled out for special treatment? The answer is complex and difficult.

A good case to discuss is residential building. This is an area where selective controls are already established. The postwar housing boom would have occurred in any case, but its strength was increased by the preferential credit treatment given to house builders in general and to veterans in particular. Moreover, it accounted for about 25 per cent of gross investment from 1950 to 1956. The strength of housing demand helped to account for the rapid recovery from the 1949 and 1954 recessions, and the apparent ending of the housing boom was an important factor in the recession. In some respects this is a repetition of the 1920's. A housing boom contributed to general prosperity in that period, and a weak housing market helped to make the economy vulnerable in 1929. To a considerable extent, housing tends to obey laws of its own and to influence rather than to follow the general course of business conditions.

From the point of view of general stabilization there is, therefore, an impressive case for reducing fluctuations in house building. The necessary machinery to do this already exists. Present forecasts of population increase and family formation suggest that it might have been possible in 1945 to set housing on a reasonably steady upward trend that would have had a good prospect of lasting until, say, 1975. As it is, we may have to wait until the late 1960's for a strong revival of housing demand.

Objections to such a course are partly economic, partly social, and, to a large extent, political. From the strictly economic point of view, housing construction above such a trend level was probably needed to accommodate the postwar labor force. From the social point of view it is obviously desirable that house construction should fluctuate in the same manner as family formation. These factors clearly justify departure from a long-term "trend" policy. But there seems no good reason why the movement to the suburbs should not have proceeded more slowly than it did—in the interests of economic stability. Despite necessary qualifications, the case for a selective policy designed to stabilize housing construction expenditures remains substantially intact.

Housing, however, is the clearest case for selective treatment. In the present state of our economic knowledge, one cannot recommend selective stabilization measures in other areas, except in cases where speculative or inflationary tendencies are clearly discernible.

Administration and Control Techniques

In this chapter an attempt has been made to emphasize that selective controls are needed not as a substitute for general controls but as an addition to them. Selective measures are likely to be of little avail unless the more general relationships among expenditures, taxation, and credit availabilities are such as to keep the economy on a course of steady growth. Selective controls have a role in modifying the character of growth, and in arresting departures from it. Consequently, the first administrative requirement is that there should be coordination in the application of the available instruments of stabilization policy, general or selective.

Within the executive branch, the policies of the Treasury, the Budget Bureau, the federal credit agencies, and the Federal Reserve Board are all interrelated, but coordination of their operations is frequently notable by its absence. The federal credit agencies have seldom attempted to reconcile their policies with those of the Federal Reserve Board. The Treasury often raises funds on the long-term market at a time when the Federal Reserve is attempting to lower long-term rates. The Federal Reserve in recent years does not appear to have recognized that its monetary restriction was being imposed in addition to severe fiscal deflation.

But coordination must not be carried too far. Whether general or selective, credit restriction arouses intense political opposition. While political support for antidepression measures is not lacking, the Federal Reserve must remain outside the main current of political forces if it is to take effective action against inflation—such as producing occasional unemployment or restricting consumer credit in the cause of price stability.

With respect to selective control techniques, some of the important instruments of policy are already in existence. The Federal Reserve System presumably knows a great deal about the technique of operating selectively in the financial markets, and combining open-market operations with control of the banking system. It has now had almost twenty-five years of experience with its stock-market credit controls. With respect to housing, the federal government's system of mortgage guarantees and insurance provides it with a flexible and effective method of regulating housing credit. In the industrial area, the techniques of direct lending and accelerated amortization are well known. In all these areas the problem is how and when to use known controls, and in what combination, rather than what kinds of control to use.

The outstanding piece of unfinished business with respect to techniques of control is to devise an effective method of controlling consumer credit—admittedly a difficult matter. Experience with the emergency controls of World War II and the Korean War has led many disinterested economists to the conclusion that administrative difficulties are so great as to present a compelling argument against the use of these controls. That experience does at least indicate that, if such controls are to be instituted in the future, new concepts and techniques should be employed.

In the first place, consumer credit controls should be permanent rather than of an emergency or temporary character. If the authority of the President or the Congress has to be invoked, or even if the Federal Reserve Board has the authority to institute such controls, it is almost certain that the controls will be applied too late. To avoid political attack, the authorities will tend to wait until the need for control is quite evident to large sections of the public as well as to the expert. This will mean waiting until an inflationary disturbance is near its peak. If imposed at that time, controls may be worse than useless.

Suppose that controls of stock market credit or bank reserves existed on a stand-by basis. The Federal Reserve might well feel that a financial panic would result from their sudden introduction. As it is, existing ratios can be increased or decreased without fear of serious psychological repercussions. Likewise, consumer credit controls should be continually in force, even though, for most of the time, they may do no more than validate the policies pursued by credit institutions in response to general credit conditions.

The other main question is whether control of consumer credit should be exercised by imposing liquidity ratios (i.e., reserve requirements) on credit institutions, or by controlling directly the terms and conditions of loans, or by doing both things.

The first method would apply to credit intermediaries the methods that have for a long time been applied to commercial banks. While this method commends itself in principle, there are doubtless many complications.

Direct control of terms and conditions of consumer installment loans has acquired a bad reputation on the basis of past experience. The main objection lies in the possibilities of evasion. To be effective the controls must prescribe the down-payment ratio for the durable goods purchased; and the regulation can be evaded by changing trade-in allowances. Suppose that a new car sells for $1,000, the old car is traded in for $400, and the consumer borrows $600. Then a regulation requires a 50 per cent down payment. This can be complied with simply by raising the price of the car to $1,200 and the trade-in allowance to $600. To enforce this method of control, it seems that price ceilings must also be imposed—and enforced—on both new and old cars.

There is, however, a way out of the difficulty. The regulation can prescribe that the maximum loan granted shall not exceed some stipulated proportion of the manufacturer's wholesale price plus freight to the point of delivery. With respect to automobiles, this method seems practicable since so few manufacturers are involved and trade-ins are most important. Such a regulation would have useful side effects. It would tend to keep dealers' margins at a uniform proportion of the wholesale price, and it would discourage the pernicious habit of insisting on "extras." The consumer could pay high profits to dealers and buy extras if he wanted to, but he would have to pay for them in cash. This kind of regulation should not be particularly offensive to believers in the forces of the competitive market.

Any proposal for selective credit controls meets objections on the ground that it increases the discretionary authority of the ex-

ecutive, and hence hastens us on the road to serfdom. The argument is therefore advanced that, if selectivity is needed, it should
be accomplished by legislation rather than administration; and a
selective excise-tax system is to be preferred to selective credit
controls. This argument ignores the needed flexibility of administrative methods. But meeting it on its own ground, our experience with selective tax legislation is not encouraging. A process
traditionally and regularly exposed to the influence of organized
pressure groups is not necessarily superior to one that relies on
administrative discretion. The history of the Trade Agreements
Act can be cited as a case in point.

We should aim at a tax system well adapted to long-run needs,
and containing selective features. But to attempt to alter the tax
structure for short-run purposes of cyclical stabilization would
expose it unduly to political pressure. Short-run tax adjustments,
when needed, should take the form of uniform and temporary
percentage changes in (income) tax liabilities. Short-run selective
effects should be achieved through selective credit controls.

CONCLUSION

It is frequently argued that given objectives of policy can be
most efficiently achieved through the use of the minimum number
of policy instruments needed for their attainment. Consequently,
it is said that a few general controls are to be preferred to a combination of general and selective controls.

The efficiency of a control system depends heavily on the degree to which mistakes are avoided in its application—in an uncertain world. Mistakes can arise from two sources. *First,* they are
likely to increase with the number of facets of economic behavior
controlled. If, for instance, the government attempts to control
consumption, investment, and government expenditures, it is likely
to make some mistakes that it will not make if it attempts to control only two of them. In the former case it must know more about
the structure of the economy than in the latter. *Second,* however,
mistakes will depend on the extent of changes (measured in terms
of their effects) in the control variables needed to achieve given
results. Presumably, most is known about economic behavior

relations in the neighborhood to which we are accustomed. The effect of small, but significant, changes in credit conditions or tax rates can be more accurately predicted than that of large ones. This consideration means that more than the minimum number of controls needed should be used to produce given results.

Selective controls are useful from both points of view. They may reduce the number of factors the government must influence. Selective credit controls, for example, permit the government to influence investment behavior without affecting consumer behavior. Their use also permits smaller changes in the control variables than does reliance on general controls. The main economic objection to many selective controls is that their availability may tempt the authorities to increase the number of things controlled, which may prove far from efficient. However, the most efficient control system involves the use of more controls than the minimum number that may prove effective, and it includes the use of selective credit controls.

4. Postwar United States Monetary Policy Appraised

HENRY C. WALLICH and STEPHEN H. AXILROD

In the nature of things, a definitive appraisal is possible, if at all, only of matters dead and gone. Monetary policy today is very much alive. All that this chapter can hope to offer, consequently, is an interim report.

Given that limitation, the present moment (the beginning of 1964) seems well chosen for an appraisal. We are, and have been for about six years, in a period marked by comparative stability in the average level of prices but accompanied by an unsatisfactory level of unemployment, slow growth, and a substantial deficit in our balance of payments with foreign countries. The persistence of these problems certainly raises the question of how well monetary policy and also other public policies have been adapted to the situation. More generally, the role that monetary policy can and should be expected to take in achieving the country's economic goals needs to be appraised. With this in mind, we first review events of the earlier postwar period for the light they shed on the functioning of monetary policy and the changing use made of the instruments of policy. We then turn to the issues raised by more recent experience.

FROM THE END OF THE WAR TO THE ACCORD OF 1951

At the end of World War II, the fortunes of Federal Reserve policy had reached their all-time low. They had been declining ever since the fateful days in 1929 and 1930, when the weight of monetary policy, at least as it was then conceived by policy-makers, had been thrown against the onrushing depression—but to no visible effect. They had continued to drop throughout the 1930's as other agencies of the federal government expanded their monetary, fiscal, and political powers—although the possibility that the Federal Reserve did not do as much as it might have cannot be denied. The nadir was reached in 1945 when the Treasury, having availed itself of the Federal Reserve for war financing, expected the System to remain a continuing and submissive instrument for solving the problems of federal debt management.

Struggle To Free Monetary Policy

With a federal debt of over $250 billion, a new phenomenon fraught, it was thought at war's end, with unforeseeable consequences, the System's chief function had become stabilization of the government securities market. The pattern of interest rates had to be preserved by appropriate purchases and sales; the Treasury's refunding operations had to be supported; in general, the market had to be watched continually and treated with the utmost circumspection, for it was thought that any attempts to raise interest rates, except perhaps on the shortest maturities, would intensify the danger of panicky market movements that might upset the economy. It must be remembered that at that time many analysts feared a postwar depression.

The situation facing the System was aptly characterized by a professor from a Middle Western college who, with a group of his colleagues, spent a couple of days being shown around one of the Reserve Banks. "I thought you tried to regulate the economy with discount rate and open-market operations," he said, "but all I have heard you talk about is how to regulate the government bond market." At this low point in its fortunes the System made two basic decisions. First, it rejected the view that depression was the country's main danger and, instead, geared its expectations to inflation; and second, it clung to the principle of general credit control as the core of monetary policy.

In its struggle to make this principle prevail, the System's chief antagonist was, of course, the United States Treasury Department. In the immediate postwar years both became concerned about inflation, but the Treasury took the view that to try to control

inflation by raising interest rates was useless at best and dangerous at worst. Given the huge debt and an overexpanded money
supply, both inherited from the war, nothing could be achieved,
short of massive measures, by trying to influence the liquidity of
the public. On the other hand, massive measures might bring
about a collapse of the bond market, the public credit, and perhaps the entire economy.

The Federal Reserve, in turn, did not at first suggest unpegging
the entire interest rate structure of the federal debt. Such an
enormity was not contemplated until about 1949, since the System
shared the Treasury's fear that without support the market might
collapse—and in those early days there may have been some
justification for the view. What the System argued for, initially,
was merely an unpegging of short-term money rates, beginning
with the 3/8 per cent rate on ninety-day Treasury bills. This arti-
ficially low rate not only blocked all freedom for monetary policy,
but also encouraged holders to play the pattern of rates—selling
short-term securities to purchase higher yielding long-term securities—and thereby forced the System to add to inflationary pressures since it had to buy the short-term securities that were being
liquidated.

Beginnings of a Flexible Policy

In the second half of 1947, the Treasury at long last agreed to
let the Federal Reserve withdraw support from Treasury bills
and certificates, the chief short-term instruments. This created
the first modest amount of "elbowroom" for monetary policy.
But the necessity of keeping the long rate from rising above an
agreed-upon level meant that monetary policy could operate
flexibly only within very narrow limits. If attempts at monetary
restraint or growth in credit demands forced commercial bank
and, in general, market sales of long-term securities, the Federal
Reserve was compelled to buy them, thus supplying reserves to
banks, to keep the rate from rising above the ceiling; since rate
pressures were for the most part upward, the ceiling was in effect
a peg of the long rate.

The revival of strong inflationary pressures at the time of the
Korean outbreak in 1950 raised, in a very pointed way, the ques-

tion of Federal Reserve independence to pursue a counter cyclical and, when required, an anti-inflationary monetary policy. At the same time, the Treasury was faced with the possibility of new large-scale federal financing, which would be facilitated by continued Federal Reserve market-support policies.

The ensuing and at times severe conflict was terminated by the Accord of March 4, 1951. The two agencies agreed that the government bond market was to find its own level subject to a number of actions designed to smooth the transition and ease the Treasury's financing problems. In effect, the peg was removed gradually, and the Federal Reserve became free to conduct open-market operations for counter cyclical purposes. Monetary policy at last had regained its freedom.

An Appraisal of Pre-Accord Policies

It may be true, but not quite fair, to say that monetary policy in the pre-Accord period accomplished a good deal less than it might have. Experience since the Accord indicates that the market risks inherent in tightening credit and letting the bond market find its own level may have been greatly exaggerated at the time. But given the undigested nature of the federal debt, much of it loosely held, the danger was, and still is, difficult to assess.

Assuming the danger was exaggerated—a tall assumption from the Treasury's point of view—how much of the postwar inflation might have been avoided by timely monetary restraints? Any answer is in large part guesswork. But bearing in mind the delayed impact of inflation suppressed by wartime controls, the increases in labor and materials costs that had occurred, the shortage of supplies, the exceptionally large overhanging liquidity of consumers and of many firms, one probably does not go wrong in thinking that monetary restraint, however skillfully applied, would have had a limited effect at best. The major part of the postwar inflation was probably unavoidable.

POST-ACCORD POLICIES

The Treasury-Federal Reserve Accord opened a new era for United States monetary policy. It allowed monetary policy to be guided by criteria of economic growth and stability, unfettered by considerations of debt management. It thereby provided for freely fluctuating short- and long-term interest rates, subject to certain Federal Reserve commitments designed to help Treasury financing, to smooth the transition to the new regime, and to contain disorderly market conditions.

Freedom for monetary policy raised many problems in the early years and as time went on. These included the impact of the Federal Reserve upon the market, interaction between Federal Reserve and other governmental policies, and achievement of balance among sometimes conflicting policy objectives. These kinds of problems can best be understood in light of economic and financial developments in the dozen years after 1951 and of policy actions affecting them.

The period from the spring of 1951 to the end of 1963 provided the Federal Reserve with an interesting, not to say puzzling assortment of situations. Three broad subperiods can be distinguished: one, roughly 1951–58, when economic cycles occurred against a background of high employment and at times creeping inflation; a second, 1958–60, which can be termed a watershed, in which old problems were abating and new ones were coming forward; and a third, 1960–63, in which the new problems of persistent balance-of-payments deficit, excessive unemployment, and (at least in the eyes of some observers) lagging economic growth required revision of older views about how policy should operate.

High Employment and Creeping Inflation, 1951–58

The first post-Accord period of high activity combined with monetary restraint ended in the summer of 1953. It might be argued that the timing of the turn was influenced by a sudden tightening of the market induced perhaps by overly hasty tightening actions—and, more particularly, intimations of tightening to come—by the Federal Reserve and the Treasury in the spring of 1953. But one would have to assign very great power to monetary effects to believe that the 1953 downturn was brought on in any significant degree through market reactions that raised interest rates—by what in terms of later experience seems a moderate amount—in anticipation, perhaps partly misguided, that a real monetary squeeze was ahead.

The 1953–54 downturn was characterized chiefly by its mildness; this, in fact, has been a characteristic of all the postwar recessions. In that period the Federal Reserve moved quickly and decisively. System actions to ease credit conditions through open-market purchases of securities and a cut in reserve requirements helped bring down rates on Treasury bills from 2.30 per cent to as low as 0.60 per cent in the spring of 1954 and on long-term government bonds from 3¼ per cent to 2½ per cent. Stimulative actions also led to rapid expansion of commercial banks' loans and investments, mainly the latter, and of bank deposits, mainly time deposits.

The System's actions were powerfully assisted at that time by a tax cut. Aided by the underlying strength of demand, these measures helped to turn the cycle upwards in the second half of 1954. The apparent success of fiscal and monetary policies may not have been without some costs, however. The increase in bank liquidity as a result of stimulative Federal Reserve policies immunized the banks to some extent against subsequent pressure. The difficulties the System encountered in exerting restraint in the next expansion are traceable in some measure to the liquidity reserves that it had supplied banks with during the 1954 period of ease.

There were, however, strong-enough inflationary forces at work in the expansion of 1955–57 and in the circumstances of the time —featuring the exuberant capital-spending boom and upward-cost pressures—so that it would have been difficult at best for the System to contain inflation more successfully than it did. Prices rose most of the time—wholesale prices from mid-1955 and consumer prices from early 1956. The steadiness of the rise through 1957 brought the term "creeping inflation" into popular use and made many wonder if inflationary psychology had become an important influence on economic decision-making in the private economy. Stock prices, which had risen sharply in 1954, continued to rise substantially in 1955 and early 1956; and real estate values again began rising after a post-Korean period of stability.

The end of the cyclical expansion and boom that began around mid-1954 came in the summer of 1957, as indicated by the behavior of gross national product in real terms. The rise in production had become quite moderate by 1956 and 1957, however, but price rises persisted. The Federal Reserve had steadily tightened money in the expansionary period in order to contain inflationary pressures. The timing of the last tightening action in this period—raising the discount rate by a ½ percentage point to 3½ per cent in the late summer of 1957—turned out to be unfortunate, for it came virtually at the top of the boom and onset of recession.

Along with the progressive tightening of money and credit, the timing of the discount-rate action made it easier to argue that Federal Reserve policy contributed significantly to the end of the boom. But the appearance of excess capacity provides a more plausible explanation of the downturn. The surge in business capital spending and a large rise in inventory accumulation seem to have created imbalances between areas of heavy business investment—such as autos and steel—and the emerging pattern of consumer expenditures.

The 1957–58 downturn was brief but sharp. Between the summer of 1957 and winter of 1958, which was the cyclical low, gross national product in real terms fell by about 9 per cent (annual rate). In efforts to reverse the decline, the Federal Reserve took actions to ease credit conditions. The discount rate was reduced by ½ point in the fall of 1957 and subsequent reductions were made in rapid order in early 1958. Member banks themselves with enough reserve funds to reduce their indebtedness to Federal Reserve Banks and to restore in some degree their reduced liquidity. As reserve positions continued to be eased through open-market operations and reserve-requirement reductions, bank credit became readily available, and money supply, after declining in the latter part of 1957, rose rather rapidly in 1958, as did time deposits at commercial banks.

In this atmosphere of active ease, market participants, who had more and more become aware of the flexible interest rate implications of anticyclical monetary policy, discounted a good part of the expected market effect of the policy of monetary ease. Demand for U.S. government securities in anticipation of still higher security prices was so strong that short-term rates dropped precipitately from about 3½ per cent to under 1 per cent and bond yields dropped from around 3¾ per cent to 3¼ per cent.

It turned out, however, that the economic outlook became more favorable more rapidly than many had anticipated and that prospects for a tightening of monetary policy seemed nearer at hand than many had thought. In this situation, market expectations reversed and security prices came under strong downward pressure, partly as a result of the previous build-up of speculative positions in longer term issues. And in July, 1958, the Federal Reserve intervened in the market to correct what is considered to be disorderly conditions.

It appears that the market's 1958 experience with discounting future interest rates introduced a note of caution into its later actions. The market became aware of the dangers involved in trying to outguess the Federal Reserve, let alone outguessing the economy. Dealers and other active participants still took positions that were influenced by bullish or bearish attitudes, but the bulls were more reluctant to run ahead of the herd and the bears tried to be a little more certain about the weather before emerging from their caves. This note of caution became more pronounced in the early 1960's, when the Federal Reserve began to make transactions regularly in all sectors of the market, not just in the short-term area. It raised questions about how far a policy of dealing in all maturities could be pushed without interfering with normal market processes, as had occurred in the pre-Accord period.

"Bills Only" Policy

During most of the decade of the 1950's, the Federal Reserve operated in the open market in accordance with an announced policy of confining transactions to short-term securities except when necessary to correct disorderly conditions. This became known as the "bills only" policy because Treasury bills were the instrument conventionally traded in the short end of the market. By dealing only in short-term securities, where the market was deepest and trading most active, the System limited its open-market operations to the supply or removal of bank reserves and left the determination of interest-rate structure to market forces.

A variety of technical advantages could be and were claimed for the technique. It helped to make the market for government securities more self-sustaining, which was an important considera- tion in view of the fact that the market for many years had be- come accustomed to large-scale governmental intervention. If the Federal Reserve, at any moment, could temporarily push the price of any particular security issue up or down, who would pay atten- tion to the underlying economic factors that ought to govern the market? "Bills only" helped to reduce the preoccupation of the market with guessing the System's next move and the consequent reluctance of dealers to take the risks necessary to an active and self-reliant market.

A self-sustaining market, in turn, supplied the System with a better picture of market forces. So long as the System dictated the rate pattern, how could it know what the market really wanted the rate pattern to be? A rate pattern set by the System would be artificial. For instance, a lower long-term rate set by the System would not necessarily reflect a correspondingly greater flow of investment funds. It was argued that the economy would benefit little from these artificialities, while the monetary authorities would have deprived themselves of a clear and immediate picture of the emerging situation. In other contexts it was argued, incon- sistently, that the operations of the System were not large enough significantly to affect the interest-rate structure.

Yet the System, by dealing only in bills, did not mean to deprive itself of all power over intermediate and particularly long- term rates. If money is fed in at the short end, arbitrage and sub- stitution will transmit the impluse to the long end. But the market will decide just how the impulse works itself out over the stretch.

The critics of the "bills only" doctrine also had a number of strong points to make, however. The chief one, perhaps, was the argument that the flow of funds from the short- to the long-term sector of the market was neither smooth nor quick. To pour funds into the bill market in the hope that they would spread, in part through the process of bank-credit expansion, to the long-term sector of the market was, some critics implied, like filling a long tank by pouring into it at one end not water, but some material of greater viscosity, like tar. To achieve a given effect in the long-term sector within a reasonable time, a disproportionately large volume of funds would have to be poured in at the short end. Otherwise the System might find long-term rates remaining "sticky" when it would like to see them move.

Both the System and the critics overstated their positions. The System admitted as much when it moved to an "all maturities" policy in the early 1960's, when, as we shall see, it found it necessary to put upward pressure on short-term rates while at the same time avoiding as much as possible upward pressure on long rates. At the same time, the critics apparently overestimated the extent to which the long rate could be affected by what were in effect System debt-management operations, given the strength of fundamental market forces and the limitations that concern for a self-reliant market and prudent management of its own portfolio set on System action.

The Watershed, 1958–60

The cyclical upswing that began in 1958 was comparatively brief—lasting but two years—and was associated with the emergence of developments that were to persist, as it turned out, into the early 1960's, and which were to distinguish the years 1958–63 sharply from the 1951–58 period. Gradually, both policy objectives and operating techniques were adapted to the new set of problems.

One characteristic of the 1958–60 upswing was that it stopped short of satisfactory levels of employment. The unemployment rate, which had averaged a little more than 4 per cent in the years 1955–57, averaged 5.5 per cent in 1959 and just about 5 per cent over the first five months of 1960, when the upswing was phasing out. At the time, it was thought by many that this problem of unemployment, whatever its immediate causes, would disappear not too far along in the next cyclical upswing. But this unfortunately did not prove to be the case.

Another emerging characteristic of the economy in the years 1958–60 was comparative stability in the average level of prices. Consumer prices rose, but at a slower pace than in the earlier upswing. Wholesale prices, meanwhile, stabilized on average. These price developments in part stemmed from the incompleteness of recovery from the previous recession, which was reflected in idle plant capacity and manpower resources. In turn, the price developments, as they continued, tended to modify the inflationary expectations that had been generated by previous price advances.

The third characteristic of this watershed period was the enlargement of the United States balance-of-payments deficit with other countries. The United States had been running a deficit for most of the postwar period but it was moderate in size and served the useful purpose of enabling foreign countries to build up their war-depleted liquidity reserves by adding to dollar holdings. There was little drain on the U.S. gold stock associated with the moderate deficits because foreign countries placed most of their new net dollar funds in deposits with U.S. banks or in U.S. government securities. But in 1958 and 1959 the deficit was substantially enlarged (from an annual average of less than $1 billion in 1951–57 to $3.6 billion in 1958–59) as our export surplus narrowed; and foreign countries, already well supplied with dollars, took a substantial portion of their net earnings in gold. In the two years 1958 and 1959, our gold stock declined by $3.3 billion to a level of $19.5 billion, whereas it had declined only about half that much in the eight years from the end of 1949, when the gold stock was close to its postwar peak of $24.7 billion, to the end of 1957.

The decline in the gold stock was less a worry in itself than it was as a symptom of too large a U.S. balance-of-payments deficit. It is not clear, however, to what extent this deficit influenced monetary policy during the cyclical economic upswing in domestic activity occurring at that time. Monetary policy was indeed tightened rather more than domestic economic conditions seemed to warrant in the latter part of 1958 and in 1959, but this seemed to have been less a response to the emerging balance-of-payments situation than it was to the experience of 1954–55, when massive easing and slowness to tighten had made it difficult for the Federal Reserve to regain control of bank credit later on. In addition, there appeared to be lingering inflationary fears. Fears of continued inflation were not without foundation, of course. For instance, stock prices rose sharply in 1958 and continued to rise, though more moderately, in the first part of 1959, reflecting widespread inflationary expectations. Also, interest rates moved sharply upward, with both short and long rates reaching new postwar peaks near the end of 1959 and in the early days of 1960, likewise indicating some continued inflationary expectations on the part of market participants.

While monetary policy may have been too tight in 1959, the Federal Reserve in early 1960 apparently did anticipate the need to combat a possible recession—or, at a minimum, the System saw that inflationary conditions were waning. This was brought home to the Federal Reserve by the sharp decline in interest rates in the early months of 1960, in response to the bearish market expectations that emerged when it became apparent that the economy was not so buoyant as many expected it would be and when it also became clear that the federal government was going to run a budgetary surplus in 1960. While money supply declined from mid-1959 to about mid-1960, banks in the first half of 1960 were able to reduce borrowings from the Federal Reserve to quite low levels. At the onset of the 1960 recession, conditions were favorable to rapid monetary expansion, in contrast with the situation at the onset of recession in 1957, when banks were still heavily in debt.

Many would argue, however, that open-market operations should have been more stimulative in early 1960, and the discount rate should have been reduced earlier than it was. The Federal Reserve discount rate, which had been raised gradually from a low of 1¾ per cent in the spring of 1958 to a high of 4 per cent in the late summer of 1959, was not reduced until June, 1960 (then by half a point), and was reduced again in August to a level of 3 per cent. More stimulative policies, it is said, would have kept the money supply from declining in the early part of 1960 and thereby kept the economy from going into recession. Whether money alone would have had so powerful an effect is, of course, conjectural. In addition, there was the risk of very heavy outflows of capital abroad from the even greater declines in interest rates that would likely have been the product of a more expansionary open-market policy at that time. In fact, a sharp rise in capital outflows abroad was a major problem in 1960, even though the yield on three-month Treasury bills did not fall below the 2.10

per cent to 2.40 per cent range, and led to increasing concern with the balance of payments by the monetary authorities.

The Domestic Economy and the Balance of Payments, 1960–63

The recession that began in the late spring of 1960 was over by the winter of 1961, by which time gross national product in real terms had fallen by only 2.5 per cent at an annual rate. From the winter of 1961 through 1963 real gross national product rose steadily, although at times hesitatingly. Nevertheless, there was considerable dissatisfaction with the performance of the domestic economy because unemployment did not go below 5.5 per cent of the labor force in almost three years of expansion. Many be-′ lieved that this unsatisfactory level could have been reduced if the economy had grown more rapidly, but some attributed the unemployment to structural maladjustments—an example being the problem of workers released by declining industries, like coal, who had neither the skills nor the mobility to be absorbed by other industries. Yet, it can be argued that even if a significant portion of the unemployment had been structural, a more expansionary fiscal or monetary policy than we had at the time still might have reduced it by encouraging faster economic growth, but at some cost to the price stability that was achieved.

While there was considerable debate in the early 1960's about whether structural, in contrast to total, unemployment was larger than in previous years, the need for price stability was neverthe-less manifest because of the persistence during the years 1960–63 of the large balance-of-payments deficits that had emerged two years before. Deficits remained in the $3–$4 billion range, even though the balance on transactions in goods and services with foreigners became more favorable than it was in 1958–59 as price stability contributed to maintaining and improving the competi-tiveness of United States exports in world markets. Our gold stock declined further, although the rate of decline slowed, and was $15.6 billion at the end of 1963.

Increased capital outflows from this country to major financial centers abroad played an important role in continuance of the balance-of-payments deficit in 1960 and for several years after.

This increased the concern of the monetary authorities with the balance of payments since a good part of the capital flowed abroad as a result of the policy of monetary ease being pursued in this country to encourage domestic economic expansion. With domestic money market conditions easy, funds flowed abroad because higher interest returns were available there or because borrowers took advantage of the ready availability of credit here. For instance, in 1960 and 1961 short-term capital outflows from this country were $1.3 billion and $1.5 billion, respectively, mostly representing bank loans to foreigners, after averaging less than $300 million a year in the previous seven years. There also seemed to be a large flow of presumably short-term capital abroad that was not reported in official statistics, insofar as can be judged by the "errors and unrecorded transactions" item in the balance-of-payments statistics and by the opinion of market experts.

The juxtaposition of a balance-of-payments problem, as intensified by rather heavy capital outflows, and a problem of domestic unemployment led to several adaptations in the operations of monetary policy. Basically, these all represented efforts to encourage domestic credit expansion without at the same time putting much downward pressure on short-term interest rates.

Faced with the need to minimize downward pressure on short-term rates, the Federal Reserve in the period of recession and recovery did not reduce the discount rate below the 3 per cent to which it had been lowered in the summer of 1960. Thus, it was not lowered by as much as in earlier recessions. In the fall of 1962, reserves were released to banks through a reduction in the reserve requirement against time deposits in the hope that this would provide reserves to banks with a minimum downward effect on short-term rates, for reserves would otherwise have had to be supplied, it was argued, through open-market purchases of mainly short-term securities. The Federal Reserve after the Accord had often reduced requirements, but usually in recessions, to provide reserves immediately to all parts of the country.

Abandonment of "Bills Only"

The principal adaptation in monetary instruments to cope with the short-term interest rate problem during the 1960–63 period was the abandonment in early 1961 of the "bills only" policy that had been followed since 1953. By late 1960 it had become apparent that open-market operations would have to be extended into the longer-term area if downward pressures were to be taken off short-term interest rates for balance-of-payments purposes while bank credit expansion was being promoted to encourage domestic economic growth. With open-market operations the most steadily used instrument of policy because of its inherent flexibility, an expansion in its operating scope would enable reserves to be provided through purchases of longer-term securities, which would relieve short rates of the immediate pressures associated with open-market purchases of Treasury bills. Of course, when commercial banks bought short-term securities in the process of using the reserves made available to them, such rates would tend to decline. However, this could be offset, at least in part, by Federal Reserve sales of Treasury bills, which would add to the market supply available for bank purchase. Such operations were in fact undertaken. In addition, the Treasury concentrated cash financings during the early 1960's in the short-term area, which also added to the market supply of short-term securities. Meanwhile Treasury trust account purchases of long-term securities were undertaken in an effort to contain upward, or put downward, pressure on long-term rates.

The policy of buying long and selling short came to be known popularly as "operation twist" because it represented an effort to move short and long rates in different directions by official actions —to get short rates up and long rates down—in opposition to historical market tendencies for such rates to generally move in the same direction, although with different amplitude and speed of movement. The Federal Reserve itself never officially admitted to a sustained effort to reduce long rates, although it was certainly clear to all concerned that this was a worth-while by-product of efforts to minimize downward, or exert upward, pressure on short rates.

Influence on Interest-Rate Structure

A brief look at interest-rate developments does not provide any clear insight into the degree of success of these Treasury and Federal Reserve operations, although it does suggest that any successes were marginal in character. Basic market forces were, it appears, quite resistant to twisting, or at least were so given the energy applied in official operations.

It is very possible that the comparative stability of short rates, though at successively higher levels, in the 1961–63 period was in part a psychological product of official policies, as the market, convinced that the Federal Reserve and Treasury had specific short-term interest-rate aims, guided itself accordingly. In addition, it can be argued with some justice that official policies served to moderate tendencies for long-term rates to rise, even though they may not have succeeded in reducing such rates for long. Yet, the moderateness of the economic expansion itself and the ample supply of long-term saving make one wonder how much real steam there could in any event have been behind a rise in long-term rates.

The impact of the large flow of saving was especially evident in 1962, when long rates actually declined. Long-term markets eased as a result of the rise permitted at the beginning of 1962 in maximum permissible interest rates payable on time and savings accounts at commercial banks. Such rates, which are established for member banks by the Board of Governors of the Federal Reserve System in accordance with the Federal Reserve Act and under provisions of administrative Regulation Q, were raised to make commercial banks competitive with other outlets for savings.*

Banks quickly took advantage of the change in Regulation Q and raised actual rates. The response of domestic investors and savers was prompt, massive, and by and large continued through 1963. Inflows to time and savings deposits had been large in 1961,

---

* Maximum permissible rates on time and savings deposits had been 3 per cent effective at the beginning of 1957. Effective the beginning of 1962, rates on savings deposits became 4 per cent for those held more than a year and 3½ per cent for those held less; for other time deposits maturing in a year or more the rate also became 4 per cent; for those in six months to a year 3½ per cent; for those in ninety days to six months and in less than ninety days it remained at 2½ per cent and 1 per cent, respectively. Effective July 17, 1963, the maximum rate on time deposits maturing in ninety days to a year was raised to 4 per cent.

when short-term market interest rates were relatively low, but the pace of expansion picked up sharply in 1962 (from an annual rate of 13 per cent to 18 per cent) and remained high in 1963. An unusually large part of the expansion represented business funds placed in negotiable time certificates of deposit issued by banks, which began to assume importance as yet another money-market instrument competitive with Treasury bills. Money supply also rose during these years at a rate that was by no means low in comparison with experience from 1952 onward.

These heavy inflows of time and savings deposits to banks, which caused them in turn to invest heavily in long-term comparatively high-yielding securities and loans, were probably the principal reason for the decline in long-term yields in 1962. Yields thus rose in 1963 in part because the initial structural adjustment of the financial system to the new time deposit rate had worn off. But they also rose because monetary policy in 1963 became less easy and pressures in the short end of the market were transmitted to the long end. The discount rate was raised to 3½ per cent at midyear, and during the year member banks came under more reserve pressure. By the end of 1963, both short- and long-term market rates were further above their 1960–61 lows, but still substantially below their 1959–60 peaks.

An Appraisal of Policy Caught Between Two Fires

Many have argued that the Federal Reserve in the 1960–63 period did not do all it could to expand the domestic economy. Others have said that the balance of payments was not attacked vigorously enough. What can we say about the two issues—recognizing that, as of this writing, the fires are still burning though it is not clear how hotly?

By many of those dissatisfied with the domestic performance of monetary policy in 1960–63, the existence of unemployment was taken, on the face of it, as evidence that policy should have been easier and that money supply should have risen even more rapidly. While it was generally admitted that the rapid rise in time and savings deposits (with a large amount taking the form of negotiable time certificates of deposit held by corporations) partially substituted for expansion in money, it was also contended that some of the growth was a substitute for other forms of savings and did not reflect any net new expansion of credit.

It was believed that greater monetary ease than was voted by the majority of the Federal Open Market Committee would have helped both the domestic economy and the balance of payments, since more rapid economic growth would presumably follow and this would entail rising interest rates. This view downgraded the likelihood of price inflation with more money and the likelihood of a deterioration in our export surplus, which might offset any gain on capital account. And the view depended on a number of other assumptions—none of which were certain—the chief one being the conclusion that more rapid growth would occur and therefore interest rates would rise. But money, as many have pointed out, is only one factor in growth, and its relative importance is an issue still to be decided; without a rapid expansion in credit demands generated by faster economic growth, more money would have led to even lower interest rates.

Those who were dissatisfied with the balance-of-payments performance of monetary policy seemed to feel that international capital flows were quite responsive to interest rates and that domestic spending and investment were not. So tighter money would not harm the domestic economy and would benefit the balance of payments.

But while certainty about the exact degree is lacking, it does seem that both domestic spending and international capital flows are responsive to interest rates and associated credit availabilities. Domestic investments in homes and plant and equipment, for instance, are generally considered to be influenced to some extent by long-term interest rates. On the international side, we can feel sure that short-term capital flows between the United States and foreign financial centers are responsive to differentials in short-term interest rates and credit availabilities, although we cannot be sure by how much or to what extent other conditions (such as confidence, or lack of same, in the currency) may be offsetting or contributory. Long-term capital outflows too are responsive to differentials in credit conditions, and, like short-term flows, were a source of balance-of-payments troubles in the early 1960's. To moderate long-term outflows, an interest-equalization tax on for-

eign long-term securities was proposed by the Kennedy Administration in 1963. This tax, which would in effect add to the
interest cost of such securities, was thought a more desirable
alternative either to direct capital controls or to an even tighter
monetary policy that might have imperiled domestic investment.

In evaluating the impact of changes in interest rates and credit
conditions on the domestic economy and the balance of payments,
the majority of the Federal Open Market Committee apparently
felt that the truth—or at least virtue, as Aristotle would have it—
lay somewhere in beween the extremes, and that neither the possible beneficial effects of rising interest rates on the balance of
payments nor their possible damaging effects on the domestic
economy could be ignored. Given the balance-of-payments problem, and the contributory role of short- and long-term capital outflows (including bank loans to foreigners) in the deficit, it seems
clear that the Federal Reserve felt constrained in what it could do
to expand bank credit and money domestically. The willingness
to undertake open-market operations in all maturities did not free
it from the balance-of-payments constraint. Neither such operations by the Federal Reserve nor Treasury debt management had
powerful enough upward effects on short-term interest rates to
enable the Federal Reserve to pursue an even more aggressive policy of bank-reserve expansion. But, by the same token, neither did
they have powerful enough downward impacts on long-term rates
to eliminate consideration of the need for a more aggressive policy of reserve expansion.

In this respect, some questions can indeed be raised about
whether the Federal Reserve operations of selling short-term securities and buying long-term ones were pursued with enough
vigor. Other questions can be raised, however, about whether
such operations as were undertaken were permitted to have their
full effect on long-term markets. In 1962 and 1963, the Treasury
took giant steps—through advance refundings—to lengthen the
outstanding debt. This was a laudable and important long-run
objective; however, the refundings may have had the effect of
keeping long-term rates higher than they would otherwise have
been, although the method by which they were carried out may
have a smaller impact on interest rates than regular refundings

or cash financings. One might say that, in a way, the all-maturities operating policy of the Federal Reserve contributed as much to the feasibility of lengthening the government's debt as it did to encouragement of private long-term financing.

A balanced judgment about the performance of monetary policy in the 1960–63 period would probably tend to be favorable because the recession that took place early in the period was mild, the ensuing expansion of the economy was sustained, and, withal, the balance-of-payments deficit was contained. But in making such a judgment it is not necessary to agree completely with those who believed that a serious deterioration in the quality of credit was near at hand (because, to cite one example commonly given, of the emphasis on speculative multifamily residential and commercial buildings encouraged by easy conditions in mortgage markets). Nor is it necessary to agree with the implicit high-level liquidity trap argument of those who contended that monetary policy domestically had gone as far as it could and that even more credit and even more liquidity would not be likely to increase spending. But it is necessary to recognize that the balance-of-payments situation added another dimension to monetary policy considerations.

While monetary policy performed pretty well (as evidenced by the continued expansion of money supply and bank credit and by the comparatively limited rises in interest rates) in a difficult situation, it was not by any means an unqualified success. In the final analysis, though, and in view of our continuing international and domestic economic problems in the period, monetary policy may well have been asked to do too much. Fiscal policy, while it was expansive, was not expansive enough. Hindsight makes it clear that a tax cut early in the period—say 1961 or 1962—might have helped the domestic economy and freed monetary policy to make a more concerted attack on the balance of payments.

Judgments about monetary policy in this period can at best be tentative, though, because at the present moment we are still in the midst of a very long period of cyclical upswing. Yet it is clear that Federal Reserve authorities showed flexibility and a degree of ingenuity in dealing with problems generated by the juxtaposition of large balance-of-payments deficits and a recalcitrant economy. Even so, the experience of the early 1960's—not to mention experience with other problems in earlier years—demonstrated the need for an even more coordinated use of all public policy instruments than was actually achieved.

COMPETING OBJECTIVES

The use of policy instruments cannot be considered apart from the objectives that policy attempts to reach. In general, we can say that public economic policy seeks economic growth at full employment, stable average prices, and over-all balance in international payments. But we have seldom, if ever, managed to have all these goals satisfied at the same time. In the short run, this is often a happenstance of the rhythms of world and national economic movements. Over more extended periods, also, there have been some incompatibilities among these objectives, given the nature of existing policy instruments and the economic and institutional environment. But competing objectives are nothing new to policy-makers, and they need not be overstressed. They should and can be regarded, after all, as a basic fact of economic life, calling for marginal adjustments rather than radical choices.

Price Stability and Growth

It was the compatibility of price stability and economic growth at full employment that principally troubled policy-makers in the 1950's, especially in the mid-1950's. In the course of the 1956–57 battle against inflation, growth of output and productivity slowed down. Yet price stability was not then achieved largely, it was argued by many at the time, because of the cost-push genesis of the inflationary pressures.

Critics of System policies felt that monetary policy was not a proper instrument to fight such an inflation. Monetary policy works by restricting demand, and if demand is not the cause of inflation, monetary restraint cannot be the cure, except at the cost of excessive unemployment. In the absence of self-restraint on the part of labor and management, such critics would tend to prefer full employment to price stability if such a choice had to be made.

Some other critics of monetary policy seemed to feel that apart from the question of whether inflation was of the cost-push or demand-pull variety, a little inflation—commonly called creeping inflation—was necessary for growth at full employment. In general, these critics thought that price stability enforced by tight monetary restraint created a sluggish economy that was hostile to growth of output and productivity.

The defenders of monetary policy could whittle down such arguments, but they could not altogether refute them. There is doubt whether the marginal unemployment that might be created by monetary restraint against inflation is a greater social evil than the inflation that might be generated in a high pressure economy. Most of the labor force is covered by unemployment compensation, only a limited number generally become unemployed, and those only temporarily for the most part—although the problem of long-term unemployment became more severe in the early 1960's. Inflation, on the other hand, hurts large numbers, perhaps less severely, but the damage done to savings and relative income position tends to be permanent. Moreover, even if inflation could be contained to a creep—and this seems doubtful over the long run—its continuation, and especially the growing expectation of still further inflation, would do harm to the economy through distortion of investment decisions, discouragement of saving, compulsion to speculate, and erosion of our competitive position in world markets. This suggests that growth stimulated by inflation is not sustainable. Finally, if inflation should ultimately lead to severe depression, we would end up with the worst of both worlds.

There were balance-of-payments deficits in the period of creeping inflation, but these created little worry. They were small in size and, as mentioned earlier, enabled foreign countries to increase their international reserves during a period characterized mainly by a general shortage of the dollars necessary to rebuilding both war-shattered economies and liquidity reserves. Moreover, those who felt that a little inflation was not a bad thing domestically may also have felt that a little inflation would gradually ease the world dollar shortage by enabling foreign countries to compete more effectively in world markets against U.S. products. It was not only inflation, however, that in fact brought on the large balance-of-payments deficits of 1958–63, when a dollar shortage turned into a dollar surplus—although inflation may have been a contributory factor. And those in favor of a little domestic inflation were clearly not also in favor of so large a balance-of-payments deficit.

The debate over inflation and domestic growth was not resolved by the events of 1958–63; it was only held in abeyance. The price stability in that period may have reflected lessened cost-push pressures, but this in turn might well have been the result of the higher levels of unemployment at which the economy was operating. Thus, the two objectives of full employment and price stability might once again be brought into conflict if the economy were in a period of more rapid growth with lower levels of unemployment. It was the attention paid to the balance-of-payments problem—and our failure to resolve the problem—that was, according to many, the main reason for the slow economic growth (relative to our needs) in the early 1960's. The compatibility of balance-of-payments equilibrium and full employment was, therefore, a major issue of that period.

Balance of Payments and Full Employment

In the nineteenth century when a country had an imbalance in international payments, its consequent loss of gold would be more or less automatically reflected in resraint on money and credit expansion and in higher interest rates at home. As a result, capital would tend to flow into the country rather than out, which would help the balance of payments. But the relative scarcity of credit would also tend to reduce domestic demands and lower domestic costs, and thereby reduce imports and raise exports. This too would help the balance of payments, although often at the expense of a rise in domestic unemployment.

Modern central banks and modern international currency arrangements were designed in part to avoid the harmful impact on the domestic economy of international payments imbalances. The central bank was capable of offsetting the restraining effect on domestic credit of gold outflows, while—with exchange rates among countries fixed—international financial institutions and currency arrangements enabled a country to supplement its foreign-exchange reserves during a deficit period through loans and other reciprocal arrangements.

Nevertheless, in a period of large and continuing payments deficits, like that experienced by the United States in 1958–63, the need for central bank credit restraint to improve the balance of payments gradually becomes more pressing, and a country may be faced with the old-fashioned dilemma of reconciling the balance of payments with a desire for faster domestic growth. The United States in 1958–63 was more fortunate than most countries would be in a similar situation. We had (and still have as of this writing) a large gold reserve and foreign countries were willing to continue holding a substantial portion of their net dollar earnings in deposits or securities. This gave us a longer period during which we could at least tolerate deficits, while a wide range of measures was being put into effect and world-wide adjustments in costs, prices, and interest rates were occurring which together, hopefully, would bring our international payments back into balance.

However, our large gold reserve did not give us as much leeway as it might seem to at first glance. Foreign-held dollars are a claim on our gold stock, for any foreign country (though no individual, foreign or domestic) can purchase gold at a fixed price from the U.S. Treasury. If confidence of foreigners in the stability of the dollar were to be severely shaken, there would be wholesale conversions of dollars into gold, which would deplete our ultimate international reserves and would have serious repercussions on our freedom to pursue domestic monetary policy.

In this respect our domestic gold reserve requirement poses a technical problem, for by late 1963 about $13 billion of our gold stock of nearly $16 billion was already required for domestic reserve purposes. The Federal Reserve does have power to suspend the requirement (with no important penalties up to a point), but this is at best a palliative. It would surely be better if Congress eliminated the domestic gold reserve requirement, as has already been done by most major industrial countries of the world. This would make it even clearer to foreigners that our whole gold stock stands behind their dollar holdings. And it would not make inflation any more likely in this country; there has been more than enough surplus gold in the past for Federal Reserve authorities to have pursued inflationary policies if they had been so inclined.

We can see that at some point, even in the United States, the monetary authorities may have to choose between domestic growth and the balance of payments. But, in an important sense, they do not have a choice, for both goals have to be pursued, as was done in the early 1960's. If we did not attempt to reduce our payments deficits, growth would surely not be long sustained because at some point the discipline of the balance of payments would make itself felt—just as the upsetting characteristics of sustained price inflation soon make themselves felt—and the longer this were delayed the worse probably would be the cumulative reaction. Thus both objectives have to be attained simultaneously. Differences among policy-makers and other knowledgeable observers in the early 1960's revolved principally around shadings of emphasis, with some critics of the Federal Reserve saying that not enough attention had been paid to the balance of payments and others saying that too much had been paid to it.

Specific Adaptations to the Balance-of-Payments Problem

The conflict between full employment and the balance of payments gave rise to specific measures that were meant to alleviate our international position so as to increase the degrees of freedom for monetary policy domestically—all in the context of a fixed exchange-rate for the dollar, which was taken as axiomatic. The proposal for an interest-equalization tax, mentioned earlier, was one of the more notable. The Administration also took a number of steps that were intended to reduce spending overseas in relation, most notably, to our overseas military commitments.

As another measure, the Federal Reserve and the Treasury also began in the early 1960's to buy and sell foreign currencies, and the Federal Reserve entered into arrangements with other central banks so that such currencies would be available when needed. These operations were not meant to be a fundamental attack on the root source of our balance-of-payments difficulties; rather, they aimed at smoothing out abrupt changes in exchange rates, discouraging speculative attacks on the dollar, and preventing temporary fluctuations in U.S. gold reserves. They bought time, in other words, and perhaps helped to keep the problem from getting out of hand.

The United States balance-of-payments problem in the early 1960's was also the occasion for a revised discussion of the problem of international liquidity. For one reason, measures taken to reduce the U.S. deficit would decrease the flow of dollar liquid assets and gold to foreign countries. At the same time, the difficulties of the United States balance of payments, together with the re-emergence of other countries as industrial powers, made it apparent that the ultimate reserve function of the dollar, and, to an extent, sterling, might well be shared by other currencies. Finally, the great expansion in world trade since the end of World War II raised questions about the need for more international liquidity in general.

The foreign operations of the Federal Reserve and Treasury and the greater cooperation among central banks of the world were steps in the right direction toward providing more international elbowroom. At a more fundamental level, expansion of the resources of the International Monetary Fund was proposed, and high-level groups were set up by the IMF itself and by leading trading countries to study this and other measures that might increase world liquidity. Meanwhile, some analysts proposed a new international reserve currency compounded out of a number of national currencies, but including principally, of course, the dollar.

Measures to increase world liquidity would tend to take some balance-of-payments pressure off our domestic fiscal and monetary policy instruments because the dollar itself might then be less in demand as an international reserve currency and might come under less speculative pressure when the balance of payments is adverse. But such measures, like official intervention in exchange markets, would only be a matter of buying time, for continued balance-of-payments deficits could still not be tolerated for long.

In general, it is unlikely that we will ever be assured that monetary and fiscal policies can be formulated without considering their balance-of-payments impact. And we will always be faced with the necessity of coordinating public policies to achieve multiple objectives.

COORDINATION OF POLICY INSTRUMENTS

As we mentioned earlier, an even more expansive fiscal policy in the early 1960's would probably have had a beneficial effect on the economy's ability to achieve both something like full employment and a closer balance in international payments. A tax cut, for instance, in those years would likely have stimulated more domestic spending. And this may have enabled monetary policy to concentrate more on the balance of payments.

In general, an easy fiscal policy and a comparatively tight monetary policy might have been an appropriate policy mix for encouraging both full employment and balance in international payments. This was especially attractive to the large body of analysts who felt that monetary policy had only a limited capacity to encourage spending in a sluggish economy, but that its effect on factors affecting the balance of payments, especially short-term capital flows, was comparatively large.

When the balance of payments is not a problem, though, different policy mixes may be more appropriate. For instance, to encourage growth, many analysts have advocated a policy of easy money and tight budgets. Low interest rates associated with easy money would presumably encourage increased investment spending that is basic to more rapid growth, while a tight budgetary policy—in which, for example, revenues run ahead of expenditures—would act as a brake on inflation, with the budgetary surplus providing the savings necessary to finance the additional investment without inflation.

How well this would work in practice depends on the buoyancy of the economy. A greater supply of saving may not always increase investment. In that case, it would tend to produce unemployment. That seems to have been the effect of the 1959–60 policy aimed at budget surpluses.

Apart from the theoretical problems in determining the right policy mix, our ability to adjust policy mixtures in practice is limited by, among other things, restraints on the flexibility of fiscal policy. These restraints on fiscal policy stem partly from the need for Congressional action to change tax rates and to obtain spending authorizations and partly at times from the clear and high-priority needs of defense.

Limitations on Fiscal Policy

Fiscal policy is regarded by many as the mainstay of cyclical action because it has the great virtue of being able to promise results in depressions, when monetary policy shows up to least advantage. But at the same time it has always been open to question whether fiscal policy has the necessary flexibility.

It became clear in 1962 and 1963, if it had not been clear before, that the political processes leading to a tax cut are so haphazard, so fraught with dispute over who is to benefit, that one has to be in a benevolent frame of mind to speak of fiscal *policy*. Stepped-up spending provides an alternative means of stimulating the economy through budgetary action, but it has defects of its own. It works slowly, and, once the floodgates are raised, all manner of undisciplined waste may pass in the name of anticyclical policy. On many occasions, moreover, the posture of the budget may be determined, not by considerations of stabilization policy, but by rising or falling expenditure needs, particularly in the defense sector.

Thus, a real dilemma is posed. Monetary policy cannot do the stabilization job alone, especially in light of the complexity and number of public policy objectives that have to be attained. Hence the almost universal call for a more active fiscal policy. But in light of recent experience and the institutional facts of life, the difficulties loom large. It is these difficulties that have led to proposals—such as a certain amount of discretionary tax authority for the President or a shelf of planned public-expenditure projects —that would make fiscal policy more discretionary in operation.

Debt Management

The executive branch of government has more discretionary control over debt-management policy than it does over fiscal or budgetary policy. And since the Treasury-Federal Reserve Accord these policies have often been well coordinated with monetary policies. The concerted attack of the Federal Reserve and Treasury on short-term rates in the early 1960's is a good example. Yet there are times when the debt manager is faced with a dilemma.

As a long-run matter, no debt manager wants to see an excessive amount of the debt in short-term securities. In the first place, he is then faced with a large and continual refinancing task. In the second place, a large short-term debt poses problems for the monetary authorities, for it provides banks and other holders with an instrument that can be readily marketed to obtain funds at times of monetary restraint. But how to lengthen the debt is quite a difficult problem, especially if interest cost is an important consideration.

In a boom, when the debt manager should issue long-term securities, he cannot, because the market will not take them at rates hitherto considered realistic. In a recession, when he can easily issue them, he should not, because it might interfere with recovery. The net result, if he stresses the anticyclical motive, is almost inevitable: He issues no long terms at all. In that case, of course, the average maturity of outstanding debt rapidly shortens, and soon once more threatens monetary as well as fiscal stability.

One possible answer, if circumstances are propitious, is the advance refundings so artfully undertaken by the Treasury in a climate of relative market stability during 1962 and 1963. Many seem to believe that these represent a way by which the Treasury can make progress toward lengthening the maturity of the debt without doing harm to stability. Nevertheless, the coordination of debt management with monetary policy, and the both of them with fiscal policy, poses major theoretical and practical problems.

A Coordinating Group?

It has often been suggested that action in the various areas of economic stabilization policy—monetary, fiscal, and debt—is easier to coordinate when the federal agencies responsible are brought together in some committee or council. For monetary policy this need is especially great, it has been pointed out, because many monetary and credit powers are exercised by agencies other than the Federal Reserve—by the Treasury, the Veterans Administration, the Federal Home Loan Bank Board, the Housing and Home Finance Agency, the Federal National Mortgage Association, and others.

During the Eisenhower Administration, an interdepartmental committee under the chairmanship of the Chairman of the Council of Economic Advisers, called the Advisory Board on Economic

Growth and Stability, performed some of the functions of coordination in a highly "advisory" way. The 1961 Report of the Commission on Money and Credit, a widely respected private group, which examined the whole range of money and credit policies, recommended that such a committee again be set up to provide the staff and interagency consultative machinery necessary to coordinate the varied governmental credit and monetary activities. But the Commission felt that establishment of a committee by statute would be undesirable, since its effectiveness would depend on such human factors as the President's willingness to use it and on the capabilities and interests of the chairman of the group, a role that should be assumed, they recommended, by the Chairman of the Council of Economic Advisers.

It is perhaps the unwieldiness—together with the peripheral role of many involved—of so large a group for coping with the complex and current concerns of monetary and fiscal policy that led to efforts to achieve coordination through more informal consultations among those most closely concerned. Toward the end of the Eisenhower Administration, and in both the Kennedy and Johnson administrations, the President held joint meetings at irregular intervals with the Secretary of the Treasury, the Chairman of the Federal Reserve Board, the Chairman of the Council of Economic Advisers, and the Budget Director. In addition, the various agencies can and do keep in close touch with one another; the Treasury and Federal Reserve, for instance, maintain contact partly through the medium of regular Monday and Wednesday luncheons attended by top policy-makers.

Meaning for Federal Reserve Independence

With respect to any fairly broad and formalized coordinating group, it would make considerable difference to the Federal Reserve whether the group had executive or only consultative powers. Executive powers, which could be exercised through presidential directives would, of course, require a change in the Federal Reserve Act and would mean the end of Federal Reserve independence. A consultative body is a more likely solution. But even that would put *de facto* restraints upon Federal Reserve independence. The Chairman of the Federal Reserve Board could not—and probably does not—easily face the President of the United States in meeting after meeting without giving some ground.

Some observers have argued that Federal Reserve independence has outlived its *raison d'être*. Congress gave the Federal Reserve independence because in 1913 it was thought that the function of a central bank was to protect the currency and that this was a highly technical affair that had to be safeguarded against political influence. Today the central bank has much broader goals. It is, moreover, just one of several agencies of the government pursuing these goals. Therefore, let us "coordinate" the Federal Reserve. As a matter of fact, the proposals by the Commission on Money and Credit concerning the structure of the Federal Reserve System would have gone some way toward reducing its independence from the President. For instance, the Commission recommended that the Board of Governors be reduced from seven to five members and that the chairman's and vice chairman's terms be coterminous with the President's; in addition, they recommended that the determination of open-market policies be placed in the Board rather than in the Open Market Committee, whose members include five Reserve Bank presidents.

But the issue of Federal Reserve independence is not basically one of organization, either within the government or within the System itself; it is a question of the substance of policy. The Federal Reserve from time to time has found itself in disagreement with the Administration—less so under the Eisenhower and Kennedy administrations than under the Truman Administration. When there was disagreement, the Federal Reserve's generally was the harder line, with greater concern for price stability and the long-run health of the economy outlook. Closer coordination, had it meant anything at all, would in all probability have meant pushing the Federal Reserve a little away from its "hard" line.

In the early 1960's, the close coordination and apparent similarity in outlook between the Administration and the Federal Reserve led to a consistent attack on the balance-of-payments and domestic-unemployment problems. This gives hope that informal processes will prove satisfactory for the needs of policy coordination and that the independence of the Federal Reserve and its ability to seek and advocate policies with a longer run perspective than may sometimes be possible for the Administration will be preserved.

THE STANCE OF MONETARY POLICY

So far, we have described monetary policy and the changing use of policy instruments over time as economic conditions change, analyzed monetary policy's role in light of multiple national economic objectives, and discussed problems in the coordinated use of all public policy instruments. In discussing monetary policy we have freely used the words "tight money" and "easy money," but have so far avoided being specific about what we mean by those terms. We have used instead a variety of credit and monetary indicators to characterize situations of ease or tightness, and this has been done partly because no simple definition seems possible.

For many observers, it is behavior of the money supply, narrowly defined as currency and demand deposits, that signals the direction of monetary policy. In support of this view, it can properly be said that the behavior of money depends in large part on Federal Reserve policy toward bank reserves, but so to a great extent does the behavior of time-and-savings deposits at commercial banks, for these have to be backed with reserves. Moreover, movements in the money supply will be affected by the public's preferences for other liquid assets, such as savings and loan shares and U.S. government securities. As these come to be preferred to money at high levels of employment and income, the Federal Reserve will tend to hold back growth in money so as to forestall inflationary pressures.

The behavior of the money supply has to be evaluated in relation to changes in time-and-savings deposits and other liquid assets for a balanced perspective. In addition, over the business cycle, changes in money supply to a great extent respond to changes in business conditions; these conditions influence money supply through their effect on business demand for bank credit, which also influences banks' willingness to borrow reserves to expand credit further. The behavior of money is an amalgam of the effects of policy and the effects of changes in the economy, i.e., of supply of and demand for money. The volume of money, therefore, is by no means an unequivocal indicator of the stance of monetary policy.

Interest rates are also taken by many as a key indication of monetary policy. They too have the disadvantage of being influenced by both demand and supply conditions, so that it is difficult to tell how much of their movement reflects deliberate Federal Reserve intentions to enlarge the supply of funds seeking investment or how much represents the effect of changes in credit demands. In conjunction with other data on borrowings and financial activity, the movement of interest rates can be interpreted, however, to indicate the preponderance of one side or the other. But if interest movements are a symbol rather than a strict measure of ease and tightness, their indication is qualitative rather than quantitative.

As a practical matter, in periods of unemployment for example, the Federal Reserve will generally attempt to add to the supply of credit in the hope that a greater availability and lower cost of credit will encourage more spending. Money supply will generally expand in the process. But if more faith is put on credit availability than on the money supply per se, exactly what happens to the narrowly defined money supply clearly becomes of secondary importance. In most of its postwar history this appears to have been the Federal Reserve view.

There are often periods in which money supply and interest rates are rising and falling together. This compounds the difficulties of interpreting monetary policy, for those who stress money may come to one conclusion and those who stress interest rates to another. Isolation of the forces of demand from those of supply is obviously necessary in coming to a judgment.

We can take the events of early 1960 as an example. Clearly, credit demands were being easily met then; it was obvious because interest rates were declining. On the other hand, money supply was also declining, while increases in bank credit were quite small. This was not necessarily bad, some would say, because banks were getting out of debt in the process, and when bank borrowings decline, this in itself makes credit conditions easier. Thus, those who stress credit availability might consider that monetary policy was taking a stance on the side of, or at least leaning toward, ease. The difficulty in this reasoning is that most of the decline in interest rates during the period was the result of a decline in credit demand and a change in expectations. Such a decline does gradually make credit easier, but it lacks the additional impetus to credit ease that would result from forceful actions on the side of supply and a consequent rise in the money supply and other liquid assets. However, as we suggested earlier, whether such forceful actions can be risked in a declining market and in the face of a balance-of-payments deficit is yet another of the very difficult practical problems that beset the monetary authorities.

At some risk of falling off a precarious perch, one might say that credit conditions are an important indicator of the stance of monetary policy, but that this may be overemphasized by the Federal Reserve itself. The trouble with the credit availability view is not that it is wrong, but that it sometimes tends to make policy-makers underestimate the need for more vigorous action in periods when interest-rate declines are being generated by market forces. Credit availability and cost cannot be considered apart from trends in the money supply; at the same time we must keep in mind that under modern economic conditions the money supply cannot be considered without reference to time deposits and other liquid assets.

Interpretation of monetary policy becomes even more complicated when the monetary authorities pursue a balance-of-payments objective that may be cast in terms of short-term interest rates. Market forces that impinge on such rates may then produce Federal Reserve actions affecting bank reserve availability. Unless the short rate can be stabilized by Treasury and Federal Reserve debt-management actions, it will have to be stabilized by actions affecting bank reserves and therefore bank credit and money. As a result, bank credit, money, and over-all credit conditions are influenced by a short-term interest rate objective held by policy-makers. While such a situation would not require anyone to change his view about what constitutes monetary ease or tightness domestically, it would require realization that the objectives and over-all stance of policy cannot be characterized by reference only to domestic credit or money variables.

SOME OTHER PROBLEMS

Monetary policy operates in an environment whose continuing change presents ever new problems. Having observed how some of the changes in the postwar period influenced the functioning of monetary policy, we turn briefly to a few other problems brought to the surface by that experience.

Unequal Impact of Monetary Restraint

During the 1955–57 boom, the impression grew that monetary restraint does not fall with equal weight on all parts of the economy. Big business, it was noted, possesses a number of defenses against restraint—large internal funds, a strong credit standing with the banks, preferred access to the securities market. Big government, of course, has virtual immunity to monetary restraint, although not to the rising interest costs that are its consequences. But small business, housing, and state and local governments are said to suffer disproportionately from credit restraint.

The impression, to be sure, in part may no more than reflect the fact that small business and the housing industry are groups not given to suffering in silence. But fairly solid evidence can be submitted, including a Federal Reserve survey taken at the time, that small business has been far less successful than big business in expanding its bank borrowings during booms, although this may also reflect factors other than a credit squeeze. The shrinkage in the volume of housing credit can be traced, apart from changes in demand, to the peculiar safeguards with which Congress has hedged the FHA and VA programs. Because it limited the rate of interest on these mortgages, they became less attractive to lenders as competing rates went up. As for state and local governments, if they have suffered from credit restraint, it has been through cost more than through failure to get their money. Yet taking all three groups together, it is hard to deny that general credit control seems to have produced somewhat selective effects. Selective effects are also apparent in periods of monetary ease. In the 1961–63 period, it was again the building industry that showed the most response to ease.

While these selective effects can perhaps be softened somewhat (for example, by greater attention to gaps in small business financing facilities), it would be unrealistic to assume that a stabilization policy that influences the economy as a whole will at the same time influence all sectors of the economy in completely the same degree. Selective controls are another matter, for they are specifically designed to affect certain areas to the exclusion of others. Without entering into the lengthy debate on their value for an economy in which we prefer to have the market allocate resources, it would seem from postwar experience that selective controls are generally not needed as an active part of stabilization policy, whatever may be the merits of having them available on a stand-by basis.

Monetary Policy Weakened by Financial Intermediaries?

A second observation concerns the growing role of financial intermediaries other than commercial banks. Some of these intermediaries—life insurance companies, savings and loan associations, pension and investment funds—have enjoyed extraordinarily rapid growth. A congeries of lenders has sprung up that, unlike banks, do not fall under immediate Federal Reserve control. They can be influenced, to be sure, by Federal Reserve–induced changes in the capital market, including the level of interest rates and the state of the securities markets. But they are not subject to pressure on reserves as are commercial banks. It has been argued that part of the financial mechanism has been getting away from the System and that the System's over-all control, therefore, is slipping. Further consequences that have been drawn from these premises are (1) that we should place less reliance upon monetary policy, or (2) that the Federal Reserve should be given power to control the lending of the intermediaries.

Those who have pressed the two criticisms that the Federal Reserve's impact is uneven and that it cannot control intermediaries do not always seem to have been aware that they are not entirely consistent with each other. The housing industry is a preferred customer of the biggest intermediaries; insurance companies and savings and loan associations invest heavily in mortgages. If credit control failed to touch the lenders, why is it that the borrowers fared so badly? Part of the explanation must be sought in the interest-rate limitations upon FHA and VA mortgages. But part of it probably is ascribable to the long arm of monetary policy, which reached the lenders via the capital market.

In addition, there is no evidence that intermediaries have been able to offset monetary restraint by obtaining more funds in periods of buoyant economic activity. In fact, like other lenders, they have been under pressure in those periods as demands for credit outran supply. As saving is restrained because individuals and businesses want to spend more, all financial intermediaries tend to be affected.

Velocity Changes

A third observation pertains to the rise in the velocity of money. The turnover of bank deposits has risen almost continuously during postwar expansion periods, partly thanks to the growth of intermediaries. The money supply was being held down by System policy, but the economy seemed to escape through a more intensive use of this money.

Sometimes this observation has been taken to imply that monetary restraint is ineffectual. That would be a misreading of the meaning of higher velocity. When velocity rises, liquidity diminishes. Lower liquidity certainly means restraint. The elasticity of this mechanism, the range over which the economy can absorb liquidity changes, does of course make a difference to monetary policy. It is worth noting, therefore, that the rise in velocity seems to represent a long-run phenomenon that was accelerated only mildly during the booms. In effect, it has been going on ever since the high-liquidity days of the war.

There is a question about whether we are likely in the future to reach a point at which velocity will have less upward flexibility because individuals and businesses will have finally reduced their cash and liquidity to minimum levels in relation to income. If that point is reached, the money supply would have to show more of an upward movement if high and rising levels of income are to be maintained.

Conclusion

Monetary policy has come a long way since the early postwar years, when many were ready to write it off. It has once more established itself as a force in our economic affairs. That is the first conclusion flowing from postwar experience.

Monetary policy, it is fair to say, has by and large been well handled—if by that we mean that the right judgments exceed the questionable ones. But in the bright light of hindsight some of the latter stand out—the excessive liquidity permitted at the start of the 1955 boom, the slow reaction to the 1957 recession, and the overestimation of inflationary fears in 1959. Some may also want to quarrel with the relative weight given balance-of-payments considerations as compared with the domestic economy in the 1960–63 period, although there is no unanimity among the disputants about which should have been given more weight.

The degree of effectiveness demonstrated for monetary policy has not, we think, produced major surprises. It has always been the common view that monetary policy has more power to restrain than to stimulate. There has also been no secret about the fact that, even on the restraining end, the risks of overshooting set limits to the use of monetary powers. In relation to the balance of payments, its effectiveness historically has been great. In an economy like ours, however, the use of monetary policy for balance-of-payments purposes is more than usually complicated by domestic considerations, and even its impact on capital movements is less clear than it is in other countries with smaller and more compact money and capital markets.

The postwar period also provides some evidence that, no matter how effective in comparison with other forces monetary policy ultimately is, policy will be better if it can anticipate future developments rather than merely react to past events. The mildness of the 1960–61 recession in comparison with the brief but deeper one of 1957–58 might in some respects have been influenced by the fact that policy began to reduce market tightness months before the onset of the former recession. But how great a lag there is in the application of monetary policy and its effect on spending is an issue strongly debated in the academic community and elsewhere—with estimates ranging anywhere from less than three months to a year. It is also a question whether the lag, however much of one there might be, is greater in boom than in recession.

In the last few years, monetary policy has had to face the problem of competing objectives in particularly severe form. Maximum growth and full employment have shown themselves capable of conflicting, at least in the short run, with price stability and balance-of-payments equilibrium. Some of the conflict is more apparent than real, however, because more and perhaps all the gain in growth that may be had in the short run by giving up price stability or balance-of-payments equilibrium will vanish in the long run. But competing objectives are nothing new for monetary policy—the competing elements change, the conflict remains. The policy-maker—or monetary policy as an instrument—is blamed by those who feel a strong attachment to one or the other of the goals.

Monetary policy in the early 1960's did show commendable flexibility in dealing with a multiplicity of objectives and in adapting its operating instruments to the needs of new situations. But monetary policy, however well instrumented, will always require the backstopping of its more powerful partner, fiscal policy. The Federal Reserve cannot do the job of stabilization alone, nor perhaps even the larger part of it. Fiscal policy, however, has not yet been fully domesticated. Far more work still needs to be done on its techniques and timing than on those of monetary management. Monetary policy has indeed carried a heavy burden.

5. Monetary Policy and the Control of the Postwar British Inflation

F. W. PAISH

THE NATURE OF INFLATION

Inflation may be defined as a condition in which money incomes are rising faster than the flow of goods and services on which to spend them—that is to say, faster than the real national income. The real national income, in turn, depends mainly on the volume of current domestic output, and though at times it may also be affected by changes in the relative prices at which part of the output is exchanged for imports, and in the amount of investment income received from, or paid to, foreign countries, these last two factors are usually of secondary importance. Broadly, therefore, it may be said that inflation is a condition in which incomes are rising faster than output.

To check inflation it is necessary either to accelerate the rise in output without a corresponding acceleration of the rise in incomes, or to slow down the rise in incomes without a corresponding slowing-down of the rise in output. Unfortunately, in conditions where inflation already exists, attempts to accelerate the rise in output tend to involve more than proportionate rises in incomes, while although the checking of a rise in incomes usually involves some check to the rise in output, the slowing-down of the rise in output is usually less than the slowing-down of the rise in incomes. Thus to check inflation it is usually necessary to slow down the rise in incomes, even though this will probably involve at least a temporary check to the rise in output.

In order to check a rise in incomes, it is necessary to check the rise in those forms of expenditure that create incomes. Not all expenditure is income-creating. If more money is spent on buying existing durable goods, or on titles to assets or to money, the rise in their prices does nothing directly to raise the level of incomes. If A buys an existing house from B, the sale in itself does nothing to raise incomes (except, perhaps, the income of the house-agent). Only if B then proceeds to spend the money by having a new house built, or in other ways that involve the creation of incomes by payments for the services of persons or of their assets, does the higher price paid by A lead to higher incomes. If it is possible to ensure that money paid for existing assets is not used except to pay for other existing assets, its expenditure is not inflationary, however far it raises asset prices; all that it does is to bring down the rate of interest. There is, however, a strong probability that the higher prices of existing assets and the lower rates of interest will make it more profitable to construct new physical assets, and that sooner or later income-creating expenditures will also rise unless they are in some way prevented from doing so.

In an isolated country, the effects of income rising faster than output will show themselves entirely in a rise in prices. If, however, there are a number of countries of which only one is inflating, the excessive rise in incomes and in demand there will not only force up internal prices, but will attract additional imports from abroad and will divert resources away from producing exports to satisfying the home demand. Internal inflation, at a rate faster than in other countries, thus tends to bring a rise in imports, a fall in exports and an adverse balance of payments. The larger amount of goods thus made available on the home market will slow down the internal rise in prices. Indeed, in an extremely open economy, with negligible transport costs, almost the whole of the effects of the inflation would be seen in the balance of payments, while internal prices would rise hardly at all until the currency was devalued. In a country such as the United Kingdom, which exports a large fraction of what it produces and imports a large fraction of what it consumes, the effects of inflation on the balances of payments often give rise more rapidly to anxiety than do those on the internal price level.

The task of checking inflation is rendered more difficult by the fact that it is frequently inconsistent with other objectives of policy, such as a maximum rate of output and a very low level of unemployment. An excess demand for goods and services leads directly to an excess demand for labor. When there are many more jobs vacant in a country than there are people genuinely looking for them, it is likely that anyone who leaves one job for any reason will quickly find another in his own line of business and his own district. If, however, the demand for labor is no greater than the supply, so that the number of vacancies is not greater than that of men seeking work, there is a much greater probability that to find work a man will have to change his job or leave his district, or both. This will inevitably take longer, and the number of unemployed will rise. If, therefore, political considerations require a government to try to maintain a lower level of unemployment than is consistent with the absence of inflation, the problem of stopping inflation may be insoluble.

TYPES OF ANTI-INFLATIONARY POLICY

If a government genuinely desires to check an inflation, it has three types of technique it may use. In the first place, it may attempt to restrict income-creating expenditure either on consumption or on the production of new assets, by means of direct controls on the spending of money. Second, it may attempt to reduce expenditure on consumption by a faster rise in tax payments by the public than in government expenditure. A third method is to try to discourage income-creating expenditure indirectly, by reducing the quantity of money (or preventing it from rising as rapidly as money incomes), and so forcing up the rate of interest.

Sometimes it is only the last of these that is classified as "monetary policy," as distinguished from direct controls and budgetary policy. All three of them, however, affect either the quantity of money or its velocity or circulation, and all three, therefore, have their monetary aspects. Further, all three have been in use in the United Kingdom, in greater or less degree, throughout the postwar period, and it is not possible to discuss the practice of any one of them without reference to the others. We shall therefore regard all three of them as coming under the heading of "monetary policy" in its wider sense, and shall proceed to consider them in turn.

Direct Controls

The first method, that of restricting the rise in income-creating expenditure by means of direct controls, was developed during the war, and has been in use, though to a steadily diminishing extent, ever since. Direct controls can be classified under four main headings: those that prevent businesses from maintaining the (money) value of their inventories; those that limit the amounts that can be spent on consumption and so enforce a rise in saving; those that restrict fixed investment directly; and those that attempt to restrict investment indirectly by restricting financial investment.

1. *Price controls.* The first-mentioned type of direct control is also the form that usually appears first in time. When a massive increase in government expenditure, usually for war purposes, simultaneously raises incomes and diverts resources away from the production of consumption goods, the first attempt to prevent the rise in consumer demand and the fall in consumer goods output from causing a rapid rise in prices is to impose direct *price control* on many types of consumption goods. This prevents retailers and wholesalers from raising prices rapidly enough to keep their sales down to the reduced level of replacement supplies. Hence, stocks of consumer goods are progressively depleted. Holders of stocks therefore find themselves in possession of growing amounts of money which they cannot spend on replacements, and which they are obliged to use for debt repayments, or to invest in government or other securities, or to hold idle.

2. *Rationing.* This stage can continue, however, only as long as stocks last. When they approach exhaustion, consumers can no longer find as much in the shops as they would like to buy at the prices fixed, and are therefore obliged to save part of their income. Under such conditions the distribution of the available supplies among consumers becomes extremely arbitrary. In order to obtain a fairer distribution, systems of *rationing* are introduced for supplies of most new goods, except for those regarded as luxuries, to the extent that these are still allowed to be produced.

3. *Fixed capital.* The third type of direct control consists of *restrictions on the creation of new fixed capital.* This control is likely to be most effective over new building, where it is possible to enforce a strict system of licensing. Output of other forms of fixed capital is more difficult to control directly, and recourse is often had to indirect methods, such as the control of supplies of iron and steel and of other materials, as well as of labor, necessary to their production. Control over the distribution and use of other types of new fixed capital is also more difficult to enforce than over new building.

The combined effect of the preceding three types of control is to limit the amount of money people can spend in ways that create additional incomes. If the restrictions are fully effective, the level of incomes can be rendered independent of the quantity of money in the economic system as a whole, and the quantity of money can be expanded indefinitely without causing inflation. If people hold money idle, the government can safely create more to take its place; while if they use it to buy existing assets, they force down the rate of interest and enable the government to borrow cheaply.

4. *Securities issues.* The purpose of the fourth type of direct control, that over new capital issues and the borrowing of money, seems to be twofold. On the one hand, this control attempts to prevent other borrowers from competing with the government for funds and so to concentrate the excess money on the market for government securities. On the other hand, it provides a second line of defense against unauthorized private investment. As long as there is a general excess of money in the system, so that very few persons or firms are short of cash, it is doubtful whether this type of control goes far toward the achievement of either of its objectives. Only when money begins to become scarce, so that many investors would have to obtain capital from someone else in order to finance investment they are not otherwise prevented from carrying out, is this type of control likely to have any appreciable effect.

5. *Limitations of direct controls.* Once the necessary machinery for enforcement has been created, the policy of checking a rise in money incomes by means of direct controls can be very effec-

tive—under certain conditions and for a limited time. As a permanent policy, effective for the control of inflation under all conditions, it is likely to break down. In the first place, its success depends on the willingness of the population to work and sell in exchange for money, part of which they cannot spend, at least on the things they want. As long as they continue to expect that they will be allowed to spend their involuntary savings in the not too distant future, they may be willing to continue to accept payment in money. But as the prospect of being able to spend freely their accumulated money savings becomes increasingly remote, they will become increasingly unwilling to add further to them, and ultimately it may become possible to obtain the use of services or to buy useful goods only if payment is made in kind. A controlled inflation pushed to extremes reaches the same ultimate result as an open inflation—money ceases to be used as a medium of exchange, and the economy resorts to barter.

A second difficulty is that the efficient enforcement of direct controls depends largely on the effective restriction of supplies. In time of war, when resources are extensively and often compulsorily employed for military purposes, it is relatively easy to prevent the substantial diversion of resources to the production of goods and services of low priority. But when, at the end of a war, large quantities of resources are released from military use, it becomes increasingly difficult to prevent their diversion to what the government regards as low-priority uses, and to prevent their products from being sold to the public. While the rationing system may continue to be effective for a limited number of essential commodities, it is likely to be much less effective for a wide range of nonessentials of which there was little production during the war. The result is that many of the resources released from the war, instead of going into high-priority uses such as capital goods and exports, or into expanding the output of essential consumption goods, tend to be absorbed into the production of consumption goods which, although officially regarded as of low priority, are in keen demand from an overliquid and luxury-starved public. The final effects of trying to maintain a system of direct controls, when it can no longer be enforced effectively, are not only an inflationary rise in incomes but a serious distortion of the structure of production.

Another disadvantage of the use of direct controls is that they keep down the amount of actual inflation only at the cost of building up behind them a very large potential inflation in the form of an excessive stock of money. This excessive stock of money was one of the main reasons why it was so difficult to control inflation in the United Kingdom after the war. In 1938, clearing bank deposits averaged £2,213m., or 46 per cent of national income; by 1945, they had risen to £4,541m., or 54 per cent; and by 1947, to £5,454m., or 64 per cent. This 50 per cent rise in the ratio of bank deposits to national income is an indication of the potential inflationary pressure built up behind the controls.

Saving Through Budget Surpluses

The second principal method of keeping down incomes is the use of surpluses in the governmental budget. In principle, the operation of this method is simple: Money is subtracted from incomes by increased taxation or reduced government expenditure, and is used for the repayment of government debt. The method is most effectively disinflationary when the budget surplus is used to repay debts to the banks, through Treasury redemption or purchase of government securities from them.

In this situation, the money subtracted from incomes is cancelled, at least until it is re-created by the expansion of other bank assets. If the surplus is used to repay government debt due to the central bank (the Bank of England), thus reducing the commercial banks' cash reserves, or if it is used to retire Treasury bills held by the discount market and the banks, thus reducing the banks' liquid assets ratios, the repayment may have not only the primary effect of reducing the quantity of bank deposits directly but also the secondary effect of obliging the banks themselves to reduce their deposits further by cutting down their nonliquid assets. The effects of debt repayment to the banks come, however, under the heading of operations on the quantity of money, which are dealt with in the next section. Here we shall deal only with the effects of budget surpluses that affect the use of money rather than its quantity.

Even if a budget surplus is used to pay off debt to (or reduce the need for borrowing from) the general public, its effects will still be disinflationary, though less so than if it had been used to cancel money. Most investors whose government securities are paid off will treat the proceeds as capital. They will therefore not spend them on consumption, but will either hold them idle or will reinvest them, usually in existing assets. Not until they come into the hands of someone who uses them to pay for the construction of new physical assets will they again become income, and this will happen only after a longer or shorter time lag. The effect of an increase in the budget surplus and its use to pay off securities held by the public will therefore be to reduce consumption and check the rise in incomes, while at the same time tending to bring down the rate of interest and usually, after a time lag, to permit an increase in investment. It is, however, possible for the higher taxes or reduced government expenditure to make business prospects so much worse that, even with lower interest rates, there is no incentive to increase the production of new assets. If this is so, the disinflationary effects of the policy will be greatly increased.

So far, the effects of an increased budget surplus seem to be identical with those of an increase in the level of voluntary saving. The truth, however, is less simple. In the first place, an increased budget surplus checks the rise in incomes only if it involves an immediate reduction in income-creating expenditure. It is unlikely that this fall in expenditure will ever be equal to the whole of the rise in the budget surplus, and in some cases it may be very much smaller. There are, for example, some taxes, such as death duties and stamp duties on the transfer of securities and property, that are normally paid almost wholly out of capital. An increase in these, yielding a budget surplus used to repay government debt to the public, merely pays back as capital money originally paid out of capital, and has little or no net effect.

Again, if very high taxes are imposed on rich men, especially those with property, they are likely to be paid in part, and often to a considerable extent, either out of capital or at the expense of a reduction in current saving. Only if the increased taxes are imposed on the relatively poor is it at all certain that they will involve an almost equal reduction in current consumption. Thus the more progressive the system of taxation, the more likely it is that increased taxes will be paid out of capital or at the expense of new savings, and the less effective they are likely to be in checking an excessive rise in incomes.

The United Kingdom is fortunate to have found two forms of tax which, although probably highly regressive in incidence, have aroused relatively little political controversy. One of these consists of the extraordinarily high excise and customs duties imposed on tobacco and on beer and most other alcoholic drinks, which together provide well over one fifth of the total tax revenue. The other is the flat-rate national insurance contribution, paid by every employed person, which at present provides nearly half the total amounts paid out by the National Insurance Funds, in retirement, sickness, unemployment, and other benefits, and to which the political objection is very much less than if it had been called by its true name of a poll tax on employed persons. If these taxes were replaced by still higher levels of progressive income taxation, there can be little doubt that, with an unchanged budget surplus, the amount of money withdrawn from the income circulation would be substantially reduced.

In addition to the difficulty that direct taxes on high incomes are likely to be paid either out of capital or at the expense of savings, there is the additional difficulty that very high marginal rates of income taxation arc likely to have undesirable effects in distorting the use of resources. This is because they diminish the incentive to earn additional taxable income. The choice is probably less between work and leisure, in the sense of idleness, than between work that produces taxable income and work that produces nontaxable benefits, sometimes in the form of unpaid services within the household. In addition, very high rates of income taxation provide a great incentive both for the legal avoidance and the illegal evasion of tax liability, and large amounts of valuable resources may be devoted to these activities, and to their prevention, instead of to increasing the real national income. When, therefore, taxation is already very high, governments may well hesitate before seeking to check inflation by raising it further. Indeed, in most Western countries a reduction rather than an increase in the proportion of national income taken in taxation would probably be desirable as a means of increasing the rate of growth of the real national product.

The economic disadvantages of seeking to check an inflation by obtaining a larger budget surplus through a reduction in government expenditure are much less marked. Reductions in expenditure through mere administrative economies, though no doubt always possible, are, however, likely to be limited. Really substantial reductions of expenditure are usually possible only through major changes in the activities or policies of the government, many of which would be almost, if not quite, as unpopular as an increase in taxation. The most popularly acceptable are likely to consist of reductions in defense expenditure, as long as these do not obviously increase the danger of war or of defeat in war. Even here, however, large and rapid reductions are likely to release highly localized and specific resources for which it is difficult quickly to find alternative uses. Hence the fall in money incomes is likely to be accompanied by some corresponding fall in national product. On the whole, the most that can reasonably be hoped for in most countries, in the absense of a major change in the international political situation, is that government expenditure should be stabilized in real terms while real national income continues to rise; or at any rate that government expenditures should rise more slowly than national income. If even this modest hope could be realized, a gradual rise in the budget surplus could be made consistent with a gradual fall in the proportion of the national income taken in taxation.

CONTROLLING THE QUANTITY OF MONEY

1. *Through budget surpluses.* So far, we have considered methods of checking an inflation in ways that involve changes in the uses of a fixed quantity of money, as between consumption on the one hand and investment and idle balances on the other. Such methods, while tending to check a rise in money incomes, also tend to reduce interest rates and so to offset part of the initial effect. We now turn to methods that affect not only the distribution of money between the different purposes for which it is used, but also its aggregate quantity. We may distinguish between three

methods: first, those that withdraw money from incomes while permitting a rise in capital expenditures; second, those that withdraw money from both income and capital expenditures together; and finally, those that withdraw it initially from capital expenditures only.

The first of these methods brings some reduction in the rate of interest, and so to some extent offsets the effect of the initial withdrawal of money from incomes. The last method exercises its effects entirely through a rise in interest rates and a consequent check to investment. The second method, while exercising a doubly disinflationary effect on incomes, has an indeterminate effect on interest rates, depending on how far the fall in the demand for money to finance investment, brought about by the reduction in the expected yield of new physical assets, offsets or outweighs the fall in the supply of money available for investment.

An example of a withdrawal of money from incomes, accompanied by a smaller rise in money available for investment, is a budget surplus used to pay off government securities held by the banks, or to repay a bank advance to a nationalized industry. The immediate effect is a fall in bank deposits, a fall in the banks' nonliquid assets, and a rise in both their cash and liquid assets ratios.* The banks will therefore be in a position to lend more or

---

* Banks in the United Kingdom keep their surplus funds in the form, not of cash reserves, but of liquid assets other than cash. These noncash liquid assets consist partly of very short loans to the discount market (call money) and partly of bills maturing in not more than three months. The loans to the discount houses are now used mainly to finance holdings of Treasury bills, while some 75 per cent of the banks' bill holdings also consist of Treasury bills. Since 1935, the banks themselves have not purchased Treasury bills directly from the Treasury, but have bought them from the market, usually when they have not more than two months to run. The clearing banks keep their cash reserves as nearly as possible at the agreed minimum of 8 per cent of deposits, but try to keep their combined holdings of cash, call money, and bills at appreciably above the conventional minimum of 30 per cent. The size of the desired excess varies with the season, being at its highest in December, reduced to 28 per cent in November, 1963, before the seasonal flow of tax payments begins, and at its lowest in March, when issues of Treasury bills are normally at their lowest.

The discount houses have the privilege of borrowing money in virtually unlimited amounts from the Bank of England at bank rate against the security of Treasury bills, though the Bank usually employs open-market operations to prevent them from having to do so as the result of merely

to buy more securities, thus tending to bring down long-term interest rates, a tendency that will be reinforced by the fall in the expected yield of capital brought about by the increase in tax receipts or the fall in government expenditure.

An example of a case where the withdrawal of money from incomes leaves the quantity available for investment unchanged is more difficult to find in a system where money consists of a mixture of notes and deposits. In a system where money is created by government decree, it might be secured by merely canceling notes to the extent of the surplus. In a check-using system, it would be necessary, in repaying government debt to the banks, to do so in a way that would leave unchanged the proportions between the different classes of bank assets. It would therefore be necessary to use an amount equal to about 8 per cent of the budget surplus to repay debt to the Bank of England, thus reducing the commercial banks' cash reserves: about one fourth to repay Treasury bills held by the commercial banks and discount houses; about one sixth to repay government securities held by the commercial banks; and about one half to repay the bank advances of local authorities or nationalized industries.

Examples of the case where money is withdrawn from both consumption and investment uses are the use of an over-all budget surplus to repay government debt to the Bank of England and its use to repay Treasury bills held by the discount houses or the clearing banks. If debt is repaid to the Bank of England, the fall in the Bank's assets will be accompanied by an equal fall in the cash reserves of the commercial banks. These will have to replenish their cash reserves by calling in loans from the market, which will be forced to borrow from the Bank at bank rate. Thus

---

accidental fluctuations: That is to say, it supplies additional cash to the market by buying bills or lending money through its agents at the ordinary market rate. If the banks are short of cash but have surplus liquid assets, they call in loans from the discount market, thus obliging the market to borrow from the Bank. If the Bank wishes to force up short-term rates, it allows the discount houses to come to the Bank and borrow at bank rate; if not, it supplies the necessary cash through open-market operations.

Up to 1958, the clearing banks holdings of securities were larger than their loans; but between 1958 and 1961, loans increased from 30 per cent of deposits to nearly 50 per cent, while securities fell from 33 per cent to 15 per cent, thus returning to the ratios of the 1920's.

the effect will be a rise in short-term interest rates and, with the depletion of the banks' holdings of call money, a fall in their liquid-assets ratio. In fact, the Treasury does not operate by varying its debt to the Bank of England (leaving that to the open-market operations of the Bank itself). In practice, if the Treasury wishes to use an over-all budget surplus in a way that will exercise the maximum disinflationary effect, by reducing the quantity of money not only in the income circulation but also in the capital circulation, it employs it in paying off Treasury bills as they mature. This has a double effect on interest rates. By making Treasury bills scarce, it tends to bring down short-term interest rates. At the same time, unless the banks and discount houses can obtain a larger share of the smaller issue, it reduces the banks' liquid-assets ratio.

In the years before 1961, when the banks' proportion of loans to securities was smaller than they would have liked, their first reaction to an inadequate liquid assets ratio was to sell securities. Since 1961, however, their ratio of loans to deposits has been nearly as high as they are prepared to see it go, and a shortage of liquid assets is therefore more likely to oblige them to restrict loans as well as to sell securities. The effectiveness of a shortage of Treasury bills for checking a rise in income-creating expenditure is therefore likely to be more direct.

In point of fact, there has been no recent year when the government has had a budget surplus, on account of current operations, large enough to cover the whole of its extra budgetary expenditure, let alone leaving a margin for debt redemption. Though there was a time, in 1948–50, when it was able to do so, in recent years it has been able to repay short-term debt to the banks, if at all, only out of money borrowed elsewhere.

2. *Debt-management policy.* Even though the government is unable to achieve an over-all surplus, it is still possible for the monetary authorities (that is to say, the Treasury and central bank acting in conjunction) to control the quantity of money by changes in the amounts and forms of their debts to banks and others. In a purely note-using economy, a reduction in the quantity of money could be achieved by the Treasury's borrowing money from the public and hoarding or destroying it. Alterna-

tively, if the notes were the liability of the central bank, the same result could be achieved by the central bank's selling assets and cancelling the notes received in exchange. In a modern check-using economy, however, the process is more complicated.

In the United Kingdom today, the vast majority of bills in existence are the obligations of the Treasury. Hence a large rise in bank rate is widely regarded as a method that, although likely to be effective if carried far enough, is an expensive one which should be reserved for moments of great emergency. The cost of high short-term money rates to the Treasury is greatly increased by the fact that very large amounts of short-term Treasury liabilities are held by overseas owners of sterling balances, who do not pay income tax and whose increased interest payments constitute an additional burden on the balance of payments.

In view of the high cost to the Treasury of large rises in short-term rates of interest, and of the belief that for checking an inflation it is a rise in the long-term rate of interest that is mainly relevant, attention has in recent years been directed to the possibility, not of making cash scarce in relation to other liquid assets, but of reducing the supply to the banks of *all* types of liquid assets taken together. This is possible because some 80 per cent of all bills in existence now consist of Treasury bills. By restricting the volume of Treasury bills on the market, it is possible to restrict the amount of liquid assets available for the banks.

There are three possible ways of cutting down the supply of Treasury bills available to the discount market and the banks: (1) to sell more of an unchanged volume of Treasury bills to holders of existing bank deposits; (2) to sell more securities to the banks themselves, using the proceeds to pay off Treasury bills; (3) to pay off Treasury bills out of the proceeds of sales of securities to holders of existing bank deposits.

In the early stages of credit restriction, when financial and other institutions are still very liquid, a moderate rise in bill rates may be sufficient to induce nonbanking investors to take up substantial quantities of Treasury bills. But as money becomes increasingly tight, it takes increasingly high bill rates to induce nonbank holders even to retain their existing holdings, and other methods become correspondingly more attractive.° Similarly, the sale of securities to the banks is possible only while they have a substantial surplus of liquid assets; so that, while this method may be useful in the initial stages of reducing their surplus liquid assets ratios, it ceases to be practicable as soon as their liquidity position becomes less comfortable. While therefore these measures may be useful in the early stages of credit restriction, to push the reduction of the banks' liquid assets ratios to the point where they will be obliged to restrict their holdings of nonliquid assets necessitates recourse to the sale of securities to the public.

The main way in which the Treasury sells additional securities to the public is to make periodical large issues on the capital market. Insofar as these are not subscribed for by the public, they are taken up by "government departments" (mainly, it is believed, by the central bank), and subsequently sold off gradually on the stock exchange as opportunity offers. Thus, in fact, government securities are kept continuously on offer to the public at market rates. The chief difficulty this policy has encountered is that the Treasury, before it can obtain funds with which to pay off its short-term bills, has to provide not only for all governmental expenditure (plus the cost of any acquisitions of gold by the Exchange Equalization Account not covered by sales of additional bills to holders of increased sterling balances), but also for the repayment or conversion of several hundred millions of medium-term securities maturing each year. Banks and other holders of these can always replenish their stock of liquid assets by allowing them to mature without replacement; and the Treasury is always under the necessity of finding new holders to take their place. Once, therefore, the restriction of the quantity of money held for investment has been carried a certain distance, it becomes increasingly difficult for the Treasury to carry it further by means of the so-called funding policy, or even to prevent the liquid assets and deposits of the banks from rising again.

° If the effect of high short-term interest rates is to attract money from abroad for the purchase of Treasury bills, there is no effect on the internal monetary position. Before the transaction, the foreigners hold gold or its equivalent and the Exchange Equalization Account holds Treasury bills; after it, the foreigners hold the Treasury bills and the Exchange Equalization Account the gold.

3. *Banking and credit controls.* It is largely because of the difficulty the Treasury and the Bank of England have found in keeping the banks' liquid assets down to a level that would compel
them to restrict their holdings of nonliquid assets, that governments have from time to time "requested" the banks to restrict
their loans, even when the banks' own liquidity positions would
have allowed them to expand them substantially. These requests
have in the main taken two forms: (1) to restrict certain classes
of loans, for uses the government regarded as of low priority;
(2) more recently, notably in the sterling crises of 1957 and 1961,
to restrict total loans, regardless of their purpose. The very rapid
rise in bank loans after the withdrawal of restrictions on bank
lending in 1958 indicates that the restrictions had been more
effective than had been believed at the time.

In 1958, at the time of the removal of restrictions on bank lending, the government introduced a new instrument for the control
of bank liquidity. The Bank of England was empowered to require
the banks to hold, in addition to their normal cash reserves,
"special accounts" at the Bank of England equal to a proportion
of their deposits that could be varied from time to time. These
"special accounts," which were to bear interest at approximately
the Treasury bill rate, were not to be regarded as part of the
banks' liquid assets, and their institution would thus reduce the
banks' liquid-assets ratios. In an emergency, it would therefore be
possible for the Bank of England to reduce the banks' liquid-assets
ratios without being forced to sell securities to the public, probably on a falling market.

The Bank first put its new powers into force in May, 1960, as
part of the measures introduced to check the overrapid rise in
money incomes, with an instruction to the banks to hold 1 per
cent of their deposits on "special account." In July, 1960, the
requirement was raised to 2 per cent, and in August, 1961, to 3
per cent. As the rate of rise of incomes slackened, the balance of
payments improved and confidence in sterling was restored, the
percentage of bank deposits to be held on "special account" was
reduced, to 2 per cent in May, 1962, to 1 per cent in October, and
to nothing in December.

A somewhat similar step, though operating in the opposite

direction, was taken in November, 1963. At that time fears were expressed that the Bank's success in taking advantage of the firm market to sell long-dated government securities to the public was reducing the supply of Treasury bills available to the market and was threatening to run the banks short of liquid assets. To prevent an undesired tightening of credit at a time when the government had no wish to check the rise in demand and output, the Bank of England announced that the minimum liquid-assets ratio that the clearing banks were expected to maintain had been reduced from 30 per cent to 28 per cent of their deposits.

With the two instruments of "special accounts" at the bank of England and a variable liquid-assets ratio, the Bank of England should in future be able to control the liquidity position of the banks irrespective of its ability to sell long-dated government securities to the public.

Operation of Anti-Inflationary Policies in Postwar Britain

Direct Controls—1945–47.

While some of the policies discussed above, and especially the financial controls over the lending and borrowing of money and the raising of new capital, have been in force in the United Kingdom with varying degrees of rigor throughout the whole postwar period, we can divide the past nineteen years (1945–64) into four distinct phases, each clearly characterized by the emphasis given in government policy to one or another of the three main classes of counterinflationary policy just described.

In the first phase, which lasted from the end of the war until nearly the end of 1947, the main emphasis was on direct economic controls. During the war, and especially in the years after 1942, there had been built up an elaborate series of controls on consumption and investment. These were effective in slowing down the rise in prices and incomes during the later years of the war. The rise in the volume of bank deposits, however, which in the early years of the war had lagged behind the rise in incomes, was accelerated in the later years; and by the end of the war the ratio of bank deposits to national money income was considerably

TABLE 1

NATIONAL MONEY INCOME, CLEARING BANK DEPOSITS, NOTE CIRCULATION, AND YIELD

ON CONSOLS

(In Pounds Sterling)

	Estimated Net National Money Income	Average Clearing Bank Deposits	Ratio of Deposits to National Income (Percentage)	Yield on Consols	Average Note Circulation	Ratio of Note Circulation to National Income
1913	2,368	740	31.2	3.39	155	6.5
1921	4,460	1,764	39.6	5.21	437	9.8
1922	3,856	1,730	44.9	4.42	400	10.4
1923	3,844	1,629	42.3	4.31	388	10.1
1924	3,919	1,622	41.4	4.39	391	10.0
1925	3,980	1,610	40.5	4.44	383	9.6
1926	3,914	1,615	41.3	4.55	375	9.6
1927	4,145	1,661	41.0	4.56	373	9.0
1928	4,154	1,709	41.1	4.47	372	9.0
1929	4,178	1,743	41.7	4.60	362	8.7
1930	3,957	1,757	44.1	4.48	359	9.1
1931	3,666	1,711	46.7	4.39	355	9.7
1932	3,568	1,745	49.0	3.74	360	10.1
1933	3,728	1,906	51.1	3.39	371	10.0
1934	3,881	1,830	47.2	3.10	379	9.8
1935	4,109	1,947	47.4	2.89	395	9.6
1936	4,388	2,156	49.1	2.93	431	9.8
1937	4,750	2,220	46.7	3.28	480	10.1
1938	4,816	2,213	46.0	3.38	486	10.1
1939	5,160	2,175	42.2	3.72	507	9.8
1945	8,480	4,541	53.6	2.92	1,284	15.1

(continued)

TABLE 1 (continued)

	Estimated Net National Money Income	Average Clearing Bank Deposits	Ratio of Deposits to National Income (Percentage)	Yield on Consols	Average Note Circulation	Ratio of Note Circulation to National Income
1946	7,950	4,922	61.9	2.60	1,358	17.1
1947	8,520	5,454	64.0	2.76	1,384	16.2
1948	9,605	5,703	59.3	3.21	1,254	13.1
1949	10,140	5,761	56.8	3.30	1,269	12.5
1950	10,701	5,800	54.1	3.54	1,287	12.1
1951	11,771	5,918	50.3	3.78	1,342	11.4
1952	12,686	5,844	46.0	4.23	1,435	11.3
1953	13,609	6,012	46.2	4.08	1,532	11.3
1954	16,447	6,225	43.0	3.75	1,630	11.3
1955	15,360	6,171	40.1	4.17	1,760	11.4
1956	16,753	5,998	35.8	4.73	1,875	11.2
1957	17,656	6,122	34.7	4.98	1,967	11.1
1958	18,427	6,319	34.3	4.98	2,033	11.0
1959	19,254	6,661	34.6	4.82	2,101	10.9
1960	20,486	6,900	33.7	5.42	2,211	10.8
1961	21,869	7,035	32.1	6.20	2,306	10.5
1962	22,631	7,228	31.9	5.98	2,326	10.3
1963 (est.)	23,750	7,560	31.8	5.59	2,397	10.1

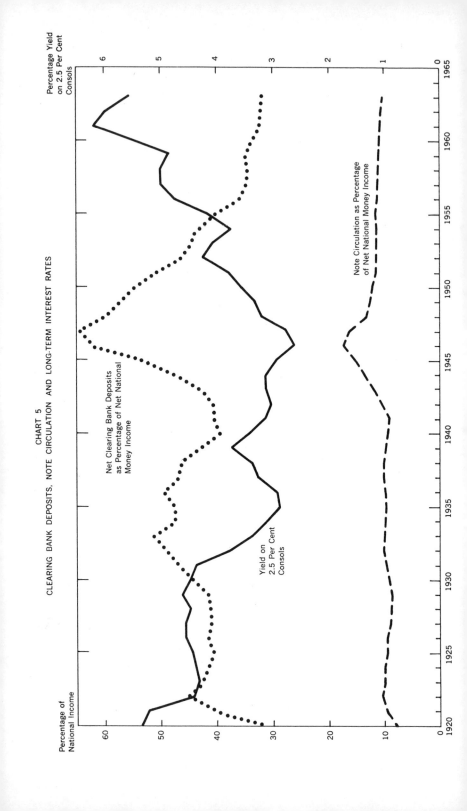

CHART 5
CLEARING BANK DEPOSITS, NOTE CIRCULATION AND LONG-TERM INTEREST RATES

Percentage Yield on 2.5 Per Cent Consols

Percentage of National Income

Net Clearing Bank Deposits as Percentage of Net National Money Income

Note Circulation as Percentage of Net National Money Income

Yield on 2.5 Per Cent Consols

higher than in 1938 (see Table 1 and the chart). Since, however, the controls were largely successful in keeping this new money out of consumption expenditures, it was possible to confine its effects almost entirely to investment in existing assets and securities, where it kept prices of assets high and interest rates low.

It was, no doubt, the remarkable effectiveness of the physical controls in the later years of the war that induced the government in the immediate postwar years to embark upon a policy of expanding the money supply substantially further, while relying on direct controls to prevent its escaping into consumption expenditures and raising incomes and prices there. The motives behind this policy seem to have been mainly four: (1) to bring down the interest burden of the national debt, especially on the securities which it was proposed to issue as compensation to the former owners of nationalized industries; (2) to promote the rapid re-employment of men released from the armed forces; (3) to provide capital on easy terms for those forms of investment approved by the government; and (4) to carry further the curtailment of investment incomes.

The budget deficit of over £850m.* for 1946 was therefore financed mainly by borrowing from the banks; so that between January, 1946, and January, 1947, clearing bank deposits rose by £900m., or nearly 20 per cent. But at levels of under 3 per cent, long-term interest rates proved resistant to even so massive an injection of money as this. Although during 1946 the ratio of deposits to national income rose from about 55 per cent to nearly 65 per cent (as compared with 46 per cent in 1938), the market yield on 2½ per cent consols fell only from 2¾ per cent to just over 2½ per cent.†

By early 1947, it was becoming clear that under peacetime conditions the physical controls could no longer be relied upon to keep the excess money out of consumption expenditures. The effects of excessive purchasing power, combined with those of

* These and subsequent budget figures are those given in the National Income estimates for the Revenue Account of the Central Government. They cover calendar years and include the cash surpluses of the National Insurance Funds.

† See Table 1. For a fuller discussion of this period, see F. W. Paish, "Cheap Money Policy," *Economica,* August, 1947.

price controls, showed themselves in a series of physical shortages, of which the most serious was coal. In spite of the controls, the rise in consumer expenditures and in labor earnings and prices began to quicken (see Tables 2 and 3). Perhaps most serious of all, the diversion of resources to meet the rising home demand checked the rise in the volume of exports, which had shown an encouraging start in the second half of 1945 and the first half of 1946.

In 1947, therefore, the attempt to hold down long-term interest rates by the creation of large amounts of new money was abandoned; the ratio of bank deposits to national income began to fall; and long-term interest rates started on their long climb that, apart from temporary checks in 1953–54 and 1958–59, did not reach its peak until 1961. The effects of the 1946 expansion, however, continued to be felt throughout 1947, culminating, in spite of heavy drawings on the North American loan, in the balance-of-payments crisis of the autumn; and in November an emergency budget inaugurated a new policy.

Budget Surpluses—1948–51.

The autumn budget of 1947, supplemented by the spring budget of 1948, imposed additional taxation at a time of falling government expenditure. They brought about the period of massive saving through central government budget surpluses associated with the name of Sir Stafford Cripps. During the four years 1948–51, the central government budget surpluses on income account aggregated over £2,400m. (see also Table 4), and on income and capital accounts combined, over £2,600m. During the same period, the local governments made capital expenditures (mainly on building small houses to rent at subsidized rates) to the extent of £1,200m., and nationalized industries to the extent of over £700m., both in excess of their own savings. Thus the aggregate net savings of all the public authorities combined were some £700m. in excess of their combined net capital expenditures. More than half this surplus was used to reduce central government debt to the banks, which fell by some £400m. between the end of 1947 and the end of 1951. This repayment of government debt was sufficient to offset the greater part of the rise of over

TABLE 2

PRODUCTION, PRICES, AND INCOMES IN THE UNITED KINGDOM
(Percentage Changes Over Previous Year)

	Production and Real Income			Money Incomes				Prices	
	Index of Industrial Production	Gross Domestic Product	Gross Real National Income	Trade-Union Wage Rates	Earnings	Gross Money National Income	Ratio of Money Income to Real Income	Prices of Consumption Goods and Services	Index of Retail Prices
1947	+ 5.4	+ 1.0	− 1.0	+ 3.6	+ 7.5	+ 6.8	+ 7.8	+ 6.9	+ 5.9
1948	+ 8.6	+ 4.5	+ 3.8	+ 5.0	+ 7.2	+ 11.5	+ 7.4	+ 7.5	+ 7.3
1949	+ 5.8	+ 4.4	+ 4.5	+ 3.4	+ 3.9	+ 5.5	+ 1.0	+ 2.0	+ 2.9
1950	+ 5.7	+ 3.8	+ 2.9	+ 1.6	+ 5.3	+ 5.6	+ 2.6	+ 4.0	+ 2.7
1951	+ 3.4	+ 1.8	+ 1.3	+ 9.1	+ 9.3	+ 10.4	+ 9.0	+ 8.4	+ 9.9
Total 1946–51	+ 32.4	+ 16.3	+ 12.0	+ 24.6	+ 37.6	+ 46.4	+ 30.7	+ 32.2	+ 31.8
1952	− 2.3	− 0.1	+ 1.8	+ 8.4	+ 8.1	+ 8.3	+ 6.4	+ 5.4	+ 8.9
1953	+ 5.7	+ 4.0	+ 4.8	+ 4.3	+ 6.8	+ 7.1	+ 2.2	+ 1.2	+ 3.1
1954	+ 6.1	+ 4.2	+ 3.4	+ 4.1	+ 7.2	+ 5.9	+ 2.4	+ 2.4	+ 1.8
1955	+ 5.2	+ 3.5	+ 3.5	+ 6.7	+ 9.5	+ 6.5	+ 2.9	+ 3.4	+ 4.3
1956	+ 6.4	+ 1.0	+ 1.6	+ 7.4	+ 7.0	+ 8.9	+ 7.2	+ 4.5	+ 5.0
Total 1951–56	+ 15.6	+ 13.2	+ 15.9	+ 34.6	+ 44.7	+ 42.4	+ 22.8	+ 17.8	+ 25.2
1957	+ 1.8	+ 1.8	+ 1.6	+ 5.0	+ 4.6	+ 5.5	+ 3.9	+ 3.2	+ 4.0
1958	− 1.1	− 0.1	+ 1.3	+ 3.3	+ 3.3	+ 4.6	+ 3.3	+ 3.0	+ 3.0
1959	+ 5.1	+ 4.4	+ 4.4	+ 2.6	+ 5.1	+ 4.3	− 0.1	—	+ 0.6
1960	+ 7.0	+ 5.3	+ 6.1	+ 2.2	+ 8.4	+ 6.2	+ 0.1	+ 1.0	+ 1.0
1961	+ 1.2	+ 1.6	+ 1.9	+ 4.1	+ 5.6	+ 6.9	+ 4.9	+ 2.9	+ 3.4
Total 1956–61	+ 14.7	+ 13.6	+ 16.2	+ 18.2	+ 29.9	+ 30.7	+ 12.5	+ 10.6	+ 12.4
1962	+ 1.0	+ 1.4	+ 1.3	+ 2.9	+ 2.9	+ 3.7	+ 2.3	+ 3.9	+ 4.2

TABLE 3

USES OF REAL NATIONAL INCOME
(At 1958 Market Prices)

	Consumers' Expenditure				Public Authorities' Expenditure on Goods and Services			Saving Plus Depreciation			Gross National Income	
		Percentage of		1958 per Head of population		Percentage of			Percentage of			
	Pounds Sterling	National Income	1958		Pounds Sterling	National Income	1958	Pounds Sterling	National Income	1958	Pounds Sterling	Percentage of 1958
1938	12,330	70.9	81.0	88.1	2,980	17.1	80.4	2,088	12.0	56.6	17,398	76.9
1946	11,840	69.9	77.8	81.6	4,410	26.0	119.0	680	4.1	18.4	16,930	74.8
1947	12,230	72.9	80.3	83.6	3,015	18.0	81.3	1,524	9.1	41.3	16,769	74.1
1948	12,270	70.5	80.6	83.5	3,000	17.2	80.9	2,123	12.2	57.6	17,393	76.9
1949	12,540	68.9	82.4	85.2	3,195	17.6	86.1	2,445	13.5	66.4	18,180	80.4
1950	12,950	69.2	85.0	87.5	3,230	17.2	87.1	2,534	13.6	68.7	18,714	82.6
1951	12,830	67.6	84.5	86.9	3,507	18.5	94.6	2,622	13.8	71.2	18,959	83.8
1952	12,797	66.2	84.0	86.1	3,866	20.0	104.3	2,640	13.7	71.6	19,303	85.3
1953	13,318	65.8	87.4	89.1	3,973	19.6	107.1	2,930	14.5	79.5	20,221	89.4
1954	13,876	66.3	91.1	92.7	3,968	19.0	107.0	3,057	14.6	82.9	20,901	92.4
1955	14,418	66.6	94.7	96.0	3,882	17.9	104.8	3,341	15.4	90.6	21,641	95.6
1956	14,551	66.2	95.5	96.3	3,868	17.6	104.4	3,553	16.2	96.3	21,972	97.2
1957	14,843	66.5	97.5	97.9	3,748	16.8	101.1	3,717	16.7	100.8	22,308	98.6
1958	15,212	67.3	100.0	100.0	3,705	16.4	100.0	3,684	16.3	100.0	22,601	100.0
1959	15,873	67.2	104.2	103.6	3,749	15.9	101.1	3,984	16.9	108.0	23,606	104.4
1960	16,476	65.7	108.2	106.8	3,831	15.3	103.3	4,751	19.0	128.9	25,058	110.8
1961	16,816	65.8	110.4	108.1	4,030	15.8	108.6	4,693	18.4	127.4	25,539	112.8
1962	17,051	65.9	112.0	108.5	4,121	15.9	111.2	4,679	18.1	127.0	25,851	114.3

TABLE 4

SOURCES OF SAVING
(Pounds Sterling at 1958 Prices)

	Persons and Unincorporated Businesses	Companies and Public Corporations	Tax, Dividend, and Interest Reserves	Public Authorities	Total Savings and Depreciation	Depreciation of Fixed Assets	Total Net Saving
1938	1,002	1,272	103	− 289	2,088	1,260	828
1946	434	944	− 16	− 682	680	1,418	− 738
1947	92	730	431	271	1,524	1,394	130
1948	− 59	1,169	208	826	2,144	1,338	806
1949	136	1,361	− 27	998	2,468	1,387	1,081
1950	84	1,410	162	890	2,546	1,443	1,103
1951	− 6	1,297	600	730	2,621	1,463	1,158
1952	460	1,631	22	527	2,640	1,501	1,139
1953	596	1,852	68	414	2,930	1,559	1,371
1954	476	1,898	278	405	3,057	1,627	1,430
1955	605	2,050	50	636	3,341	1,678	1,663
1956	902	1,923	204	524	3,553	1,718	1,835
1957	941	1,964	88	724	3,717	1,771	1,946
759	2,181	20	− 20	764	3,684	1,841	1,843
1959	1,000	2,278	4	702	3,984	1,921	2,063
1960	1,396	2,473	431	451	4,751	2,004	2,747
1961	1,824	2,279	115	475	4,693	2,100	2,593
1962	1,568	2,342	− 68	837	4,679	2,172	2,507

£700m. in bank loans, and net deposits rose by less than £350m., or about 6 per cent. This rise was substantially less than that in real national income, which, in spite of the worsening of the terms of trade, was about 13 per cent for the period (see Table 2). If, therefore, velocities of circulation of money had remained constant, it could have been expected that inflation would have been checked and prices stabilized.

In fact, however, the effects of the preceding monetary expansion continued to work themselves out; the rise in prices, though slowed down for a time, was never wholly checked. The rise in national money income, which was 11½ per cent from 1947 to 1948, slowed down to only 5½ per cent from 1948 to 1949; as the rise in real national income was about 4 per cent in each year, the rise in the price level slowed down* from 7½ per cent in 1947–48 to only 1 per cent in 1948–49. The devaluation of the pound during that year, however (which was necessitated by the difficulties of the rest of the sterling area rather than by those of the United Kingdom itself), together with the worsening of the terms of trade due to the (partly consequential) rise in import prices, brought some intensification of inflationary pressure in 1950 and still more in 1951, when prices rose by something like 9 per cent.

Over the whole four years, prices rose by some 21 per cent and national money income by about 37 per cent. This rise in national money income, accompanied by a rise of only 6 per cent in bank deposits, reduced the ratio of deposits to national income from 65 per cent at the end of 1946 and 63 per cent at the end of 1947 to about 50 per cent at the end of 1951. This fall in the ratio, reflecting an increase in velocity of circulation of money, was accompanied by a considerable rise in long-term interest rates. The yield on 2½ per cent consols came up from 2½ per cent at the end of 1946 and 3 per cent at the end of 1947 to 3¾ per cent in September, 1951. This rise in interest rates, however, would still have been quite inadequate to equate with saving an otherwise unrestricted level of investment. Hence, even at the higher level

---

* Except where otherwise stated, the phrase "price level" refers to a price index obtained by dividing the index of money national income by the index of real national income. It is, therefore, an index of prices at factor cost of all goods and services (including imports) used in the country, both for consumption and for investment (see Table 2).

of saving established in 1948, severe controls on domestic investment were maintained throughout the period. These were less
effective for the control of investment in inventories than in fixed
assets; and in 1951 the rise in import prices caused by the Korean
War induced a major inventory boom. It was largely this additional source of internal demand that, together with drawings on
London balances by sterling area countries, brought on the balance-of-payments crisis in the second half of 1951 (see Table 6).

While the policy of budget surpluses ultimately proved inadequate to cope with the inflationary pressures induced by the
pound sterling devaluation of 1949* and by the Korean War, it
had considerable success for a time. Personal consumption per
head, which had risen sharply in 1947, remained almost unchanged
thereafter in spite of the progressive relaxation of rationing. It did
not rise much above the 1947 level until 1953. The proportion of
real national income devoted to personal consumption thus fell
from 73 per cent in 1947 to 71 per cent in 1948 and 68 per cent in
1951. In 1948 almost the whole of the rise in real national income
was saved, and the proportion of the (gross) national income available for (gross) investment rose from 9 per cent to 12 per cent
(see Table 3). This permitted not only a much needed increase in
the pace of industrial re-equipment, but also a marked improvement in the balance of payments. With the help of generous aid
from the United States, this enabled the most urgent capital needs
of other sterling area countries to be met without a further depletion of the gold reserves.

After 1948, however, a large part of the resources withheld from
private consumers was devoted to financing increased government

* Many observers at the time thought that the extent of the devaluation,
from $4.04 to $2.80 to the pound, was excessive. It is believed that the
lower rate was decided on in the expectation that the moderate United
States business recession of 1949 would develop into a major depression.
In fact, at the moment of devaluation the United States downturn had already come to an end, and even before the outbreak of the Korean War, in
mid-1950, there had been a considerable recovery. It is arguable that if the
devaluation had been to a rate of, say, $3.20 to the pound, it would have
been sufficient to bring sterling area costs and prices into line with those in
the United States and other countries, and that the subsequent inflations in
the United Kingdom and other countries of the sterling area would have
been correspondingly less marked.

expenditure on goods and services, first on the health service and later on defense. For the rest of the period, therefore, saving rose only slightly faster than national income, and the proportion of national income available for investment increased only from 12.2 per cent in 1948 to 13.8 per cent in 1951. Not until 1951, however, when to the rise in rearmament expenditure was added a very large investment in inventories, did the level of saving again prove seriously inadequate to meet the demands on it, and the policy broke down in a new wave of inflation and a balance-of-payments crisis.

Monetary Policy—1952–58.

The first period of tight money—1951–52. On taking office in October, 1951, the new Conservative Government was faced with a difficult situation. The combined effects of the United Kingdom's own adverse balance of payments, and of heavy withdrawals of sterling balances by other countries of the sterling area, were causing the gold reserves to fall at an alarming pace; at the same time, in spite of the downturn in import prices, both wage rates and retail prices were rising rapidly. Some action to check the loss of gold and the internal inflation was urgent. Possible measures available were the intensification of physical controls, a further increase in saving through budget surpluses, and a return to the traditional methods—in abeyance for nearly twenty years—of checking an outflow of gold through a restriction of the quantity of money and a rise in short-term interest rates.

Any attempt to secure a larger budget surplus was rendered difficult by the very high existing level of taxation and rising expenditure on defense. In fact, apart from the largely political and much criticized excess-profits levy, no very serious effort to do so was made. Direct controls were certainly intensified, especially over the volume of imports (to the great hardship of foreign exporters) and over some types of investment. But the main innovations were the raising of the central bank discount rate, first to 2½ per cent and then to 4 per cent, and the "persuasion" of the banks to convert some £500m. of liquid assets into short-dated government securities, thus reducing their liquid assets ratio from 39 per cent in October, 1951, to 33 per cent in December and 32 per cent in January. The results of these policies were seen in rises in Treasury bill rates from ½ per cent in September, 1951, to nearly 3 per cent in June, 1952, and in the yield of 2½ per cent consols from 3¾ per cent to nearly 4½ per cent. Further, by June, 1952, bank advances were falling rapidly and bank deposits were £100m. lower than they had been twelve months before, bringing their ratio to national income down from 51 per cent to 46 per cent, the same figures as in 1938. At the same time, a marked check to internal demand was shown by a fall in the volume of personal consumption and by a perceptible rise in unemployment, especially in the textile industries. Most important of all, the balance of payments improved sharply and, in spite of continued withdrawals of sterling balances, the fall in the gold reserves, which was still large in the first quarter of 1952, almost ceased in the second quarter.

This dramatic change in the situation within a period of a few months was widely acclaimed as a great success for the new monetary policy. Subsequent information, however, seems to show that, while the introduction of a restrictive monetary policy was no doubt of great importance in influencing international financial opinion and checking speculative sales of sterling, its internal effects were no more than to reinforce and perhaps accelerate the operation of two other factors. The first of these was the continued fall of import prices, which improved the balance of payments not only directly through its effect on the terms of trade, but also indirectly by helping to bring to an end the accumulation of inventories. The second was a quite unforeseen and probably largely autonomous rise in personal saving (see Table 4). Ever since its decline at the end of the war, personal saving had been very small. Its virtual disappearance had been widely ascribed to permanent causes, and especially to the great redistribution of personal incomes brought about by inflation and high income taxes. The causes for its sudden rise from nothing in 1951 to £460m. in 1952 are still by no means clear. The most generally accepted explanation is that it marked the exhaustion of many of the involuntary wartime savings, the spending of which, as supplies became available, had hitherto been offsetting most of the positive saving, which had been carried on largely through such institutions as life insurance offices and building societies. In retrospect, it seems likely that the fall in import prices and the rise in personal saving would have brought a considerable check to the demand both for inventories and for consumption goods, even without the change in monetary policy.

The expansion of investment—1952–54. After the middle of 1952, the check to the internal inflation and the much improved balance-of-payments position encouraged the authorities to permit a relaxation of their restrictive monetary policies. Bank holdings of government debt rose steadily, and, in spite of the fact that loans continued to fall for some time, bank deposits began to expand again, rising by some £200m., or 3 per cent, during each of the next two years. Although bank rate was not reduced until October, 1953, the yield on consols fell from 4½ per cent in June, 1952, to just over 4 per cent in June, 1953, and to 3¾ per cent in June, 1954. At the same time, the government relaxed its administrative restrictions on investment.

The combined effects of easier money and the relaxation of restrictions appeared first in house-building, where the government was under an election promise to increase the number of houses built from 200,000 to 300,000 a year. The number of houses completed by public authorities, mainly for letting at subsidized rents, rose from about 175,000 a year in 1951 to about 260,000 in 1953 and 1954, while privately built houses, which had previously been kept down by licensing restrictions to under 30,000 a year, increased to 65,000 in 1953 and over 90,000 in 1954, thus enabling the government to more than fulfill its promises (see also Table 5).

The housing boom of 1953–54 brought with it a period both of prosperity and of relative stability. After the check to demand in 1952, the rate of rise in national money income declined from nearly 8½ per cent between 1951 and 1952 to 7 per cent from 1952 to 1953. At the same time, the recovery in production and the improving terms of trade brought the rate of rise of *real* national income up to nearly 5 per cent, so that the rise of prices slowed down from 9 per cent in 1951 and 6½ per cent in 1952 to 2 per cent in 1953. In fact, from March, 1953, to June, 1954, the level of retail prices was almost stationary. In spite of the fall in the average annual budget surplus from £600m. in 1948–51 to £250m. in

TABLE 5

GROSS DOMESTIC FIXED CAPITAL FORMATION

(Pounds Sterling at 1958 Prices)

	Vehicles, Ships, and Aircraft			Plant and Machinery			New Dwellings			Other Buildings, etc.			Total		
	Pri-vate Sector	Public Sector	Total	Pri-vate Sector	Public Sector	Total	Pri-vate Sector	Public Sector	Total	Pri-vate Sector	Public Sector	Total	Pri-vate Sector	Public Sector	Total
1938	—	—	330	—	—	610	—	—	702	—	—	698	1,642	698	2,340
1946	—	—	—	—	—	—	—	—	—	—	—	—	—	—	1,590
1947	—	—	465	—	—	598	—	—	521	—	—	372	—	—	1,956
1948	319	85	404	570	195	765	65	421	486	206	274	480	1,160	975	2,135
1949	305	119	424	578	267	845	79	397	476	258	330	588	1,220	1,113	2,333
1950	277	114	391	630	312	942	71	394	465	301	360	661	1,279	1,180	2,459
1951	252	95	347	611	415	1,026	72	384	456	260	380	640	1,195	1,274	2,469
1952	230	78	308	535	440	975	112	434	546	238	412	650	1,115	1,364	2,479
1953	270	93	363	515	471	986	192	519	711	247	441	688	1,224	1,524	2,748
1954	302	88	390	595	501	1,096	258	478	736	312	448	760	1,467	1,515	2,982
1955	335	107	442	681	501	1,182	286	380	666	389	449	838	1,691	1,437	3,128
1956	355	133	488	735	492	1,227	305	344	649	452	487	939	1,847	1,456	3,303
1957	373	163	536	834	491	1,325	304	319	623	463	533	996	1,974	1,506	3,480
1958	401	149	550	829	495	1,324	322	269	591	460	561	1,021	2,012	1,474	3,486
1959	449	150	599	837	541	1,378	400	270	670	486	619	1,105	2,172	1,580	3,752
1960	504	169	673	909	557	1,466	484	278	762	579	644	1,223	2,476	1,648	4,124
1961	477	146	523	1,049	618	1,667	527	281	808	690	696	1,386	2,743	1,741	4,484
1962	403	121	524	963	633	1,596	514	315	829	688	743	1,431	2,568	1,812	4,380

Sources: "National Income and Expenditure, 1963," Tables 51 and 59.

1952–54, and of the rise in house-building, the much higher level of personal saving and the low rate of inventory accumulation kept total domestic investment well within the limits of total saving, and the balance-of-payments surplus remained reasonably adequate (see Table 6).

About the middle of 1954, just after bank rate had been reduced to 3 per cent, signs began to appear that the period of stability was coming to a close. Early in 1953 the government had become concerned that the rise in fixed investment was confined to house-building, and that no increase was occurring in industrial and commercial investment. Steps were therefore taken, by tax concessions and the removal of restrictions, to encourage investment in assets other than houses. For many months these measures seemed ineffective. But from the middle of 1954 industrial and commercial investment began to expand rapidly; and by the end of 1954 it was clear that total investment was again beginning to outrun the level of saving and that inflationary pressure, which had been dormant for over a year, was beginning to appear again. In the second half of 1954, retail prices, which had been stationary since April, 1943, rose by over 2 per cent, while the stock-exchange recovery quickened toward a boom. After the beginning of 1955, a marked rise in inventory accumulation, which had been very small during the past three years, reinforced the rapidly rising level of domestic fixed investment (see Tables 5 and 6). Imports increased sharply; the balance of payments on income account became unfavorable; and the gold reserve began to fall.

The second period of tight money—1955–58. Encouraged by its apparent success in 1952, the government at first placed the whole responsibility of checking the renewed inflation on a purely monetary policy. At the end of January, 1955, bank rate was raised from 3 per cent to 3½ per cent, and at the end of February to 4½ per cent. At the same time, successful efforts were made to keep down issues of Treasury bills by sales of securities. Security sales, both by the Treasury and by the banks, brought a sharp rise in long-term rates, and the yield on 2½ per cent consols rose from rather over 3½ per cent in October, 1954, to nearly 4¼ per cent in June, 1955. No doubt remembering 1952, the government was so confident of its power to check inflation by purely monetary means

TABLE 6

SOURCES AND USES OF INVESTIBLE FUNDS
(Pounds Sterling at 1958 Prices)

	Investible Funds		Errors and Omissions	Total Investible Funds	Gross Domestic Fixed Capital Formation	Surplus Available for Stock Accumulation and Foreign Investment	Use of Surplus	
	Gross Saving	Capital Grants and Transfers from Abroad					Physical Increase in Stocks	Net Foreign Investment
1938	2,088	—	—	2,088	2,340	− 252	—	− 252
1946	680	286	—	966	1,590	− 624	− 219	− 405
1947	1,524	257	—	1,781	1,956	− 175	+ 350	− 525
1948	2,123	346	+ 115	2,584	2,135	+ 449	+ 227	+ 222
1949	2,445	279	− 100	2,624	2,333	+ 291	+ 87	+ 204
1950	2,534	239	− 11	2,762	2,450	+ 303	− 231	+ 534
1951	2,622	101	+ 57	2,780	2,469	+ 311	+ 615	− 304
1952	2,640	41	+ 21	2,702	2,479	+ 223	+ 65	+ 158
1953	2,930	19	+ 195	3,034	2,748	+ 286	+ 135	+ 151
1954	3,057	1	+ 107	3,165	2,982	+ 183	+ 54	+ 129
1955	3,341	1	− 58	3,254	3,128	+ 156	+ 315	− 157
1956	3,553	—	+ 197	3,750	3,303	+ 447	+ 243	+ 204
1957	3,717	—	+ 212	3,929	3,480	+ 449	+ 242	+ 207
1958	3,684	—	+ 244	3,928	3,486	+ 442	+ 100	+ 342
1959	3,984	—	+ 82	4,066	3,752	+ 314	+ 174	+ 140
1960	4,751	—	− 304	4,447	4,124	+ 323	+ 592	− 269
1961	4,693	—	+ 54	4,747	4,484	+ 263	+ 297	− 34
1962	4,679	—	− 130	4,549	4,380	+ 169	+ 96	+ 73

that it made substantial reductions in taxation in its April budget, taking 6*d*. off the income tax rate.

The conditions of 1955, however, were very different from those in 1952. Import prices, instead of falling, were rising; the country was feeling the reaction from several years of understocking; and plans for increased industrial and commercial investment were still only beginning to take effect. Therefore, despite the government's technical success in squeezing the liquidity of the banks, and in checking, in July, the rise in prices of equity securities, internal demand, wage rates, and retail prices continued to rise rapidly. Meanwhile, the level of imports remained high and gold reserves fell at an increasing rate. In October, the government introduced an emergency budget, increasing the purchase (sales) tax, and announcing drastic restrictions on installment sales finance, the discontinuation of further housing subsidies, and reductions in investment by public authorities. In February, 1956, bank rate was raised to 5½ per cent.

The year 1956 saw a new development almost as surprising as that of 1952. Personal saving, which in 1955 had already shown an appreciable rise above the 1952–54 level, took a new upward leap to nearly twice its 1954 total (see Table 4). A minor part of the rise can be attributed to the restrictions on installment selling. The remainder can probably be attributed to the effects of the rise in the rate of growth of real personal incomes per head, after tax, from less than 1 per cent a year in 1947–51 to 3½ per cent in 1951–56. Whatever the cause, the higher level of personal saving, together with an increase in the budget surplus from an average of £250m. in 1952–54 to one of over £400m. in 1955 and 1956, brought a major improvement in the economic situation. Although, in spite of higher interest rates, industrial and commercial fixed investment continued to rise rapidly, while house-building fell only slightly, the rise in total saving was large enough to provide a much larger margin for other forms of investment, such as inventory accumulation and foreign investment (see Table 6). Therefore, despite a continued high level of inventory accumulation, an adverse balance of payments on current account of £156m. in 1955 was converted into a favorable one of £207m. in 1956. This balance, while still smaller than what the weakness on international capital account would have made desirable, would probably have been large enough to ensure the stability of sterling but for the Suez crisis. This gave rise to heavy speculative sales of sterling and was prevented from having a disastrous effect on an already weak capital position only by a loan of £200m. from the International Monetary Fund. In spite of the rise in saving and the improvement in the underlying economic position, no relaxation of monetary restriction was possible. By the end of 1956, the yield on 2½ per cent consols had almost reached 5 per cent.

In the early months of 1957, the government took advantage of an improvement in market sentiment to undertake a vigorous funding policy, which in February enabled bank rate to be reduced to 5 per cent without causing much fall in long-term money rates. Personal and total saving continued to rise, but fixed investment rose equally fast, and with the rate of inventory accumulation maintained, the balance of payments showed no further improvement.

In the late summer, fresh speculative sales of sterling, perhaps partly due to expectations of a revaluation of the German mark, together with heavy withdrawals of sterling balances by India, caused further heavy outflows of gold and a new sterling crisis. This time the government overcame its dislike of high short-term interest rates sufficiently to allow bank rate to be raised to the crisis level of 7 per cent. At the same time, the banks were asked not to allow their total advances to rise further for any purpose.

While the rise to 7 per cent in bank rate was probably more important for reassuring foreign holders of sterling about the British Government's determination to check inflation than for its direct effects on the internal position, it marked the turning of the tide. In the second half of 1957, the pressure of demand was checked, initially by slower private fixed investment and reduced inventory accumulation and later by a fall in the volume of exports, caused by the fall in world commodity prices and a sharp improvement in the United Kingdom's terms of trade. Output fell in the last quarter of 1957 and showed no recovery for nearly a year, but the increase in money incomes was also checked; and after the middle of 1958 prices ceased to rise, while despite the fall in exports the balance of payments improved.

Partly, perhaps, because the rise in unemployment lagged a long way behind the check to output, the government was slow in relaxing restrictions on demand. Bank rate was maintained at 7 per cent until March, 1958, restrictions on hire-purchase finance and bank loans were retained until October, and the tax concessions in the 1958 budget were small. Apart from a gradual reduction in bank rate to 4 per cent by November, no real effort was made to bring down long-term interest rates, and at the end of 1958 the yield on 2½ per cent consols had fallen by only ½ per cent from its 1957 crisis peak of 5½ per cent. It thus remained far above the level of 3¾ per cent at which it had stood before the start of the 1955 credit squeeze.

The withdrawal of restrictions on bank advances and hire-purchase finance brought a rise in output of durable consumption goods in the last quarter of 1958, but, with its usual time lag, unemployment continued to rise. This was probably the main cause for the very large tax and other concessions made in the 1959 budget, at a total cost to the Exchequer of nearly £400m. This degree of demand stimulation proved excessive, perhaps because it was accompanied by a rise in clearing bank loans from less than £2,000m. in August, 1958, to over £3,300m. in July, 1960. That the main instrument of expansion was intended to be budgetary policy is, however, shown by the fact that the banks were not enabled to expand their deposits as fast as their loans and were obliged to sell some £900m. of securities. Long-term interest rates therefore never fell much below 5 per cent and by the end of 1959 were beginning to rise above it.

The immediate effect of the 1959 budget was to stimulate consumption, but in the second half of the year industrial fixed investment began to rise rapidly, and early in 1960 there was a sharp expansion in inventory accumulation. In consequence, gross domestic product, at constant factor cost prices, which had risen by only 3½ per cent in the three years ending in the first quarter of 1959, rose by no less than 8 per cent in the following twelve months. Meanwhile, although the fall in unemployment had, as usual, lagged behind the rise in output, earnings and national money income had begun to rise with increasing speed and the balance of payments deteriorated sharply. Early in 1960, therefore, the government felt obliged again to take steps to check the rise in demand and incomes.

These measures followed the familiar pattern. Tax increases in the 1960 budget were very small, but bank rate was raised to 5 per cent in January and to 6 per cent in June, while restrictions were reimposed on hire-purchase finance. In May, the new powers of the Bank of England to restrict bank liquidity were put into effect, and the banks were required to place 1 per cent of their deposits on special account at the Bank of England; in July, this was raised to 2 per cent. By the middle of 1960, the yield on 2½ per cent consols was back to 5½ per cent—its level at the time of the 1957 crisis.

These measures brought a temporary relaxation of pressure. The rise in output was checked, mainly by a reduction in consumption, accompanied by a sharp rise in personal saving, while balance-of-payments difficulties were solved for the time being by a heavy inflow of short-term money from Europe, attracted by the rise in interest rates. In October, therefore, bank rate was reduced to 5 per cent.

Return to Policy of Restraint by Fiscal Means

The budget of 1961 introduced a major change of policy. Although the actual net changes in taxation were small, with a substantial (and overdue) reduction in surtax offset by increased company and other taxes, the Chancellor was given powers to increase (or reduce) the general level of indirect taxes by 10 per cent whenever he thought it necessary. His use of these powers was not long delayed. The first half of 1961 saw an accelerated rise in money incomes, a premature recovery in output, and the first substantial rise in retail prices for over two years. Meanwhile, heavy withdrawals of foreign-owned sterling balances were prevented from depleting the inadequate gold reserve only by heavy borrowings, estimated at £300m., from European central banks.

By July, it was apparent that the country was facing a sterling crisis even more serious than that of 1957. Bank rate was again raised to 7 per cent, the banks were required to raise their special accounts at the Bank of England to 3 per cent of deposits, and restrictions on bank lending were tightened. At the same time a

loan of £500m. was negotiated with the International Monetary
Fund, to repay the temporary loans from European central banks
and to strengthen the reserves. But on this occasion, for the first
time since 1951, the monetary measures were supplemented by
substantial fiscal measures of restraint, and the general level of
indirect taxes was raised by 10 per cent, yielding an extra £130m.
in the current financial year and over £200m. in a full year.

This combination of measures again proved effective. During
the second half of 1961, the rise in money incomes was reversed,
the rise in output was checked, and the balance of payments improved. Before the end of the year the government was able to
begin to relax restraints, at first all monetary. In November, bank
rate was reduced to 6 per cent, and then by stages to 4½ per cent,
in April, 1962. At the same time the restrictions on hire-purchase
finance and bank lending were removed, and the special account
requirements reduced to 1 per cent. On the other hand, the 1962
budget was almost neutral, with the withdrawal of the 10 per
cent general surcharge (which remained available for future re-
use) almost exactly offset by increases in particular indirect taxes.
The monetary and financial measures alone were, however, enough
to bring a steady rise in output during the first three quarters of
1962, though unemployment, with its usual time lag, continued to
rise, and the margin of unused capacity was perhaps rather higher
than necessary. In the last quarter, the rise in output was checked,
mainly by a further fall in private industrial fixed investment and
in inventory accumulation, in spite of a continued rise in consumption demand, especially for durable goods. At this point the
government had the opportunity, if it had wished to take it, to
conduct a "cheaper money" policy, by issuing short-dated securities in order to buy up long-dated ones. In fact they limited their
monetary measures to a further reduction in bank rate to 4 per
cent (which they took steps to prevent from having a corresponding effect on bill rates) and to the release of the last 1 per cent of
the banks' special accounts. Instead, they turned back to tax reductions as a means of stimulating demand. In consequence, the
long-term rate of interest, which had already fallen from its crisis
level of 6½ per cent to 5½ per cent, did not go below that level.

It is impossible to say how far the failure to take the opportunity to reduce the long-term rate of interest below 5½ per cent was the result of deliberate policy; but a case can be made for it on balance-of-payments grounds. The high rates of interest now ruling in the United Kingdom make it much easier to attract and retain foreign long-term, as well as short-term, capital. It has therefore been possible to export long-term capital, especially to other countries of the sterling area, in amounts greatly in excess of the favorable balance of payments on current account, without either incurring dangerous increases in foreign-owned short-term debt or depleting the gold reserve.

The fiscal measures introduced in the last quarter of 1962, at a total cost to the Exchequer of some £200m., included another special release of postwar credits, heavy reductions in purchase tax on automobiles and other consumer durables, and substantial tax concessions on industrial fixed investment. In addition, large extensions were announced to the program of public-sector fixed investment. But before they had time to become effective, output, especially in the construction trades, was checked by an unprecedentedly severe winter, and unemployment rose to the highest level recorded since the coal crisis of 1947. It was probably this high level of unemployment that persuaded the Chancellor to give large additional tax and other concessions in his 1963 budget, at an estimated further cost to the Exchequer of £270m. The extent of the combined concessions may be judged from the fact that an "above-the-line" surplus of £353m. in 1962–63 was converted into an estimated deficit of £90m. in 1963–64. In addition, further increases were announced in the public investment program.

By the end of 1963 the indications were that the government had repeated its mistake of 1959 and, misled by the temporarily high level of unemployment, had again overstimulated demand. Between April and October the index of industrial production rose by over 5 per cent, between April and December the seasonally corrected percentage of unemployment fell from 2.7 per cent, in the second half of 1963 imports were rising faster than exports, and money incomes appeared to be rising with excessive speed. If these indications can be trusted, it can be expected that before long the familiar symptoms of excess demand will have reappeared. If whatever government is then in power repeats the policies of 1952 and 1955–57 and uses mainly monetary means to check the overrapid rise in incomes, the long-term rate of interest may well be forced even above the 1961 crisis level of 6½ per cent. If, however, the government reverts to the policy of 1947–48, and uses mainly fiscal measures, or even to that of 1962, and uses a combination of fiscal and monetary measures, the long-term rate may continue to fluctuate within, say, ½ per cent of its end-1963 level of 5¾ per cent.

6. Limitations of Monetary Policy

HOWARD S. ELLIS

Since all conceivable economic policies have their limits, the task of appraising any specific policy, in a world that falls short of perfection in a number of ways, implies an estimate of how important its limitations are when compared to available alternatives.

Bearing in mind this relativism, I shall approach the subject of the limitations upon monetary policy from three angles: the effectiveness of its operation, the desirability of the ways in which the policy works, and the value and mutual compatibility of its aims. These three categories cannot always be completely separated, but they will serve well as an ordering device for the appraisal.

The Effectiveness of Monetary Policies

The limitations ascribed to the effectiveness of monetary policy may be divided for purposes of study into two major groups. One of these groups embraces objections or limitations of a general theoretical nature. The shortcomings of monetary policy are supposed to be inherent in the nature of things, including the normal reactions of individuals and firms. The other group is concerned with institutional developments, particularly recent developments in the United States. The limitations of monetary policy are due to historical and specific reasons, and not necessarily to the operation of the monetary mechanism. Perhaps these two groups can be designated as "general" and "institutional" limits on the efficacy of monetary policy.

"General" Limits upon the Efficacy of Monetary Policy

1. *Income, assets, and spending.* J. M. Keynes lent the great authority of his name to the idea that *income* is the central eco-

nomic phenomenon and that the influence of varying rates of investment upon economic activity can be traced by exclusive attention to the division of *income* between consumption and investment. Some of Keynes's followers have deduced from this that government tax and expenditure policies are potent because they bear directly on income. But monetary policy, they believe, at best exercises a milder, more circuitous, or slower effect on economic activity because its impact is primarily or originally upon the value and composition of *assets*.

More recent followers of Keynes, such as Don Patinkin, in *Money, Interest, and Prices,* have repudiated this idea. Every money outlay, they argue, involves the individual person or firm in a decision as to how much money should be retained; and every retention or holding of money involves a decision as to whether it is best to hold wealth in this form or in the form of securities or productive equipment that yields income. Thus the background of asset holdings may be as important and pervasive as income in determining expenditures. If this is true—and it seems impossible to avoid the logic of the position—then monetary policy through its effect upon *assets* may abstractly have just as strong and immediate results on spending, employment, and prices as does fiscal policy through its effect upon *income*. Whether fiscal or monetary measures have, in fact, the greater potency depends upon a variety of factors that differ considerably from one situation to another.

2. *Interest elasticity of the demand for and supply of capital.* One of the channels—it will later transpire that it is not the crucial one—by which monetary policy is supposed to be able to influence economic activity is the effect of central bank discount policy on market rates of interest and thus on investment. But just how elastic the demand for capital may be with regard to interest rates has been debated for decades without producing a simple or conclusive answer. Econometric studies of investment behavior have yielded unsatisfactory results.[1] We can be fairly certain that long-term borrowers—for residential and industrial construction and for public utility investment—are more sensitive to interest cost, borrowers for investor purposes less so, and consumers and all types of "speculative" borrowers least so. These conclusions reached in 1952 by the Chairman of the Board of Governors of

the Federal Reserve Board[2] were reflected a decade later by Samuelson, who added that "the evidence does seem inescapable that
increases in the cost and tightening of the availability of credit do
have substantial effects on investment spending."[3] Recent attempts
by the Federal Reserve to raise short-term interest rates for the
sake of the foreign balance, while holding down long-term rates
for the sake of domestic investment (the so-called twist operation)
must rest on a conviction of the Board that interest cost is significant for investment.

In the early 1950's, John H. Williams and Robert V. Roosa ex-
pounded a theory that central bank action operated only secondar-
ily upon borrowers and savers, but primarily upon the positions
and decisions of lenders. This effect, which has been known popularly as the "freezing-, pinning-, or locking-in" of bank holdings of
government securities, was thought to follow from a reluctance of
banks to sell securities at less than par values when interest rates
advance. Thus the rise of the Federal Reserve discount rate was
believed to have an immediate and potent effect in restricting
bank lending.

Subsequently, however, doubts arose as to the strength of the
"Roosa effect." Banks, it was pointed out, feel an obligation to
take care of their regular customers and may accept some losses
in order to extend loans and retain patronage. Furthermore, the
federal income tax provision peculiar to banks that permits them
to deduct full net capital losses in calculating taxable income reduces the penalty on taking losses from the sale of securities. Statistical studies by John H. Kareken and Warren L. Smith bear out
the scepticism regarding locking-in.[4] It has been pointed out,
however, that a substantial *de facto* locking-in exists for some
banks in the requirement of collateral for public deposits and un-
invested trust funds.[*] While this explanation of the lock-in is new,
it operates, as Roosa had argued, to transmit Federal Reserve discount policy to the market without much slack. The really residual

---

[*] As of June 29, 1963, all commercial banks held government deposits of
all categories of $31,341.2 million, but held federal, state, and local securi-
ties of $94,533.7 million, or three times the amount of deposits. However, it
is reported on good authority that some important banks have a rather
narrow leeway between collateral required and securities actually held for
this purpose.

quantity for the banks thus locked-in is not government securities but mortgages. Obviously, the rapidity with which mortgages can be shifted to nonbank owners is limited when compared with government securities, particularly in view of the lack in this country of a well-developed secondary market for mortgages.

Beside the somewhat narrower meaning of locking-in as applied to the commercial banks, the term has been given a broader meaning: high rates of interest operate to lock-in *any* owner of a bond, and the longer the maturity the greater the leverage exercised by the high rates. This universally recognized and by no means novel fact reported by the Radcliffe Committee has become the keystone of central banking and of monetary control. In the United Kingdom, the Bank of England apparently no longer controls the volume of bank reserves through the traditional channels of open-market operations and the discount rate. It has taken on the obligation, presumably as a consequence of the increased role of government in the total of investment, to provide the Exchequer with residual finance according to need.[5] In place of the usual controls over bank reserves, the authorities have attempted to limit liquidity (in general, not simply money) by funding short- into long-term debt, i.e., into "consols," the key securities in the gilt-edged market. Thus the Radcliffe Committee has come to rely almost exclusively upon debt management and to regard the supply of money as merely incidental; and it has not hesitated to endorse whatever high interest rates might be supposed to be necessary to control private liquidity in this way.

Against this "Radcliffism" even Professor Gurley, whose philosophy the committee undoubtedly thought they were espousing, is compelled to protest that the "money income ratio, modified by the presence of other liquid assets, and within the context of real variables, was the principal determinant of the level of interest rates in Britain during the postwar period."[6] In fact, the attempt in the United Kingdom to put the opposite view into effect, by operating on interest and leaving the money supply to the "needs" of the Exchequer, failed to control liquidity. "Credit was dear but not scarce," and inflationary pressures prevailed. The upshot of the British experience is that "what happens to the money supply is much more significant than what happens to interest rates."[7]

This conclusion, which would seem to be unavoidable, does not say that interest elasticities are completely unimportant, but it does sign the death warrant of Radcliffism in its attempt to control spending through interest rates alone.

Commercial bankers and central bank authorities have always attached as much significance in a tight-money policy to what they call "availability" as to the interest rates. Now "availability" may be variously interpreted, with corresponding variations in its significance. In the Radcliffe view, the quantity of lending (or at least of long-term lending) is uniquely related to the interest rates on gilt-edge; in this view availability plays *no role*. But in the bankers' view, lending is always associated with more or less risk, and the lender always decides not only whether he is prepared to lend, but also whether he is prepared to lend as much as the borrower wants. Unlike potatoes, loans are not available to the single demander in unlimited quantity. Thus an "unsatisfied fringe" of borrowers appears as a permanent feature of credit markets; lenders never offer unlimited sums to individual borrowers, whatever the rate of interest may be.

This rationing of credit, or what may be called the "quality of credit" varies in intensity in the course of the business cycle; the variation is greater than customer loan rates, but because it does not lend itself easily to quantitative reporting, it is ignored in econometric models. At the close of the 1955–57 tight-money episode, a survey of bankers on the effects of Federal Reserve policies elicited the response from only 1 per cent of those replying that the increased cost of borrowing "appreciably" discouraged borrowing; 42 per cent said the effect was "very little," and 57 per cent stated that they were giving more attention to the past records of applicants; 42 per cent said they paid increased attention to maintaining balances on account; 38 per cent required faster payment schedules; 25 per cent scaled down the size of loans from amounts requested.[8] The full effect of a tight-money policy can never be shown by the behavior of interest rates. Still more important is the reduction of availability, and the outcry against the Federal Reserve policy of tight money during 1956–57 and still more in 1959 seems to bear eloquent witness to the fact that the policy "took hold" on the conditions of commercial bank lending.

3. *Perverse reactions of the market.* The increase of monetary velocity during periods of business expansion and its decline during contractions is a natural consequence of changes in certain main economic variables that operate in one direction. Dishoarding in boom periods occurs naturally as the result of improved investment prospects, rising prices, increased employment and output, and rising interest rates, which increase the cost of holding idle balances. A procyclical behavior of velocity is clearly observable throughout the present century; as long ago as 1936, it led Professor J. W. Angell to conclude that greater stability in the money supply would result in greater stability in velocity and money incomes.[9] It was generally recognized that induced changes in velocity rendered efforts at stabilization through monetary devices more difficult, though not impossible if complemented by appropriate fiscal measures.

The general tenor of the Radcliffe Report in England and the Eckstein Report in the United States, however, has been to regard induced velocity changes in the course of economic fluctuations as rendering monetary controls impotent or virtually so.[10] This extreme conclusion seems to result from (1) the confusion of secular with cyclical developments, and (2) the altogether human weakness, to which economists have always been vulnerable, of projecting a recent trend into the indefinite future.

With regard to the first point, there can be no doubt that velocity has increased secularly since 1946 under the influence, first, of a gradual dishoarding of cash balances accumulated under rationing during the war, and second, of a gradual increase in the volume of near-moneys called into being through the growth of nonbank financial intermediaries. But even the doubling of income velocity, from about two to four per annum, should not swamp a monetary authority when distributed, as it has been, over nearly twenty years. The *cyclical* variations of velocity, which are of more immediate concern in both the Radcliffe and Eckstein reports, do not appear more formidable than in earlier periods. Indeed, an important conclusion of Milton Friedman's massive statistical enquiry into United States monetary history is that, "In response to cyclical variations, velocity has shown a *systematic* and *stable* movement about its trend, rising during expansion and falling during contraction."[11] With regard to the upward trend of velocity since 1946, the conclusion of the Commission on Money and Credit seems warranted:

> . . . this does not mean that a restrictive monetary policy does not have a restrictive influence. It means only that to restrict lending by a given amount, the growth of the money supply must be more limited than if velocity did not rise. The increase of velocity need not negate the effectiveness of monetary policy.[12]

With regard to the second point, against two decades of secularly rising velocity are to be set the preceding seventy-five years of declining velocity. Prediction is a hazardous business; but the least that can be said is that a reversal of the upward trend since 1946 is a distinct possibility, and some rational grounds exist for expecting it. More important, however, is the reflection that if cyclical velocity variations around the trend do not appear to be growing larger, the trend would merely influence the relative difficulty of controlling booms compared with depressions. In either event the gradualness of the change scarcely appears to be a menacing limit to the efficacy of monetary policy.

4. *Lags in effects of monetary policy.* The conventional view concerning lags has been that, while they impair the efficacy of monetary policy, they take effect within a sufficiently short time to be at least contracyclical in operation. Professor Friedman has, indeed, taken the position that the lags are so long and so variable that monetary policy does not necessarily stabilize, but may as often contribute to the violence of economic fluctuations.[13] The Eckstein Report reaches the somewhat more conservative conclusion that the lags are long and "create difficult problems";[14] and the Commission on Money and Credit concludes that general monetary controls since the war have required from six to nine months to produce a change in the direction of ease and a further six months for their maximum effect.[15] Actual evidence concerning lags is scant and the judgment of informed observers fails to provide the policy-makers with much illumination. In this uncertain state of affairs, it is well to recall that other stabilization de-

vices, such as changes in taxes and in government expenditures, also involve serious lags, particularly in the United States where the absence of responsible cabinet government forces the Congress to undertake the laborious task of determining fiscal policy. The history of the tax reduction proposed in 1963 is a case in point.

Uncertainty concerning timing has caused Professors Friedman and Shaw to abandon discretionary monetary control altogether, and they are joined in large measure by Professor Angell. Not many other economists, however, have been able to convince themselves of the merits of the alternative they propose—a fixed annual increment to the money supply. This is particularly difficult to accept in view of the plurality of objectives of monetary-fiscal policy and the necessity for adapting to new situations as one or other of these goals seems, for the time being, to be more important from a national viewpoint.

Rather than abdicate monetary policy altogether, which would seem to leave a vacuum into which direct controls would be bound to rush, it would seem preferable to concentrate upon devices to reduce the lag of monetary-fiscal measures, and to improve the setting in which these policies operate. This important subject is discussed in other chapters in this volume.

Institutional Developments Adverse to Effective Monetary Policy

The preceding sections have considered difficulties encountered by monetary controls arising out of the economic behavior patterns of households or firms. By contrast, certain other difficulties arise from institutional developments, and these are constantly changing. In the early 1950's, the member banks' resort to borrowing from the excess reserves of other member banks—the use of "federal funds"—was usually mentioned as a source of embarrassment to monetary control. In the course of a decade, this has largely dropped from view, following the general realization that these borrowings represented a "once-over" increase of the commercial bank credit superstructure on a given amount of Federal Reserve deposits. Monetary policy could easily take account of this fact and compensate for it. Currently, commercial banks are making extensive use of "certificates of deposit" as a means of increasing the volume of lendable funds. The "negotiable CD" has enhanced the substitutability of time deposits for demand deposits, with the result that a greater amount of total deposits, and lendable funds, is related to a given level of primary reserves. In this sense, further "economy" in the use of reserves has been achieved.* This is also a once-over change and also does not present a progressive source of difficulty for the monetary authorities.

Another institutional limitation, the "bills only" rule, which the Federal Reserve created for itself, has now apparently passed into desuetude after a short life extending from 1953 to 1958. Economists outside the Board of Governors generally regarded this rule as a gratuitous narrowing of the field and efficacy of open-market operations. Eventually the Board, without formal retraction, disavowed the rule in deeds, for instance, in the late summer of 1958 to "correct a disorderly market,"[16] and thereafter to hold down long rates for domestic purposes while raising the short rate to aid in coping with the loss of gold abroad.

Another institutional obstacle that faded away was the belief, held in the first postwar years, that a large national debt placed limits on monetary policy. Reactivating monetary controls after the support of the government security market during the war would, it was feared, spell a collapse in their values and usher in a depression. Federal Reserve action in cautiously easing the supports and finally, after the Accord of 1951, in abolishing them, produced no such effect. Nowadays the *size* of the debt is not regarded per se as causing difficulties for monetary policy. There would probably be a consensus among economists that the maturities are too short for desirable leverage effects from Federal Reserve discount rates; and the interest ceiling on long-term

* According to a special survey conducted by the Federal Reserve, negotiable time certificates of deposits outstanding at 410 member banks amounted to $6.2 billion by December 5, 1962, compared to about $1 billion at the end of 1960. At the end of 1963, the total of these certificates outstanding was $9.92 billion. Mr. Charles F. Haywood, Director of Economic Research, Bank of America, San Francisco, called to my attention the parallel of this phenomenon with the growth of the use of federal funds in the early 1950's. I am indebted to him for a number of valuable suggestions and criticisms.

securities is a nuisance for effective policy. But these are relatively less important matters than those we are about to consider.

1. *The growth of nonbank financial intermediaries.* More important, at least in the current literature, is the discussion of the growth in recent decades of financial institutions other than commercial banks. Resting upon earlier researches by Goldsmith into financial intermediaries in general, Shaw and Gurley proclaimed the superior importance of the "state of liquidity of the whole economy" over the supply of money, which was only one component of liquidity and a dwindling one at that. While monetary theorists had for many years spoken about near-money, the challenging presentation of Shaw and Gurley led to extreme reactions. On the one hand, some people were (and some still are) prepared to argue that monetary stringency calls new financial intermediaries into being or activates the economizing of cash through the creation of near-moneys, making velocity indefinitely extensible and rendering monetary controls impotent.[17] On the other hand, orthodox economists continued to insist on the uniqueness of money as a means of payment, however much the securities of nonbank institutions might contribute to liquidity.

Appeal in these circumstances to *a priori* arguments as to whether other intermediaries are like or unlike banks are apt to be bootless. It is clear that money and near-money are within certain ranges and under certain circumstances substitutable assets, and the practical problem is the empirical investigation precisely of this substitution.

It is probably too early to look for conclusive results, but a substantial number of investigations, such as that of Warren L. Smith, point to a greater degree of substitution between the demand and time deposits of the commercial banks than between demand deposits and money on the one hand, and accounts with savings and loan associations and mutual savings banks on the other.[18] The implication of this finding is, fairly clearly, the greater importance of being able to cope with the destabilizing portfolio adjustments of commercial banks than with controls over other financial institutions. One device, suggested by Professor Alhadeff, for securing greater stability in bank holdings of governments would be to make all bank-eligible government securities nonmarketable. Compared with the complexities of regulation of nonbank intermediaries, this device is simpler, but would entail a drastic reduction in the bank demand for government securities as secondary reserves. General monetary controls are probably the best answer to bank portfolio adjustments.[19] The time could conceivably come when the nonbank intermediaries can be shown to contribute so much to the short run instability of velocity as to require regulation akin to the banks. This would not appear to be highly probable, however, because commercial banks "specialize in providing the marginal fluctuating portion of the financial requirements of the private sector of the economy. Intermediaries are more specialized in providing long-term funds for mortgage finance, fixed capital investment, and capital improvements by state and local governments."[20]

Meanwhile, however, there would be a good case for more extensive and more stringent supervisory control over nonbank financial institutions, trust, and private pension funds, as recommended by the Commission on Money and Credit.[21] This move can be recommended not only on grounds of equity and equalizing in some measure the conditions of competition among financial intermediaries, but also in removing an existing institutional bias toward investment in real estate. In the interest of economic growth, this bias is unfortunate.

2. *Federal lending policies.* As long ago as 1912, the Aldrich Commission had discussed the problem of an effective coordination of various federal departments and agencies concerned with credit, but without concrete results. In 1957, three economists again examined the theme, with particular reference to federal lending and guaranteeing agencies, concluding that these activities were then "at least as influential as determinants of total demand as were federal fiscal operations," and that these operations were often in direct conflict with Federal Reserve policy.[22] Since the Treasury–Federal Reserve Accord of 1951, the coordination of credit policies has improved, not only in that area, but generally. Nevertheless, it is probably true that the lending agencies have a natural expansive bent, based on their interest in a particular segment of the economy. While this is not a matter of immediate concern, it would be well to follow the recom-

mendation of the Commission on Money and Credit in making explicit provision for some kind of consultative machinery to secure unified credit policy. The responsibility lies with the executive branch of the federal government.

3. *Cost-push inflation.* The prevalence of periods of general expansion and inflationary pressure in the United States (and elsewhere) since the war has led to widespread concern with the problem and to the identification of and emphasis upon cost-push types of inflation, in contrast to older theories which ran—at least implicitly—largely in terms of demand-pull. As is frequently the case, the inruption of a new theory produced extreme views. The pure cost (or wage) explanations of price-level behavior took root first in Europe—for example, in England, with Abba Lerner, and in Denmark, with Jørgen Pedersen. Perhaps its most straightforward advocate in the United States is Sidney Weintraub.[23] The opposite extreme is represented by the "Chicago School" economists, who have generally denied that trade unions significantly raise real wages and who have attributed inflation to monetary factors rather than to the influence of wages.[24] Our analysis rejects both of these extremes, as well as extremes in another sense, namely, that all cost inflation devolves into demand inflation, or vice versa, or that it is conceptually impossible to separate the two. One good reason for admitting or insisting upon the presence of both cost and demand elements is the plausibility attaching to another somewhat new approach—Schultze's demand-shift theory of inflation—which involves both sides of the market.

The masterly review of inflation theory, in general and in all important varieties, written by Bronfenbrenner and Holzman makes it undesirable to repeat the performance here in an unsatisfactorily sketchy fashion.[25] From this review it seems clear that most economists (including the present writer) consider cost-push inflation to be important in the contemporary scene, and that most economists assign active roles to both labor unions and to oligopoly and monopoly pricing of commodities. Most economists (again including the present writer) consider cost-push to be a most serious limitation of or threat to the efficacy of monetary control. Although some die-hard "monetarists" believe that the

Federal Reserve could break the cost-push by a sufficiently tough restrictive monetary policy, this seems to be completely unrealistic from any practical view of the political scene, particularly with a background of a persistent 5 or 6 per cent residual unemployment rate.

Despite the critical importance of cost-push, there are good reasons, both theoretical and practical, for insisting upon the *admixture* of cost and demand that characterizes the inflations of the late 1950's and the early 1960's. Most important, the facts seem clearly to point that way: ". . . the inflation appears to have been due to excess demand in certain sectors, notably capital goods, together with sharp increases in wages at a time when productivity was rising only very slowly."[26] Moreover, cost inflation, though economically distinct, does indeed pass rapidly into demand inflation and vice versa; statistically they are difficult to disentangle. Also, the "new" kind of demand-shift inflation is—despite the author's denial of the relevance of either cost-push or demand-pull to the 1955–57 inflation—actually a compound of both.[27] Thus the evening-up of wage differentials, markup pricing, and the existence of oligopolistic product markets are given as reasons why wage-push can flourish. But these same factors figure prominently in making demand changes inflationary in Schultze's exposition. Indeed, in a purely competitive situation it is doubtful whether demand-shifts would be inflationary.

A practical reason for emphasis on the *de facto* mingling of cost-push, demand-pull, and demand-shift inflation is that a large part of the remedies against one type are—simply by reason of the mutually reinforcing character of the different types of inflation—effective against each and every one: Antitrust may hold down monopoly and oligopoly profits and thus restrain the push for higher wages; antitrust applied to gratuitously restrictive labor practices would reduce the inflationary effect of demand-shifts, and so forth. Possibly most important, however, is the fact that restrictive fiscal and monetary policies act not only via demand-pull, but on the other types as well.

While these reflections may be somewhat reassuring, they do not suffice to guarantee that monetary (and fiscal) measures may not break down from sufficiently strong pushes on the cost side.

There is a definite need for *wage policy;* and the most generally available and defensible policy is resistance against wage increases exceeding the national *average* increase in productivity. Despite the fact that this criterion has been derided as ridiculous,[28] it quite properly commands widespread respect, is understandable to the layman, and can with equal justice be applied to profits.

Authoritarian wage determination would be repugnant to the traditions of democracy and freedom in this country, but this does not preclude an administration wage policy. The mere announcement of such a policy would presumably exercise some influence on collective bargaining. But government influences upon wages are in fact manifold: legal minimum wage legislation, the adjudication of wage disputes, the scale and duration of unemployment compensation, the prices paid government contractors, and the wage and salary scale of an ever-increasing number of government employees. It is scarcely to be expected that a wage policy would be perfectly achieved, but it would supply a powerful support to fiscal-monetary measures and a logical complement to antitrust.

THE DESIRABILITY OF MONETARY CONTROLS FROM THE ANGLE OF THEIR "MODUS OPERANDI"

Does Monetary Policy Discriminate Unfairly?

Some economists, such as Leon Keyserling, J. K. Galbraith, and S. E. Harris, have argued that the incidence of monetary controls is discriminatory and that this limits their usefulness and should limit their use. These economists have objected to what they consider unfair discrimination, as evidenced in the tight-money policy of 1955–57, against residential construction and borrowing by local governments, small business, and consumers. They lament what they regard as the social injustice of limiting the credit available for building homes, schools, and small business premises and equipment, and for the durable consumers' goods required by low-income families, which are insensitive to interest charges.

Moved by criticisms of this sort, the Federal Reserve conducted a full-scale inquiry in 1957 and 1958 into the financing of
small business;[29] and subsequent investigations have extended
the coverage to other fields supposed to be at a disadvantage
from tight-credit policies.[30] These extended empirical studies have
reached the conclusion that "Discrimination amongst borrowers
was apparently largely on traditional banking standards of credit-
worthiness and goodness of borrowers."[31] To those who basically
do not believe in the allocation of capital by its cost in interest,
there is nothing to recommend the meeting of inflation by screen-
ing out the less important uses of capital by its price. This position would then necessarily involve the allocation of capital by
authoritarian decision, which in some quarters would be feared
as potentially more discriminatory than allocation by price.

Interest Cost to the Treasury of Flexible Monetary Policy

Another objection to monetary controls (opposed to the way
they operate rather than to their efficacy) is the complaint that
tight money raises the cost of borrowing to government itself.
This factor seems to assume importance in contemporary conditions in which, in the United States, the service of the publicly
held national debt runs to nearly $8 billion annually, or less than
7 per cent of the federal budget.

The truth in this matter lies somewhere between one extreme
view, which would assess the cost of debt service simply at its
face value, and another extreme, which counts the real cost of
internally held public debt at nil, i.e., a pure transfer cost. The
real costs of the $8 billion service on the publicly held debt—
assuming that the loss in want-satisfaction of those taxed approximately equals the gain to those to whom interest is paid—are the
costs of the processes of tax collection and interest disbursement
and the impairment of production incentives through taxation.
In addition, if government securities are held preponderantly by
the well-to-do, and if the tax system is not correspondingly progressive, there may be a loss in aggregate utility in the transfer.
But these costs, which are by-products of the $8 billion debt serv-
ice, will strike many persons as modest, when one considers one

of the two or three available stabilization mechanisms for the
$600 billion–income economy of the United States.

The rational attitude is that the payment of interest is the cost
of avoiding inflation. Concerning the coupon rate on a security
of given maturity, the higher interest rate presumably results in
firmer holding in the hands of the public. Concerning contrasting
costs of different maturities, shorter term debt is generally cheaper,
but—being more liquid for the holder—less restrictive upon spending.[32] But, of course, varying the mix of debt maturities is only
one way of raising or lowering the average rate paid on the national debt.[33]

The Strength and Weakness of Monetary Policy Viewed from the Angle of Plural Goals

Whether and in what sense monetary policy is to be regarded
as effective depends upon the purposes it is supposed to serve,
and upon the mutual compatibility of these purposes. Is it possible to discern some priorities among imaginable goals? In what
respects are the goals complementary or contradictory?

From the history of central banking, it is evident that the regulation of the balance of payments came very early—in the case of
the Bank of England, not later than the first quarter of the eight-
eenth century. Price stability as an objective lagged not far behind, although the Federal Reserve was loath to recognize this
as a responsibility long after Irving Fisher elevated it to a primary aim. High-level production and employment were certainly
emphasized in the business-cycle theories of the twentieth century, though it remained for Keynes and the Employment Act to
make them parts of the economists' creed. Finally, the emphasis
on growth, though no more novel than the *Wealth of Nations,*
received its current impulse from the Cold War and from the
aspirations of the poorer peoples for economic development.

To these objectives of monetary policy, recognized fairly generally as basic,[34] others have been added, such as preserving or
securing equity in the distribution of wealth and income, providing adequate support to national defense, and the encouragement
of economic freedom and private enterprise. To avoid an impos-

sible overload on one set of control instruments, however, these latter goals generally have to be regarded as ancillary. True enough, inflation and deflation, overly full employment and un-employment undesirably bias the distribution of wealth and income. But monetary policy can, at best, avoid these distortions of distribution; it cannot be expected to achieve equity, which depends basically upon real factors, modified in some measure by fiscal arrangements. Much the same can be said concerning economic freedom and private enterprise. They flourish in a relatively stable economic setting to which monetary policy can contribute; but they are not themselves its product. With respect to national defense, the larger its claims the more difficult is the task of monetary control, but the marshalling of resources is primarily a problem for public finance and for government administration in general. We therefore relegate these objectives to other control mechanisms, or make them paramount for monetary objectives in unusual circumstances only.

Among the four basic objectives—price stability, high and stable output and employment, growth, and balance-of-payments equilibrium—it is currently fashionable to assign to the first and fourth an importance subordinate to the others; but there are good reasons for caution on this score. In the first place, rather substantial attention must always be given all four and special circumstances can make any one for the time being the great national issue. Second, within certain limits the attainment of each of these objectives may condition the realization of the others or of another. Third, it may be that a certain purpose which seems to be an overriding one from a national viewpoint is not primary among the objectives to which *monetary* control may reasonably aspire. This is the case with the objective of growth. I proceed in reverse order with these points.

Fostering Economic Growth

Economic growth or progress is frequently given an honorific place in the objectives of monetary policy, and it would certainly be folly to deny that monetary controls do have such a purpose. But how does monetary policy promote progress? As ordinarily understood and practiced, monetary control does not and should not involve the authoritarian direction of resources into particular uses, including those most intimately conjoined with progress. How then does monetary control make a contribution in this direction? The answer would surely have to include that this control make whatever contribution it can to high-level employment and price stability. In this way, the tempo of progress is accelerated through the avoidance of the wastes of speculation and of misdirected production. If, in addition, a liberal or free enterprise system is desired, either for the sake of freedom itself or for the sake of the economic progress that has been linked with capitalism, then monetary control may be viewed as making a further contribution toward progress by facilitating the operation of a liberal economic regime. Nevertheless, the mainsprings of economic advances do not lie in the monetary system but in saving, investing, innovating, trading, organizing, etc. Active policies to further growth and development are oriented toward these (and possibly other) "real" factors. When we have covered the aims of promoting a free-enterprise economy, securing full employment, and maintaining price stability, we have exhausted the contributions of general monetary policy to progress.

Stable Prices and Stable and High-Level Output

It is common in current discussions to say that the choice between stable prices and stable and high-level output presents a dilemma: Indeed, this idea has been formalized into a "dilemma model" in theory.[35] There are important elements of truth in the idea of a dilemma in the face of these two objectives, but it is not *all* a matter of dilemma. Both sides need to be understood.

In the first place, it should be emphasized that stabilizing prices in some contexts serves also to stabilize output and employment. Thus, if the choice is between strong cyclical ups and downs and marked abatement of these fluctuations through monetary policy in a matrix of proper complementary policies, there is no dilemma. Similarly it would be difficult to deny that the stoppage of marked and chronic price inflation or deflation could improve output and employment. Thus by no means all actual cases involve a policy dilemma between stable prices and stable output.

In the second place, there can be no dilemma for monetary policy in choosing whether to effect prices or output. As Paul Samuelson has cogently pointed out, if an expansionary monetary or fiscal policy is pursued:

> . . . the resulting change in P x Q will get distributed between expansion in Q as against P, depending upon how much or how little labor and capital remains unused to be drawn on, and how strong or weak are the cost-push upward pressures that come from the institutional supply conditions of organized and unorganized labor, of oligopolistic price administrators, and more perfectly-competitive enterprises.[36]

The monetary authority cannot face a dilemma of choice as to the impact of its action if there is no choice. Furthermore, it is generally recognized that in deep depression an expansionary monetary policy might not increase either P or Q, but go in large part to the graveyard of idle cash balances.

The real "dilemma" of the monetary policy-maker is thus not the question of whether to direct his efforts more in one of these two directions than the other, but rather how much of a sacrifice of one objective to accept for a gain in the other, in case of incompatibility. A statistical study by Dewald and Johnson has reached the conclusion that monetary policy in the United States in the decade following the Treasury–Federal Reserve Accord did not sacrifice high employment and growth to price stability or balance-of-payments equilibrium.[37] But the fact that a substratum of unemployment persisted through the greater part of 1962, 1963, and into 1964, accompanied by a tendency of prices to rise rather than fall, seems to show that monetary policy had for the time being reached the end of its string. Since *aggregative* fiscal policies do not operate in a far different way from general monetary measures, the same conclusion must be reached here also, though the *tax reform* approach to growth and lessened unemployment has yet to be fully tested.

Balance-of-Payments Equilibrium

Much the same considerations as those treated in the preceding paragraphs apply to this objective in comparison with others. But in this case, the foreign balance is a less vital matter for the United States than for many (probably for most) other countries, and the foreign balance can be influenced by many measures other than monetary policy. During the closing months of 1963 the outflow of gold decreased, and part of the credit for this improvement should probably go to the rise of short-term interest rates without corresponding increases in long rates. But the vigorous use of restrictive monetary and fiscal policies scarcely seems to be indicated by the domestic or international situation. If these policies can restrain the rate of inflation in this country behind the one abroad, the effect will be favorable on the gold situation. For the rest, a variety of other measures of a remedial character are available.

A judicious summing up of the evidence would seem to indicate that monetary controls are neither so potent as its most zealous advocates in the past decade have believed nor so limited as has been argued by the skeptics, particularly those of the Eckstein and Radcliffe committees. Debt management directed toward the behavior of long term gilt-edged securities does not suffice: The quantity of money has to be controlled. Fiscal policy in the more general sense is an indispensable and powerful complement of monetary policy; but in the United States today there is not sufficient flexibility in taxes or expenditures to make fiscal policy a dependable, unique channel for stabilization.

The review of supposed limitations on monetary policy points to an upward cost-price spiral as the only really insurmountable obstacle to the effectiveness of conventional monetary controls when combined with appropriate fiscal measures. Skeptics of monetary policy seem to be torn between the beliefs that they are too potent and too little effective; sometimes both ideas are combined into the contention that controls fail to operate until a certain point, at which they "take hold" with sudden violence. But a discrete or "all or none" operation of monetary controls has in fact been conspicuously absent in recent history.

7. Making Monetary Policy More Effective

ALBERT GAILORD HART

The machinery of American monetary policy was designed long ago, in the light of economic theories now obsolete, to meet situations very different from those we confront today. It is a testimonial to the flexibility of our political institutions that United States monetary policy has, nevertheless, been fairly effective. But it would be surprising if an objective inquiry could not find many barriers to effective policy in our inherited monetary institutions and attitudes, and many ways of improving monetary performance.

Origins of the Monetary Policy Structure

Important parts of the current United States monetary structure go back to the National Banking Act of 1863, and to nineteenth century legislation on coinage and paper money. But what has been called our "monetary constitution" was shaped chiefly by the Gold Standard Act of 1900 and the Federal Reserve Act of 1913. Both these underlying statutes were drastically amended in 1933–35. Since then, our basic internal monetary arrangements have remained unchanged. It should be noted, however, that the establishment and evolution of the International Monetary Fund has changed the international aspects of our monetary structure. And at home the wider field of "credit" has seen a sprawling and uncoordinated growth of private operations, federal lending and credit insurance, and a limited degree of regulation.

The very real effectiveness of our monetary structure is all the more surprising when we remember that both the Federal Reserve Act of 1913 and the amendments of 1933–35 were largely reactions to financial panics. The panic of 1907—coming on top of a long series of nineteenth-century panics—was believed to show the need of some monetary organization that could correct the "inelasticity" of paper money supply by issuing notes based on "commercial paper" in the hands of banks. (One way to look at the Federal Reserve System is as a regularization of the arrangements for emergency issue of "clearinghouse certificates" by joint action of commercial banks, which had proved a useful palliative in these panics.) The prolonged series of bank failures that culminated in the banking holiday of 1933 was taken to show the need for an organization to shield depositors against banking collapse, and for a stronger control of credit with its centers of power further from the commercial bankers and Wall Street.

Both diagnoses obviously made sense up to a point. But it is equally obvious that they focused public attention on only a few sectors of the monetary problem; and in the light of present views on economic stabilization, the initial emphasis on "elasticity" of the money supply would seem dangerous—like enhancing the tendency of bank operations to accentuate upswings and downswings of economic activity.

It is remarkable that the resulting changes in the central banking structure have on the whole proved helpful in solving the broader problems of monetary policy. In fact, the 1961 report of the Commission on Money and Credit suggested no basic changes. As will appear below, I do not share this complacency about the existing structure. But to say that it can be improved is not to deny that it has served us well. We have had neither financial panics nor significant bank failures for over thirty years (an unprecedentedly long period in United States economic annals); and while the contribution of monetary control to stabilization is debatable, we must not forget that the over-all record since World War II is extremely good. The longest previous period of substantially uninterrupted full activity was 1923–29; since the end of World War II, we have had no recessions more intense than those within the 1923–29 period, and since 1952 we have enjoyed essential stability of prices. Monetary reform today is a question of making minor improvements in a good over-all performance, of curing certain latent weaknesses before they have a chance to do serious damage, and of improving the *world* (as opposed to the internal) monetary structure.

CHANGES IN UNITED STATES ECONOMIC STRUCTURE, DIAGNOSTIC CAPACITY, AND ECONOMIC OBJECTIVES

The probability that there is room for substantial betterment of our inherited monetary organization is plain if we review the changes during recent decades in the general structure of the American economy, in the stock of economic information and ideas with which to diagnose monetary problems, and in the objectives appropriate for monetary policy.

Economic Structure

As compared with 1913, or even 1933, the United States today is much more industrialized and urbanized, and carries on its economic activities much more through corporate and governmental organizations. On the financial side, there has been a considerable growth of such institutions as life insurance companies, savings and loan associations, installment finance houses, and (most recently) credit unions (relative to the growth of banks). These institutions have become highly competitive with banks—both in attracting funds from individuals and corporations, and in types of lending that used to be bank specialties. The nonbank credit institutions have developed lending practices different from those traditional in banking (notably the fully amortized home mortgage, the "term loan" and "private placement" of new securities), and have drawn bankers into competing by using similar methods. Thus the field of *bank credit* has become part of a progressively more integrated field of *financial-intermediary credit*. This interpenetration of different financial markets has been intensified by the widespread holding of government securities—highly liquid, and regarded as suitable assets for individuals and corporations as well as for banks and other financial intermediaries. Furthermore, these assets and corporate bonds link across to two other new major types of financial institutions that are not exactly in the "credit" field—mutual funds invested primarily in common stocks, and pension funds.

Many observers feel that this broadening and integrating of United States financial markets has left the monetary authorities (in particular, the Federal Reserve) in the position of trying to influence the whole financial situation from one narrow corner. To regulate activities carried on by commercial banks, while essentially the same activities are carried on by other financial institutions beyond direct Federal Reserve control, would seem awkward. Other observers feel that the greater importance of government debt, widely held, has enlarged the sphere of influence of the Federal Reserve and the Treasury, enabling them to influence all kinds of financial institutions by open-market operations in federal securities. These observers hold that banking continues to be the pivotal financial activity through which everything else can be steered. The difficulty in interpreting this situation is shown by the fact that the Commission on Money and Credit had to report an unresolved disagreement among its members.

Economic Information and Concepts

Despite the extensive studies by the National Monetary Commission after the panic of 1907, information about the way the American economic and financial system operated was scarce (by today's standards) when the Federal Reserve System was established. Even at the time of the banking amendments of 1933–35, following the crisis of the Great Depression, many types of information we now take for granted were difficult to find. To illustrate, we were just beginning in 1933–35 to get a statistical picture of installment credit and mortgage operations, and little systematic information had been assembled about credit institutions other than banks. Even for banks, the admirable collection of monthly financial statistics on which we now rely so heavily began to be put together only during World War II. (By a heroic effort of reconstruction, Friedman and Schwartz have recently assembled monthly figures of money supply back to 1907 in their *Monetary History of the United States;* but we had no such compilation in the interwar period.) As regards broader economic statistics, as late as the 1930's we had only fragmentary information on the course of business sales and inventories, on consumer purchases, on construction activity, and even on government operations. We had no figures on business intentions to install plant and equipment, or on the relation of broad aggregates of economic activity to available capacity.

Even today, we are seriously handicapped in economic diagnosis by inadequate knowledge of the past. This makes it hard to distinguish structural changes in the economy from ephemeral aberrations. But if the evidence is thin in spots today, it was grossly inadequate when our present monetary policy structure was designed.

In view of the lack of information, it is scarcely surprising that the theories used in economic and monetary diagnosis were inadequate. The basic concept underlying the original Federal Reserve Act seems to have been the "needs of trade" theory. According to this theory, a bank could do no wrong so long as its loans were of the right *quality*—"sound" in the sense of being genuinely devoted to financing inventories (of finished goods, goods in process, or raw materials) on their way to sale. This theory was qualified only by the recognition that the Federal Reserve at times might have to impose high costs of borrowing to check an expansion that threatened the nation's monetary reserves. This view was unrealistic. It ignored the large and growing part of bank operations devoted to other kinds of financing. It did not deal with the effect of *quantitative* changes in credit; and it ignored the strategic feedback relation that tends to make expansion in inventories and in bank credit mutually reinforcing. In the light of today's monetary theories and information, the "needs of trade" doctrine sounds like a rule to intensify economic instability.

No clear monetary theory can be found in the legislation of 1933–35. It was recognized that the credit deflation of 1929–33, though it could have been rationalized by the "needs of trade" doctrine and by changes in our international reserve position, had been a major disaster. The general tendency of the 1933–35 legislation was therefore to increase Federal Reserve power to regulate the over-all volume of bank credit. Power was given to the Federal Reserve to vary reserve requirements of commercial banks; and the open-market power, which had been used informally since early in the 1920's, was codified. "Selective" credit control was introduced in the form of regulation of stock-exchange "margins" by the Federal Reserve. (Incidentally, this regulation was set up to apply to "banks and brokers"—recognizing the effect of parallel operations outside the banking field on regulation that work only upon banking.) The theories implicit in this legislation are (1) that quantitative changes in bank credit influence business activity and prices in the direction of the credit change, and (2) that certain key sectors of the United States economy may be centers of infection for general economic instability. Few economists today would regard either view as erroneous, although an oversimplified version of either may be misleading.

Economic Objectives

There has been a marked evolution in the standards or objectives set for monetary policy by responsible opinion. The initial objectives were too timid (by present-day standards); those of the 1920's too ambitious; those of the period from 1933 to 1951 too timid; and those since 1951 again possibly too ambitious.

The standard explicit in the Federal Reserve Act of 1913 was to "accommodate commerce and industry"; it was understood as well that the Federal Reserve was to prevent financial panics and protect our international reserve position. The standard of the 1920's was less definite. "Accommodate commerce and industry" was reconstrued to mean checking upward movements of credit and business that threatened to become inflationary, and checking downward movements that threatened to induce inflation. In addition, the Federal Reserve System (under the leadership of Benjamin Strong, head of the Federal Reserve Bank of New York) tried to exercise a stabilizing influence on monetary systems abroad. In short, the monetary authorities took on a half-defined responsibility for the whole area of economic stabilization—the domain today of monetary, credit, fiscal, price, and wage policy.

The collapse of this policy (and the abandonment of ambitious objectives for monetary policy) constituted one of the most notable bankruptcies of the Great Depression era. The reasons for the collapse were primarily forces beyond the control of the Federal

Reserve—the stock exchange collapse of 1929, the end of the long building boom of the 1920's, and adverse developments in Europe. But the Federal Reserve itself contributed—specifically by imposing extremely tight money in the autumn and winter of 1931–32. In contrast, the monetary-policy objectives of the period from 1933 to the celebrated Treasury-Federal Reserve Accord of 1951 were extremely timid. An over-all responsibility of government (including the monetary authorities) for high employment and stable prices was registered by enactment of the Employment Act of 1946. But the Federal Reserve's basic power to affect bank-reserve positions by open-market operations was mortgaged to the secondary objective of maintaining prices of government securities. During the Korean War inflation of 1950–51, the position of the Federal Reserve was essentially a passive one. While in fact the expansion of the public's holdings of "means of payment" (that is, the sum of "pocketbook money," in the form of coins and paper currency, plus "checkbook money," in the form of demand deposits at commercial banks) was modest, there was a sharp expansion of bank credit. Attempts were made to brake the expansion of credit by more rigorous down payments and periods of payment on consumer installment contracts and on mortgages (regulated by the Federal Reserve under special legislation) and by "voluntary credit restraint" at commercial banks, guided by Federal Reserve suggestions. But these actions took definite shape only late in the Korean War inflation, and did not bite very deep. Furthermore, the emphasis on financing production in the "voluntary restraint" guidelines (including validation of loans to permit financing inventory at higher prices) harked back to the needs of trade theory, and positively encouraged use of bank credit to support the inflation.

The famous Accord of March, 1951, between the Federal Reserve and the Treasury relieved the Federal Reserve of the incubus of price-fixing for government securities. The transfer from the Treasury to the leadership of the Federal Reserve System of William McC. Martin (a former President of the New York Stock Exchange) did not represent the importation into the Federal Reserve of Treasury inhibitions about debt management, but increased "independence" in Federal Reserve leadership. In fact, this change inaugurated an era when Treasury leadership was much more responsive to Federal Reserve influence. With the arrival of Secretary Douglas Dillon (a sophisticated Wall Street financier) and Under-Secretary Robert Roosa (an officer of the Federal Reserve Bank of New York, who had for years managed the open-market account), it could be argued that Federal Reserve leadership had infiltrated the Treasury.

Since the signing of the Accord (or, at least, after a transition period of a year or so during which the bond market was weaned of its habit of relying on Federal Reserve "pegs"), the Federal Reserve has again been free to use its open-market powers for general monetary control. During the Eisenhower Administration, operations were somewhat hampered by a self-denying ordinance (the "bills only" policy) that barred sales and purchases by the Federal Reserve of any but the shortest maturities of government securities. This may well have been a necessary step to encourage the market to set its own bond prices rather than to base them on what the market thought that the Federal Reserve thought. But in recent years, the Federal Reserve has again felt free to deal in all maturities and has in fact operated largely in medium-term securities.

During this period, the Federal Reserve has carried what would seem an undue share of the responsibility for economic stabilization. There has not been much flexibility in the management for economic stabilization of fiscal policy (that is, of taxes and government expenditures), so that Federal Reserve management has been the most important flexible instrument available to stimulate the economy in recessions or slow it down when inflationary tendencies appeared. In addition, the Federal Reserve has had to reconcile the claims of domestic economic stability with policies to check the nation's loss of international monetary reserves through a balance-of-payments deficit, which in the early 1960's assumed menacing proportions. In these circumstances, the good over-all record of economic stability does the Federal Reserve great credit. But it must also be admitted that the problem has been simplified by the large scale of government outlays for defense, and by a practically continuous optimistic revision of values on the stock exchange. Neither of these supports can be expected to continue as strong as it has been in recent years, and we should be concerned as to whether the economic situation will be manageable when they weaken.

Timing and Impact of Monetary Policy

Before going on to suggestions for changes in the structure and strategy of monetary policy, it is worth while to examine in some detail the timing and impact of monetary policy in the post-Accord period—that is, from 1952 onward. This is done in the apparatus of charts that accompany this paper.

Response of Policy to Unemployment and Inflation

The responsibility of monetary policy for economic stabilization implies that it should work to stimulate the economy when there is heavy unemployment, and to brake the economy when there is an inflationary drift in the price level—hoping always that the two objectives will not come into conflict. The problem is neatly summed up in a jingle by Kenneth Boulding:

> Divergent policies we seek
> For markets strong and markets weak—
> But hoping to avoid this crisis:
> Too weak for jobs, too strong for prices:

The record of reactions in monetary policy is shown in Chart 1. The tendency of Federal Reserve policy can be fairly well summed up at any time by a single figure—the size of "free reserves." This measures the excess of reserve funds actually held by the commercial banks that are members of the Federal Reserve System over the debts of these banks to their Federal Reserve Banks. If free reserves are substantial, banks have incentives to expand credit and enlarge the public's stock of money; if free reserves are small or negative (as they may be if the debts represented by "discounts and advances" at Federal Reserve Banks are large), banks have incentives to contract, or at least to check, expansion. The Federal Reserve can enlarge free reserves by buying securities on the open market or by lowering legal reserve requirements for member banks; it can shrink free

CHART 1

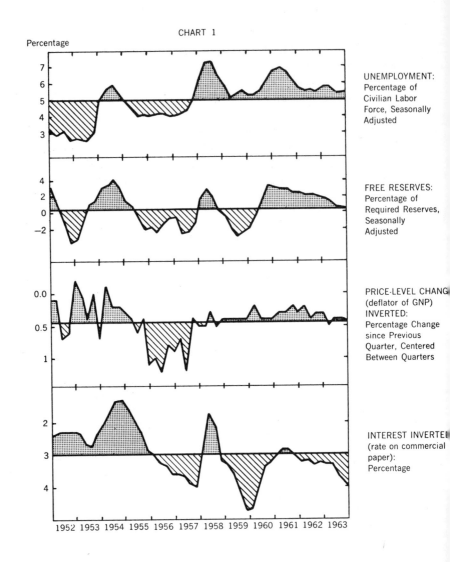

Percentage

UNEMPLOYMENT:
Percentage of
Civilian Labor
Force, Seasonally
Adjusted

FREE RESERVES:
Percentage of
Required Reserves,
Seasonally
Adjusted

PRICE-LEVEL CHANGE
(deflator of GNP)
INVERTED:
Percentage Change
since Previous
Quarter, Centered
Between Quarters

INTEREST INVERTED
(rate on commercial
paper):
Percentage

1952 1953 1954 1955 1956 1957 1958 1959 1960 1961 1962 1963

reserves by selling securities or raising requirements. Free reserves are affected also by some changes beyond Federal Reserve control (for example, the outflow of gold to foreign countries, and the growth of domestic circulation of paper money); but these changes can if desired be *offset*. If we look at any period as long as a month, we may be sure that the level of free reserves is what the Federal Reserve authorities *decide* it should be.

In the chart, free reserves are traced in the second curve from the top. Since the strength of the incentives offered to banks by a given dollar amount of free reserves depends on the height of reserve requirements, I have stated free reserves as a percentage of required reserves. The curve shows that the Federal Reserve was presenting the commercial banks with incentives to expand in 1954, in 1958, and on a considerable but diminishing scale since 1960. Free reserves were negative (that is, banks had incentives to contract credit) in 1952–53, 1955–57, and 1959–60. On the whole, the transition from one situation to the other has been rather abrupt.

The overshadowing responsibility for economic stabilization is represented by the top curve of the chart, which shows unemployment as a percentage of the civilian labor force. The responsiveness to unemployment of the Federal Reserve is shown by the fact that the peaks of unemployment in 1954, 1958, and early 1961 are matched so neatly by peaks in the free-reserve curve. It will be noted that, if anything, the peaks in free reserves come a little ahead of those in unemployment—a tendency that would be still sharper if we used monthly instead of quarterly figures— so that the Federal Reserve has apparently been vigilant. On the other hand, the intensity of the Federal Reserve response seems to have fallen off: The strongest movement of free reserves, in 1954, was in response to the lowest of the three peaks of unemployment. Furthermore, the restrictive policy of 1959–60 and the steady reduction of pressure toward monetary expansion since the peak in late 1960 both came despite unemployment levels well above 5 per cent.* It would appear that Federal Reserve

* To give definite shape to the curves, I have drawn horizontal lines at the average levels for 1952–63 of the variables measured. The average unemployment level happens to be almost exactly 5 per cent. It should be

responsiveness to unemployment has been weakening.

The anti-inflation criterion of policy is measured in the third curve, which shows *percentage changes* from quarter to quarter in the price index known as the "deflator for gross national product." Because a rise in prices should suggest contraction, and a fall in prices should remove inhibitions to expansion, I have turned the price curve upside down. The restrictive policy of 1955–57 reflects rather rapid price increases; since unemployment was low at this time, there was no conflict of objectives.* On the other hand, it is hard to see in the price record any basis for the restriction of 1959–60 or for the drift toward restriction in 1961–63.

The pervasive effect of the balance-of-payments difficulties of the early 1960's must be presumed to be the main reason why free reserves were reduced in 1961–63. Counterpart of this movement is the rise in interest rates in 1961–63, which is shown in the bottom curve of the chart. (The movement of the curve is downward, since the curve is turned upside down because high interest rates correspond to low or negative free reserves.) The Federal Reserve has felt bound to keep short-term interest rates in this country in line with rising rates abroad, so as to limit transfers abroad of short-term capital.

Transmission of Monetary Policy Through Bank Operations

While it is the Federal Reserve that sets the stage by determining the reserve position of the commercial banks, it is the commercial banks and their customers who are the actors in the drama. The relation between free reserves and actual operations at the commercial-bank level is shown in Chart 2.

The top curve of Chart 2 represents the active side of opera-

---

stressed that these average levels should *not* be assumed to be *satisfactory*. In the case of unemployment, nobody seems to argue that a percentage above 4 per cent is satisfactory, and many economists would feel that a satisfactory percentage would be well below 4 per cent. For my part, I should aim at a satisfactory target level in the next few years between 3 per cent and 3½ per cent.

* As with unemployment, the average rate of price change that is used to calibrate the diagram (about 0.4 per cent per calendar quarter) is too high to be entirely satisfactory. But few economists would regard a rise at this rate as fast enough to be a major evil.

CHART 2

Percentage

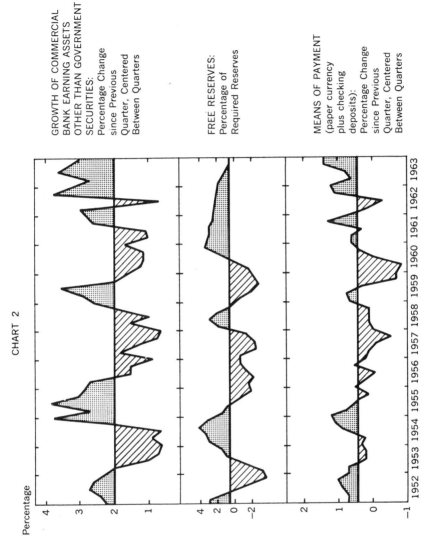

GROWTH OF COMMERCIAL
BANK EARNING ASSETS
OTHER THAN GOVERNMENT
SECURITIES:
Percentage Change
since Previous
Quarter, Centered
Between Quarters

FREE RESERVES:
Percentage of
Required Reserves

MEANS OF PAYMENT
(paper currency
plus checking
deposits):
Percentage Change
since Previous
Quarter, Centered
Between Quarters

tions in bank credit: It measures percentage changes from quarter to quarter in the average level of commercial bank "loans and investments" excluding from investments their holdings of government securities. Each of the three phases of high free reserves has its counterpart in a phase of rapid expansion in bank credit, and each of the three phases of low free reserves has its counterpart in a phase of slow expansion.* But there is a marked difference in timing, with corresponding points in the top curve in most cases a year or more behind their counterparts in free reserves. And the decline in free reserves in 1961–63 had not brought on by the end of 1963 any decline in the rate of credit expansion. It might be inferred from this last fact that there has been a fairly satisfactory reconciliation in the early 1960's of international and domestic objectives, with domestic credit expansion somehow insulated from the Federal Reserve's reaction to the international reserve situation.

Below the middle curve of the chart, which reproduces for reference the free-reserve curve of Chart 1, the bottom curve traces quarter-to-quarter percentage changes in the stock of "means of payment"—that is, hand-to-hand currency plus checking deposits. These changes, though smaller and more irregular, also show counterparts to the fluctuations of free reserves. The time lag behind changes in free reserves is smaller for the stock of means of payment than for the credit curve at the top of the chart. This is possible because fluctuations in means of payment arise not only from changes in the loans and investments measured above, but also from changes in bank holdings of government securities, and from decisions of depositors to hold their funds in checking accounts or as time deposits. The lags of changes in means of payment behind free reserves are irregular, ranging from almost instantaneous response to over a year in different episodes of the record. Furthermore, the intensity of fluctuations in the expansion of means of payment seems to lack a clear relation to the intensity of fluctuations in free reserves.

* The average quarter-to-quarter expansion in 1952–63 was almost exactly 2 per cent calendar quarter, and the low points of the curve come above 0.5 per cent.

Impact of Monetary Changes on Transactions

The process may be traced a step farther—into actual economic operations—in Chart 3. Here the top and bottom curves are carried forward from Chart 2. But the middle curve shows quarter-to-quarter percentage changes in "transactions," which involve money payments. I have measured "transactions" by private gross product (that is, gross national product less the services of "general government" employees), excluding changes in inventory (that is, excluding the part of output that is not currently sold).

We may best start with the fluctuations in the rate of growth in transactions in the middle curve, and look for counterpart movements in the other curves. For convenience, I have tagged with a capital letter each point of most rapid increase or decrease in transactions.* A considerable proportion of these tagged maximum-increase and minimum-increase points have counterparts on the means-of-payment curve—either at the same date, or with the means of payment moving earlier than transactions. But there are not quite enough high and low points on the means-of-payment curve to match all those on the transactions curve, so that we have to play a sort of musical chairs in attributing counterparts to the changes in transactions. Furthermore, the apparent counterparts often differ radically in intensity, and the apparent lead of changes in means of payment is highly variable. Thus the correspondence between the curves has to be seen rather impressionistically.

Turning to the comparison of transactions with commercial bank credit, it is easier to find definite counterparts, though there are still some points that one cannot match up. Amplitudes of fluctuations in rates of growth of credit are much more like those in the growth of transactions. But it must be noted that fluctuations in credit seem to come later than corresponding fluctuations in transactions.

* Note that the points so tagged are not identical with *peaks and troughs* in transactions. Even though the rate of growth has begun to slacken, transactions go on growing till the rate of growth drops below zero. Thus in 1952–53 the peak rate of growth (point S on the middle curve) came with the rise of 3.3 per cent between the third and fourth quarters of 1952; but there were three further positive changes (of 2.6 per cent, 1.0 per cent, and 0.3 per cent), bringing transactions to its peak in the third quarter of 1953.

CHART 3

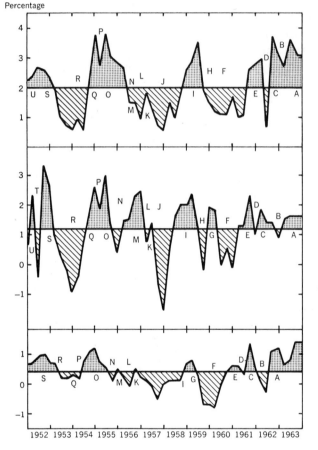

Percentage

GROWTH OF COMMERCIAL
BANK EARNING ASSETS
OTHER THAN GOVERNMENT
SECURITIES:
Percentage Change
since Previous
Quarter, Centered
Between Quarters

GROWTH OF
"TRANSACTIONS":
INCREMENTS OF PRIVATE
GROSS PRODUCT EXCLUDING
GOVERNMENT:
Percentage Change
since Previous
Quarter, Centered
Between Quarters

GROWTH OF
MEANS OF PAYMENT
(paper currency
plus checking
deposits):
Percentage Change
since Previous
Quarter, Centered
Between Quarters

The presence of an arbitrary element in these comparisons is evidenced by the differences we meet when we try the effect of different measures of the stock of money (Chart 4). In the top curve of this chart, we trace quarter-to-quarter changes in money, as Professor Milton Friedman prefers to define it—including, along with the means of payment, the public's time deposits in *commercial* banks, but excluding other time deposits. This traces quite a different course from the curve for means of payment, with again some indications of a rather indefinite lead over changes in transactions.* The picture is different if we adopt the widest measure of all in common use (bottom curve of Chart 4) and consider "liquid assets," including the public's holdings of savings deposits, saving and loan "shares," and government securities. Here there seems to be a lag of liquid assets behind transactions—presumably because the forces that generate a bulge in transactions also set up operations in government debt, mortgages, and the like, which generate a bulge in liquid assets.

Diagnosis

One way to read this record is to stress the lag mechanism, assuming that monetary policy works through its effects on the liabilities of the banking system (which, of course, are cash assets for the nonbank public). According to this argument, if monetary policy starts to move so as to "lean against the wind" of any recession or boom as soon as the recession or boom is clearly identified, we first have a lag that the effects work through into bank-credit operations that generate money, and then a further lag while the changed stock of money takes effect on substantive economic activity. These two lags add up to well over a year; and their duration is not only long but uncertain. Hence the effect of

* A prominent feature in the top curve of Chart 4 is a peak in early 1958, which is not to be found either in the curve for the stock of money or in the curve for liquid assets, and which has no counterpart in the curve for free reserves.

This conspicuous high point, which, if valid, is interesting because it offers a monetary "explanation" of the rapid growth of transactions in 1959, seems to be an effect of the arbitrary boundary between time deposits in commercial and other banks. At this moment, there happens to have been a strong *relative* growth of time deposits in commercial banks—a fact that cannot carry too much weight in general monetary analysis.

CHART 4

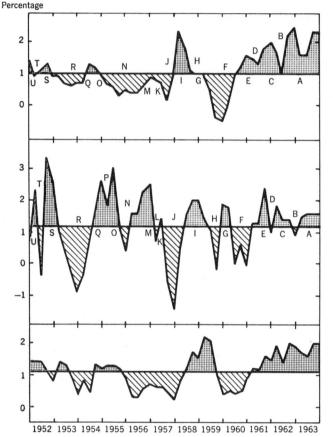

Percentage

GROWTH OF FRIEDMAN'S MONEY (means of payment plus time deposits in commercial banks): Percentage Change since Previous Quarter, Centered Between Quarters

GROWTH OF "TRANSACTIONS": Percentage Change since Previous Quarter, Centered Between Quarters

GROWTH OF LIQUID ASSETS (Friedman's money plus claims on savings banks and savings and loan associations, plus government securities): Percentage Change since Previous Quarter, Centered Between Quarters

1952 1953 1954 1955 1956 1957 1958 1959 1960 1961 1962 1963

trying to counter a current fluctuation of business is to leave the
current substantive economic situation almost unaffected, while
setting forces at work that will act a year or so later—in a direction and intensity that may be appropriate or may produce undesired economic events at that time. If this diagnosis is accepted,
the part of wisdom would be not to try to be too clever, but to
hew to some such line as Milton Friedman's proposed constant
rate of increase in money stocks. Monetary policy would then
have to admit that it was not counteracting economic fluctuations
—but could claim that at least it was not *generating* fluctuations,
and that the feedback from its steady rate of monetary expansion
should exert a calming influence on the economy as a whole.

Another line of diagnosis of short-term fluctuations is to look
at the *asset* side of banking, and consider the effects of credit
extension, illustrated by the close relation of bank earning assets
and transactions shown in Chart 3. The fact that these earning
assets fluctuate behind instead of ahead of fluctuations in transactions forbids us to adopt anything like a mechanical causal theory
in which credit operations generate activity. But it seems likely
that credit plays a permissive role, and that if credit can be held
more stable, sharp movements of activity will tend to damp out.
The lack of a credit follow up to the abortive upswing in the
winter of 1959–60 (point G in the middle curve of Chart 3) may
illustrate such a permissive role. It is striking also that over the
six-quarter inflationary period from mid-1950 to the end of 1951,
the money stock as measured by Milton Friedman rose by only
6.6 per cent, as compared to a rise of 21.8 per cent in transactions,
and of 25.0 per cent in credit.

In the second diagnosis as well as the first, there is a substantial
lag to worry about, as may be seen from the top two curves of
Chart 2. Thus this diagnosis tends to agree with the first in sug-
gesting that the tendency of the Federal Reserve to adjust free
reserves to the current business situation may have deferred
effects much stronger than its immediate effects, and may contribute to later fluctuations. The counsel not to try to be too
clever may well apply as much under this diagnosis as under the
one that tries to explain everything by changes in the money
stock.

Where the two diagnoses differ is that the credit diagnosis suggests that the composition of bank assets as well as their size is an influence on the business situation. If this is the case, it is not enough to have a policy toward free reserves, but monetary policy must have other instrumentalities with which to influence asset composition. Furthermore, if the general movement of bank assets other than government securities affects the course of events, it is interesting to consider the possibility of stabilizing various components of activity by operating on types of credit especially related to those areas. Consumer installment credit and housing credit are well-known examples of such types of credit with pervasive influence on major sectors of the economy; and probably there are others.*

SOME POLICY PROPOSALS

At this point, it is obviously my responsibility to suggest changes in structure and strategy that could make monetary policy more effective. Despite the negative conclusions of the Commission on Money and Credit, I find that the possibilities are very rich.

International Monetary Relations

The first requisite of a really effective monetary policy is to recover our freedom of action on the international front. Through much of the interwar and postwar periods, the United States has simply been so generously provided with international reserves that we had nothing to worry about: If a monetary policy geared

---

* In the first edition of this volume, I noted the interesting relation between the time-shape of business loans of commercial banks and that of business inventories. Mr. William J. Frazer, Jr., points out that a large fraction of the inventory is in lines of manufacturing where loans are relatively trifling ("The Financial Structure of Manufacturing Corporations and the Demand for Money: Some Empirical Findings," *Journal of Political Economy*, April, 1964, p. 183). There is still an interesting relation if we subtract most branches of manufacturing from both inventories and business loans; but the possibility of influencing inventory by moves toward stabilization of business loans is manifestly much more remote than I had suggested.

to domestic needs involved a loss of reserves, we could simply let reserves go. Incidentally, our share of the world's reserves was so large that a moderate change here could be a relatively enormous change abroad, setting up forces abroad that would correct our balance of payments. With our recent losses of gold, and with the enormous build-up of foreign monetary reserves held in dollars, we no longer have this security. The fact that in the early 1960's our economic expansion has not been strong enough to pull unemployment below 5½ per cent of the labor force suggests that inhibitions arising from our international position have held us back appreciably.

One obvious move toward international freedom of action is to repeal the 25 per cent reserve requirement in gold that now applies to notes and deposits of Federal Reserve Banks. This limit simply immobilizes a large share of our gold.

A second possibility is to reform the world monetary structure so as to assure a reasonably rapid growth of "world liquidity." This would create an uptrend in the total monetary reserves of the world's industrial countries, and the United States could reasonably expect to share in that uptrend, since we possess a good deal of export capacity that is underutilized for lack of demand.*

A third possibility is to get into a position where we can devalue our currency by 5 or 10 per cent if we find ourselves confronted with a "structural disequilibrium," as we seem to have been during the early 1960's. This possibility also bears on international monetary reform, since the evolution of the "key currency system" has tended to set up undesirably rigid links between the dollar and the currencies of other industrial countries. Many proposals for international monetary reform are designed so as to intensify this rigidity.

---

* In collaboration with Nicholas Kaldor and Jan Tinbergen, I laid before the United Nations Conference on Trade and Development, in March, 1964, a paper on "The Case for a Commodity Reserve Currency." This proposal aims at an expansion of world monetary reserves through a monetary standard based on a composite of primary materials—generating income for primary producing countries, and expanding the demand for exports of the industrial countries.

General Controls of Bank Credit

It would not be difficult to design generalized control mechanisms that would stand in the way of any rapid shifts in the composition of bank assets. This could be done from either of two sides. One possibility would be to relate bank reserve requirements to assets rather than (or in addition to) liabilities. The other would be to revive the proposals for "security reserves" that were under study some years ago, and that have counterparts in other countries.

There is something anomalous about basing our monetary controls upon reserve requirements that apply to the holding of deposits, in view of the fact that a bank typically does not make a decision about its volume of deposits, but simply accepts all it can attract. A requirement related to "loans" (for example, to the total amount of earning assets other than government securities) would have the obvious merit of addressing its incentives to the point of decision: For each bank does have to have a policy of expanding or not expanding such assets. To link the bank's permitted volume of "loans" to its cash reserves and set limits to those cash reserves by the established procedures of open-market operations and variation or reserve-requirement percentages would be an effective method of checking an expansion.

Note that when we speak of "checking" an expansion, we do not mean to cut off permanently the demands for goods and services that power an economic expansion. But a properly applied slow-down of loan expansion in a situation like, say, 1955 can lead to *postponement* of demand. Whether a check to expansion is likely to produce such a postponement at times when there would otherwise be an inflationary excess of demand is a good touchstone of sound policy.

The other alternative for preventing undue surges of loan-financed demand would be to have security reserve requirements that required banks to hold a certain proportion of their deposits in government securities. Such a scheme would mean that when banks came up against the limits of their cash reserves, they could not expand lending power by transferring their government securities to nonbank holders.

Neither of these devices would suffice to generate an expansion of loans if enough qualified borrowers failed to appear at the banks. But this is not a new hazard: The possibility that banks may not be able to use all their lending power exists already, and was a serious problem in the late 1930's. To the extent that a more stable monetary policy managed to get loan-financed projects postponed, it would transfer a certain amount of demand into what would otherwise be less active periods.

Selective Controls

The possibility of going inside "loans" in the very broad sense just used, and instituting more specific controls, has been often examined. Such controls could not well be limited to commercial banking: As experience with stock market controls and wartime experience with installment credit have demonstrated, such credits if regulated at all must be regulated not only at banks but also at competing institutions.

Professional opinion is divided on the usefulness of such controls. I venture to suggest that the difficulty is in good part the fussy character of rules on down payments, number of installments to be paid, and the like. An alternative would be to set up a system of transferrable permits to have loans of such types outstanding, and limit the supply of credit by limiting the number of permits. To prevent this system from degenerating into one where government officials have to give away valuable privileges to some and refuse them to others, such a system should rest upon prices for the permits—ideally, prices determined at short intervals by auctioning off the permits.

Conclusion

Fruitful social invention in the monetary field is not a thing of the past. Because of the natural conservatism of the financial community and the need for clear definition of rights and duties in debt contracts, it is inevitable that there should be great stress on the advantages of following established lines in the control of financial operations. But in fact the recent period has been full of useful innovations in the design and adaptation of financial institutions and financing patterns—including (within the framework of the Bretton Woods agreements) a radical redesign of the world's international reserve system. Domestically, our monetary system has been doing well. But it could do better, and it could be better secured against possible difficulties when some of the favorable factors that have given us the all-time record postwar prosperity begin to weaken. Specifically, we should apply the test as to whether arrangements will serve in case we get simultaneously (1) a substantial cut in armament expenditure, (2) a more sober view of stock market values, and (3) a slightly higher vacancy rate in housing and commercial premises.

Despite the complacency of the Commission on Money and Credit, it is hard to believe that existing organization in the monetary field will pass these tests. At the very least, some measure of international monetary reform and some adaptation to the need to influence "credit" as well as "money" are called for. In addition, we need a re-evaluation of monetary strategy. Monetary policy needs to be unloaded by the provision of a partner in the form of a more flexible fiscal policy. At the same time, monetary policy itself needs to aim at smoothing out the movements in the composition of bank assets, and contributing to stabilization of the economy by helping stabilize some of its more volatile components.

Notes

CHAPTER 1. TOOLS AND PROCESSES OF MONETARY POLICY
(pp. 24–72)

1. In connection with these and other actions referred to in this section, see the "Open Market Policy Record for 1953" in the *Annual Report* of the Board of Governors for that year.

2. A defense along these lines is given in an article by W. W. Riefler, "Open Market Operations in Long-Term Securities," published in the *Federal Reserve Bulletin*, September, 1958. See also Ralph A. Young and Charles A. Yager, "The Economics of 'Bills Preferably,'" *Quarterly Journal of Economics*, LXXIV, August, 1960.

CHAPTER 2. MONEY SUPPLY AND STABLE ECONOMIC GROWTH
(pp. 73–93)

1. *January 1961 Economic Report of the President and the Economic Situation and Outlook*, Hearings, Joint Economic Committee, 87th Cong., 1st sess. (March 7, 1961), p. 483.

CHAPTER 3. USES OF SELECTIVE CREDIT CONTROLS
(pp. 94–115)

1. This method of posing the problem is that adopted in the 1958 Rockefeller Report, *The Challenge to America: Its Economic and Social Aspects*.

CHAPTER 6. LIMITATIONS OF MONETARY POLICY
(pp. 195–214)

1. Cf. Karl Brunner, "The Report of the Commission on Money and Credit," *Journal of Political Economy*, December, 1961, p. 613.

2. *Monetary Policy and the Management of the Public Debt*, Joint Committee Print, Joint Committee on the Economic Report, 82d Cong., 2d sess. (Washington, D.C., 1952), Part I.

3. Paul A. Samuelson, "Reflections on Monetary Policy," *The Review of Economics and Statistics*, August, 1961, p. 267.

4. Cf., respectively: "Post Accord Monetary Developments in the United States," Banca Nazionale del Lavoro (Rome), *Quarterly Review*, September, 1957, pp. 344–45; "On the Effectiveness of Monetary Policy," *American Economic Review*, September, 1956, pp. 588–607.

5. Samuel I. Katz, "Radcliffe Report: Monetary Policy and Debt Management Reconciled," Banca Nazionale del Lavoro (Rome), *Quarterly Review*, June, 1960, pp. 148–70.

6. John G. Gurley, "The Radcliffe Report and Evidence," *American Economic Review*, September, 1960, p. 680.

7. Katz, *op. cit.*, pp. 165, 168. It is interesting to observe what Alfred Marshall said long ago: "I do not myself put the rate of discount in the first place; my own way of looking at it was rather to lay stress upon the actual amount of money in the market to be loaned." ("Evidence Before the Gold and Silver Commission [1887]," *Official Papers* [London, 1926], p. 48.)

8. E. Sherman Adams, "Monetary Restraint and Bank Credit," *Banking* (Journal of the American Bankers Association), September, 1957. The poll covered 1,400 banks with two thirds of the total assets of commercial banks of this country.

9. J. W. Angell, *The Behavior of Money* (New York, 1936), pp. 162–63.

10. *Report of the Committee on the Working of The Monetary System* (London, 1959), pp. 132–33. *Staff Report on Employment, Growth, and Price Levels,* Joint Committee Print, 86th Cong., 1st sess. (Washington, D.C., 1960), pp. 343–61.

11. Milton Friedman and Anna Jacobson Schwartz, *A Monetary History of the United States, 1867–1960* (Princeton, N.J., 1963), p. 682. It should be noted that a *"stable* movement about its trend" is a somewhat different matter from simple stability of velocity, which is attributed by Lawrence S. Ritter to "quantity theorists." Cf. *Banking and Monetary Studies,* Deane Carson (ed.) (Homewood, Ill., 1963), p. 150.

12. *Money and Credit: Their Influence on Jobs, Prices, and Growth,* The Report of the Commission on Money and Credit (Englewood Cliffs, N.J., 1961), p. 49. Cited henceforth as CMC Report.

13. Milton Friedman, *A Program for Monetary Stability* (New York, 1960), p. 87.

14. *January 1961 Economic Report . . .* , p. 394.

15. CMC Report, pp. 244–45.

16. Young and Yager, *op. cit.*, pp. 364–65.

17. Cf. Radcliffe Report, *passim;* H. P. Minsky, "Central Banking and Money Market Changes," *Quarterly Journal of Economics*, May, 1957, pp. 171–87; Ritter, *op. cit.*, pp. 148–50.

18. Warren L. Smith, "Financial Intermediaries and Monetary Controls," *Quarterly Journal of Economics*, November, 1959, pp. 542–46; similarly, David Fand, "Intermediary Claims and the Adequacy of our Monetary Controls," *Banking and Monetary Studies*, pp. 234–53; H. G. Johnson, "Monetary Theory and Policy," *American Economic Review*, June, 1962, pp. 373–74; David A. Alhadeff, "Credit Controls and Financial Intermediaries," *American Economic Review*, September, 1960, pp. 655–71.

19. The so-called Heller Report (*Report of the Committee on Financial Institutions to the President of the United States* [Washington, D.C., 1963]) recommends the imposition of reserve requirements on mutual savings banks and savings and loan associations; but this is explicitly said not to be necessary for effective monetary policy, but is justified on the basis of equity.

20. Smith, *op. cit.*, p. 550.

21. CMC Report, pp. 174–80.

22. R. J. Saulnier, Harold G. Halcrow, and Neil H. Jacoby, *Federal Lending: Its Growth and Impact,* Occasional Paper 58, National Bureau of Economic Research (New York, 1957).

23. *Classical Keynesianism, Monetary Theory and the Price Level* (Philadelphia, 1961).

24. E.g., Richard T. Selden, "Cost-Push *versus* Demand-Pull Inflation, 1955–57," *Journal of Political Economy*, February, 1959, pp. 1–20.

25. Martin Bronfenbrenner and Franklyn D. Holzman, "Survey of Inflation Theory," *American Economic Review*, September, 1963, pp. 593–661.

26. Warren L. Smith, "Monetary Policy, 1957–1960: An Appraisal," *The Review of Economics and Statistics*, August, 1960, pp. 269–72.

27. Charles L. Schultze, *Recent Inflation in the United States*, Joint Committee Print, 86th Cong., 1st sess. (Washington, D.C., 1959). Demand shift as a cause of expansion and price-rise figures in D. R. Robertson, *Banking Policy and the Price Level* (London, 1926), chaps. ii and iii; and William Fellner, *Monetary Policies and Full Employment* (Berkeley, Calif., 1946), chap. iv.

28. Bronfenbrenner and Holzman, *op. cit.*, p. 639.

29. *Financing Small Business*, Report to the Committees on Banking and Currency and the Select Committees on Small Business, U.S. Congress, by the Federal Reserve System (Washington, D.C., April 11, 1958), Parts I and II.

30. Cf. G. L. Bach, "How Discriminatory Is Tight Money?," in *Banking and Monetary Studies*, pp. 254–90; James R. Schlesinger, "Monetary Policy and Its Critics," *Journal of Political Economy*, December, 1960, pp. 608–12; CMC Report, pp. 57–60.

31. Bach, *op. cit.*, p. 289.

32. Earl R. Rolph, "Principles of Debt Management," *American Economic Review*, June, 1957, pp. 302–20. If long-term rates are lower than short, then both economy and restraint of inflation would be best served by a complete shift to long; but these situations (e.g., 1957) are generally too brief to be significant.

33. It is undoubtedly true, as Warren L. Smith contends, that marginal changes in the maturities of the debt do not have important consequences; cf. his *Debt Management in the United States*, Study Paper No. 19, Joint Economic Committee (Washington, D.C., 1960). Here we are not concerned with these changes per se, but with the absolute height of the interest structure.

34. E.g., by the Commission on Money and Credit; cf. CMC Report, pp. 12–13, and chap. viii.

35. Cf. Bronfenbrenner and Holzman, *op. cit.*, p. 627.

36. Paul A. Samuelson, "Reflections on Central Banking," *National Banking Review*, I, No. 1 (September, 1963), p. 23.

37. W. G. Dewald and Harry G. Johnson, "An Objective Analysis of the Objectives of American Monetary Policy," *Banking and Monetary Studies*, pp. 171–89.

Notes on the Contributors

STEPHEN H. AXILROD is Chief of the Government Finance Section in the Division of Research and Statistics of the Board of Governors of the Federal Reserve System. He has held a variety of positions at the Board in the areas of banking, flow of funds and savings, and international finance. The views expressed in his article are not necessarily those of the Board of Governors of the Federal Reserve System.

HOWARD S. ELLIS is Flood Professor of Economics, University of California, Berkeley. In addition to teaching and lecturing both here and abroad since 1920, Dr. Ellis has been at various times: Assistant Director of Research and Statistics, Board of Governors of the Federal Reserve Board; Consultant to the House of Representatives Committee on Postwar Planning; and a member of the Economic Policy Committee, United States Chamber of Commerce. He has served as president of the American and of the International Economic Association and has written and edited a large number of books and articles on economic theory, money and banking, fiscal policy, and international finance.

ALBERT GAILORD HART is Professor of Economics at Columbia University. In 1943–53, and since 1963, he has been a consultant to the United States Treasury, and he has served as "fiscal economist" for international agencies concerned with Latin American problems. He is the author of several books, including, in the field of money and credit, *Debts and Recovery 1929–1937* (1938), *Defense and the Dollar* (1953), and *Money, Debt and Economic Activity* (1948; 3d ed., in collaboration with Peter B. Kenen, 1961).

NEIL H. JACOBY is Dean of the Graduate School of Business Administration at the University of California, Los Angeles. From 1938 to 1948 he was at the University of Chicago, becoming Professor of Finance and Vice President. He served as President of the American Finance Association in 1949. From 1953 to 1955 he served as a member of President Eisenhower's Council of Economic Advisers. During 1957 he served as United States Representative in the Economic and Social Council of the United Nations. He is well known as the author of

242

Can Prosperity Be Sustained? Federal Lending and Loan Insurance, and *Bank Deposits and Legal Reserve Requirements,* and as co-author of *Business Finance and Banking.*

FRANK WALTER PAISH is Professor of Economics with special reference to Business Finance at the London School of Economics, University of London. He is former secretary and editor of the London and Cambridge Economics Service and former Deputy-Director of Programmes, Ministry of Aircraft Production. His publications include *Insurance Funds and Their Investment, The Post-War Financial Problem and Other Essays,* and *Business Finance,* as well as numerous articles.

EDWARD S. SHAW is Professor of Economics at Stanford University. Currently a consultant to the Board of Governors of the Federal Reserve System and the Department of the Treasury, he is also a Research Associate at the Brookings Institution and a Director of the Teachers Insurance and Annuity Association of America. Among his recent publications are (with John G. Gurley) *Money in a Theory of Finance* (1960) and *Savings and Loan Markets Structure and Market Performance* (1962).

ARTHUR SMITHIES has been an economist in the Australian Treasury Department, Chief of the Economics Bureau, United States Bureau of the Budget; and Director of the Fiscal and Trade Policy Division of E.C.A. Since 1949, Dr. Smithies has been Professor of Economics at Harvard University.

HENRY C. WALLICH is Professor of Economics at Yale University. He has written widely in the field of monetary problems and economic development and has served as economic consultant to a number of foreign central banks and to several United States Government agencies. From 1941 to 1951 he was with the Federal Reserve Bank of New York, and from 1958 until recently he was Assistant to the Secretary of the Treasury.

RALPH A. YOUNG is currently Adviser to the Board of Governors of the Federal Reserve System and Director, Division of International Finance, as well as Secretary of the Federal Open Market Committee. He has held numerous academic and research posts and has published extensively on monetary policy and the Federal Reserve System.